ISLAM,
GUERRILLA WAR,
AND REVOLUTION

ISLAM, GUERRILLA WAR, AND REVOLUTION

A Study in Comparative Social History

—————— HAIM GERBER ——————

LYNNE RIENNER PUBLISHERS • BOULDER & LONDON

Published in the United States of America in 1988 by
Lynne Rienner Publishers, Inc.
948 North Street, Boulder, Colorado 80302

and in the United Kingdom by
Lynne Rienner Publishers, Inc.
3 Henrietta Street, Covent Garden, London WC2E 8LU

Library of Congress Cataloging-in-Publication Data
Gerber, Haim.
  Islam, guerrilla war, and revolution.
  Includes index.
  1. Revolutions—Religious aspects—Islam. 2. Islam
and politics. 3. Communism and Islam. 4. Revolutions
and socialism. 5. Islam and politics—Middle East.
6. Middle East—Politics and government. 7. Revolutions—
Middle East. 9. Guerrillas—Middle East. I. Title.
HX550.I8G43 1988   321.09'0917'671   88-11673
ISBN 1-55587-128-3 (alk. paper)

British Library Cataloguing in Publication Data
A Cataloguing in Publication record for this book
is available from the British Library.

Printed and bound in the United States of America

The paper used in this publication meets the requirements of the
American National Standard for Permanence of Paper
for Printed Library Materials Z39.48-1984.   ⊗

Contents

CHAPTER ONE

Revolution and Revolutionary Guerrilla Warfare

This study brings together my interests in several fields. First and foremost it is an effort to contribute to the field of comparative social history, a young sister of historical sociology, and to introduce this field into Islamic studies. My preoccupation with such topics has existed ever since I discovered Barrington Moore's famous study,[1] which converged in my mind with a prior interest in long-range movements of change, involving mainly agrarian forces, which I owe to the late Professor Gabriel Baer.

I have written this book to demonstrate the great explanatory value of comparisons for Middle Eastern history and political sociology. Except for Clifford Geertz's brilliant small volume covering Morocco and Indonesia,[2] the comparative approach has not so far been attempted on a serious scale. In this book I also seek to make a contribution toward elucidating the relations between Islam and communism or Marxism, basing my investigation on studies of the two extant Muslim-Marxist regimes, Albania and South Yemen. Because the coming to power of these two regimes was intimately connected with the dynamics of guerrilla warfare, I was led to the main topic of the book—the theoretical and actual relations between guerrilla warfare and political radicalism in general and communism in particular, a subject that has been surprisingly neglected in comparative social history. Even a casual look at the inventory of radical revolutions that have taken place in the twentieth century will show that several of them happened as part of a guerrilla war against an occupying foreign power. Was this simply fortuitous? As I shall show, the answer is probably no.

The main body of the book consists of four case studies of guerrilla campaigns—in Albania in 1939-1944, in South Yemen in 1963-1969, in Algeria in 1954-1962, and in Afghanistan beginning in 1979. These provide insights on radical revolution, guerrilla warfare, and the connection between them. I shall try to outline a middle-range theory distilled from the cases of Albania and South Yemen and then test this theory in light of the facts relating to Algeria, Afghanistan, and additional case studies, some within the world of Islam and some outside it.

* * *

Thus, my interest is the comparative social history of revolutions and the relations between Islam and communism. There is, in the literature on the Middle East, an ongoing debate on the nature of these relations. In the 1950s, it was suggested that, perhaps because of their similar logical structure, Muslim societies were apt to embrace Communist regimes.[3] To the surprise of many, a generation later not much of this prophecy has come to pass, and there is now a tendency to suggest that Islam may be a bulwark against communism.[4]

Few people are aware that two Muslim societies actually did undergo a Communist transformation—Albania in 1944 and South Yemen in 1969. It occurred to me that these cases might yield some interesting insights about the processes by which communism may come about, and thus I was prompted to undertake this study. The outcome of my original foray into the extant documentation surprised me immeasurably. First, the processes leading to the formation of the Communist regimes seemed completely unrelated to the worldview or ideology of Islam. Second, the underlying structures of these processes in both countries seemed astonishingly similar—enough so that I was convinced that a theory about the connection between certain preexisting conditions and the resultant Communist outcome might be developed from these findings. Characteristics common to both countries were a deeply skewed class structure and a successful guerrilla war against a foreign occupier. A theory emerged: in part, that a successful guerrilla war waged by a society riven by class differences and conflicts is the type of situation likely to produce a radical, Communist, or Communist-like regime—exactly as happened in Albania and South Yemen.

Construing my findings as part of a general theory was entirely different from conducting a straightforward empirical historical study. A theory, or a generalization, must apply to cases other than those from which it has been extracted. This study therefore became a comparative one. In some cases—China and Vietnam—the same set of preconditions obtained as in Albania and South Yemen, and the results were similar. But I had also to take stock of cases that were ostensibly similar, but that resulted in a completely different type of regime. Of these, the most important were the Algerian war of independence and the 1930s Palestinian revolt. The Algerian war, in terms of casualties, was one of the largest and bloodiest guerrilla wars in history. Yet, contrary to the expectations of many contemporary observers, the sociopolitical regime that emerged was no more radical than a sort of Arab socialism, which is really a form of state capitalism. One major component vital to creating a radical regime out of a guerrilla campaign was missing in Algeria: Such was the penetration of the French into indigenous Algerian society that by 1954 no Algerian upper class worthy of the name existed; the upper class was virtually made up of French nationals. Another aspect of my theory concerns the connection between Islam and communism. I believe the evidence shows that Islam in itself is not a bulwark against communism. This assertion can be treated only indirectly in relation to Albania and South Yemen, as no Islamic resistance to the establishment of those two regimes was detected. In Afghanistan, however, the guerrilla war that began in 1979 provides an ideal case study for investigation of this point, as this has been a campaign against a Communist foreign occupier and a local Communist regime. Widespread opinion claiming that the Afghan resistance has been mainly or inherently Islamic is less than convincing; it seems better explained by the country's tribal social structure than by Islam.

Walter Laqueur, whose book on communism in the Arab world remains the most important treatment of this subject, argued in 1956 that, as Islam became increasingly less relevant as a competitor for people's souls, communism was becoming correspondingly more so.[5] Indeed, Laqueur reached the empirical conclusion that after World War II communism in the Arab world was becoming a force to be reckoned with.[6] Membership figures could easily mislead: In no country did party members number more than a few thousand— fewer than in some European countries (such as Austria), where the strength of the party was nevertheless considered marginal relative to other parties—but in the Middle East other parties were just as small as the Communist party.[7] Moreover, and significantly for my study, the membership of the Russian Communist party on the eve of the 1917 revolution was no bigger, relatively speaking, than that in the Middle East in the late 1950s.[8] Laqueur predicted an important role for Communist parties in the major Arab countries in the feverish days the Arab world was experiencing in the late 1950s and the 1960s.[9]

Sound as this analysis may have looked in the 1950s, the late 1980s brings a new perspective. After an unexpected and unpredicted resurgence of political, mainly oppositional, Islam, the Islamic worldview seems more potent today than ever before. Exactly what this means for the relations between Islam and communism in the long run is not as yet clear, but it is widely agreed that a major reason for the rise of radical Islam involves the process of socioeconomic modernization and its attendant predicament. In fact, some scholars conclude that radical Islam is borne of the failure of modernism in the Arab world,[10] but the validity of this view seems doubtful to me. It would be difficult to demonstrate the exact nature of this failure, and it is also not clear why such a realization should come exactly now. Rather, radical Islam appears to be the outcome of the economic problems that have been plaguing the world since the oil crisis of 1973. It cannot be only chance that exactly the same kind of coincidence between radical Islam and a particularly severe economic crisis occurred in Egypt in the 1930s. Extreme social insecurity and widespread suffering, resulting from a shrinking volume of economic activity, have led to renewed racist fascism in some Western countries, to religious fascism in others, and to radical Islam in the Arab world.

That extreme economic dislocations have led to the rise of radical Islam rather than to radical secular ideologies (such as communism) may be a source of wonder for the political philosopher and of despair for the leftist activist, but it is not (or should not be) too surprising to the social historian. Even in China and Russia, after centuries of bitter class struggle and rebellion in the countryside and decades of untold suffering for millions of people, the Communist party, employing only Marxist ideology, had not made much headway among the masses. Only after the class struggle was grafted onto the anti-Japanese national struggle—which amounted to something quite different in nature—did the party obtain a following. Perhaps there is some sort of mass psychological block against adopting a Communist ideology, possibly because of its open rebellion against the social order. As I will try to demonstrate in this book, radical left-wing solutions are likely to be resorted to only in a combination of unusual circumstances; they are rarely the free choice of masses of populations, even where large-scale repression is present.

* * *

Social revolution—a fast, violent, and total revolution that involves far-reaching changes in power and class relations—seems in recent years to have again become a subject unto itself. Whereas for many years it tended to be submerged in broader topics, such as violence and discontent, with the studies of Barrington Moore and Theda Skocpol it would seem that the "great revolution" has come back into its own.[11] In this book, I wished to place the revolutions I investigated in a wider theoretical context, so I sought in the mass of sociological theories on revolution those that would be fitting for the cases at hand. Among those theories, the best starting point for my purposes was Skocpol's States and Social Revolution. Less important for my needs, but quite useful, were the theories of Jeffrey Paige[12] and of Moore.[13] It is also necessary to mention in some detail the work of Rod Aya.

Aya's theory—possibly the most comprehensive sociological theory of revolution[14]—in which I find much that is commendable, is flawed by a fundamental problem. Aya's strong point is his rejection of the theories of those social scientists who see revolution as something exceptional and unusual (hence a little illegitimate), the work of small groups of extremists who have been unable to adapt to their surroundings. Although such scenarios cannot always be ruled out, Aya is correct in arguing that revolutions are regular and normal forms of political action; they can, and must, be analyzed for their causes, principles, and sociological significance. However, I cannot agree with Aya's most basic argument that a revolution is an open-ended conflict between two forces—open-ended in the sense that the act of revolution is to be separated from its consequences. He raises a historical problem of enormous importance, but his solution complicates rather than solves it. Aya justifiably notes that the truly radical changes brought about by the big revolutions were effected years after the revolution succeeded, and therefore it is problematic to see the revolution as consisting of these far-reaching changes. But this approach implies that a two-hour demonstration that changed nothing has the same meaning as a demonstration that started a revolution, such as the Russian Revolution.

Although Skocpol's theory is also unsuitable in various respects, it seems to me the most important breakthrough toward the sociological understanding of *actual* revolutions—an understanding that meticulously avoids the trappings of the versions of the revolutions' most loyal supporters and most ardent adversaries. I follow Skocpol's theory, in the first place, because I accept her definition of the term.[15] Social revolution is distinguished from coup d'état, from mere political shuffle that does not affect the class[16] structure of society, from revolution in the sense of value reorientation, and from similar concepts—all important and legitimate, but not the sense of social revolutions in which we are interested here.

A further important feature of the concept of social revolution as employed by Skocpol is the fact that such a revolution is by definition a *successful* revolution; failed social revolution is a contradiction in terms. A third point is that Skocpol treats revolution as a total event from its beginning to its successful completion and is not content with analyzing various elements of it, such as the cause for eruption. The rationale behind this consideration is that a revolution as a historical event is more than the sum-total of its various facets.

Unlike cases of revolt, insurrection, and collective violence, the number of successful revolutions has been amazingly small, a fact that has rendered their study by social science techniques quite difficult. Only the application of a comparative approach allows this topic to be treated as a serious scholarly pursuit.

Among the theories of revolution, an unusually popular one attributes revolutions to short-term factors such as relative deprivation, as in the common example of long-term economic development followed by a hiatus and downturn.[17] Although such analyses may be useful and important in explaining smaller eruptions, they seem woefully insufficient to deal with full-scale revolutions. Nor does it convince to claim that such short-term crises were observed in France in 1789 or in other notable cases just before a big revolution. Many societies have experienced such crises without an ensuing revolution. What is common to the big social revolutions—and which I find worthy of emphasis—is the existence of widespread and deep-seated discontent, borne of deep societal cleavages and class antagonism. Because special circumstances are necessary for it to succeed, revolution has to be treated as a category apart rather than as a revolt, coup d'etat, or collective violence that happened to capture power.

Most theories of revolution are characterized by an emphasis on reasons or preconditions for the revolution. Possibly as a revenge, Skocpol places strong emphasis on the special conditions needed for success. This may be viewed as the quintessential contribution of her theory.[18] She seems to neglect the social-preconditions aspect of the issue, apparently assuming these to be present in every society— an assumption that does not appear to me to be true. And in this book, I have considered it supremely important to keep an even balance between these two aspects of a revolution: the necessary societal background and the actual and practical ability to stage the revolution. Insistence on this balance of factors is not arbitrary or merely logical. Such a balance arises naturally from a study of the empirical cases and is likely to be relevant to other—possibly all—social revolutions as well.

Appropriate societal background, in particular, seems to be a strangely neglected topic in the study of social revolution. Yet, not every society in which tax appropriation exists is ripe for radical revolution. Rather, it seems that a revolution needs as a prior precondition an appropriate class structure, characterized by particularly deep cleavages and gaps. A situation in which there is a visible and personal process of exploitation of the lower class by the elite enhances such a possibility, and vice versa—that is, a society riven by class differences but in which massive economic exploitation is not obvious would be less sensitive to revolution. In any event, a situation in which the elite fulfills some tolerably objective function for the lower classes will tend to be less sensitive to revolution. I am aware of the inherently problematic nature of this statement, but I nevertheless believe it to be true: In the long run, and on the whole, masses of people know where their interests lie.

Marx notwithstanding, a close look at the social revolutions of the twentieth century will show that the major type of society that has given rise to social revolutions is one torn by agrarian cleavages. Is it possible that peasants are inherently better placed to rebel?[19] I can think of several grounds for replying yes. First, the presence of the government in the countryside is much weaker than in the cities. Moreover, the villager or tribal member in many countries, certainly within Islam, often possesses firearms, which are needed for protection in the normal course of (peaceful) life, and villagers—and certainly tribal members—are often expert in fieldcraft. Furthermore, at least in view of the empirical evidence available, the proletariat appears to have been "bought" by substantive progress in its level of living. In this regard, Paige goes one step further and claims not only that an agrarian regime of landlords and tillers is sensitive to agrarian revolt but that certain of these regimes are particularly so.[20] Paige's theory is also the only one that tries to predict the type of political regime that will emerge from the revolution according to the preexisting agrarian regime—a venture somewhat akin to what I am trying to do in this study in a different context.

According to Paige, every agrarian regime that is not capitalistic—that is, based not on income derived from capital but on income from the produce of the land—is bound to see severe friction between tillers and landlords, because the entire relationship rests on a zero-sum game: the more one party gets, the less there is left for the other. Especially prone to radical revolutions are those agrarian societies based on decentralized sharecropping, in which each individual peasant works a piece of land and is expected only to hand over to the landlord an agreed share of the produce.[21] For reasons that are not entirely clear, Paige limits this category to export economies—a restriction that is problematic because, in the first place, it excludes from the picture some radical regimes (such as Russia and China) that became so without substantial export sectors. On the other hand, some agrarian sectors seem to fit Paige's logic perfectly, yet no agrarian revolution took place in them. In fact, the Middle East is famous for its regime of decentralized sharecropping, which prevailed until the middle of the twentieth century.

Paige analyzes the case of Egypt in this context and points out that cotton did not lead to an agrarian revolution because it was grown in special estates under the close supervision of an estate overseer, who allowed the peasants no day-to-day independence.[22] This argument is convincing, yet one is led to ask why no agrarian uprising took place in Syria and Iraq, where grains were produced under entirely decentralized sharecropping, but which experienced something substantially milder than a radical social revolution. It is thus clear that Paige's theory, important as it is, can account only partially for social revolutions. It may help to locate situations in which agrarian eruptions are possible or even likely, but it does not tackle the problem of how such potentialities are turned into realities.

At this juncture, Skocpol's theory is particularly valuable. A revolution does not occur in every appropriate situation. When the political center is powerful enough, it is able to prevent a revolution no matter what the prevailing social structure; massive weakening in the structure of the central government is a precondition for the appearance of an alternative government. Such a weakening is exactly what took place in Russia—largely as a consequence of its massive defeats in World War I—and in France and China. Several variants of this theme are possible. In Albania and South Yemen, for example, the functional equivalent was great weakness of the central government to begin with.

That we are dealing with a combination of two factors (a particular type of social structure and an ability to revolt) raises a serious methodological problem. In the real world, there are varieties and nuances in class cleavages and class conflict, and in possibilities of action. One can envisage a state of "trade off" between these two factors: Sometimes possibilities of action may be particularly opportune, so that they compensate for a less socially polarized society.

Another aspect of revolution Skocpol examines is the process of its actual unfolding. What is striking about most, if not all, revolutions is the incompatibility between after-the-fact ideological explanations and what actually took place. There is a strong tendency to enhance the role of the leaders and an unwarranted downplaying of the role of the masses of supporters. I have found this to be true for the case studies of Albania and South Yemen, and it is equally true for most or all of the major social revolutions. Upon probing the secondary literature with this realization in mind, I found that only Skocpol's theory was sensitive to this point.

Indeed, one of Skocpol's theoretical breakthroughs lies in her argument that it was not only the revolutionary elites that made revolution.[23] Even those revolutions that appear to have been planned were in reality much more complex. Revolution is a subtle sociological process in which elite and masses interact. Skocpol demythologizes the role of the revolutionary vanguard, which is often portrayed as having really made the difference. Needless to say, revolutionary leaders were in communion in this with researchers. The truth is, however, that both were misled by the course of events into believing that everything was the leaders' making. It has aptly been said in this context that "revolutions are not made; they come."[24] In my own understanding, the crux of the matter is not that a revolution never proceeds according to someone's prior plans (which are also important), but that all sorts of political currents have their own scenarios for revolution and only one of these plans is actually put into effect. What are the circumstances that bring a certain plan rather than another to fruition? Crucial to a particular outcome is the often unconscious role of the masses.

All of these points are quite clear even in that archetype of vanguard revolution, the Bolshevik Revolution. It is surprising how the role of unintending masses in the making of this revolution has been underestimated or even overlooked. Lionel Kochan and Richard Abraham are sensitive to this point, though possibly not sensitive enough.[25] They underscore the fact that in the first stage of the revolution, the Bolsheviks, rather than leading the masses, were actually following them. After the February revolution, a low-level social revolution, which nobody created and nobody controlled, occurred throughout the country. It had two main components, one of which was the emergence of a large number of local people's councils, called soviets, which actually ruled the country, taking orders from no one:

> Elected, as they were, by workers in factories and soldiers in the
> barracks, the Soviets—and soon they spread across the length and

breadth of the former Empire—enjoyed much more prestige in the minds of the masses than the provisional government. "The provisional government", said one minister, "possesses no real power and its orders are executed only in so far as this is permitted by the Soviet of Workers' and Soldiers' Deputies, which holds in its hand the most important element of actual power, such as troops, railroads, postal and telegraph service."[26]

From the point of view of pure Leninist theory, it is surprising that one of the first acts of the Bolsheviks in power was to legitimize the power of the soviets.

The second main component of the self-propelled social revolution in the countryside was the large-scale seizure by village communities all over the country of all aristocratic estates. Again, although such an act was theoretically in conflict with avowed Bolshevik ideology, one of Lenin's first moves upon assuming power was to legitimize these seizures:

> This was seemingly the most far-reaching agricultural reform in Russian history. In actual fact it merely recognized a fait accompli. The peasant seizure of the land had been in full spate for months before Lenin spoke and would continue throughout the early part of 1918. It was a movement unchallengeable by any force that the Bolsheviks could conceivably have mustered. It expressed, as nothing else could have done, the dual nature of the October revolution. On one side, the Bolsheviks—on the other the peasants.[27]

In the same vein, sociologist Alvin Gouldner observes that

> The consequential revolutionary struggles of the twentieth century involved the peasantry as much or more than the proletariat. Clearly the case in the Chinese Revolution, it was also what happened in the Soviet Revolution. It was mostly the *peasantry* who, hating the war and yearning for land of their own, was the core of the Petrograd garrison which was the main fighting force that overthrew the Czarist government and who made the October Revolution. It was mostly the peasantry, concerned to secure its new lands, that was the core of the Red Army which thwarted the forces of the counter-revolution.[28]

But was the role of the vanguard party crucial to the seizure of power itself? Moore casts serious doubt on that possibility as well.[29] He analyzes the day-to-day unfolding of the events of the October Revolution and finds that Lenin's role in it was marginal. Lenin was in hiding when the workers in Petrograd arose and forcibly changed the guards at some key positions in the capital. When he emerged from hiding, all that was left for him to do was to order the further change of guards at some additional spots—hardly a master plan.

An opposing theory is proposed by Sidney Hook in his famous book on the role of the hero in history. Hook sets out to prove that this role is more substantial than is held by ardent social historians.[30] The main thesis is demonstrated in a chapter in which the role of Lenin in making the Bolshevik Revolution is treated as a test case. Hook sees Lenin's role as essential. Although the downfall of the tsarist regime was widely expected, nothing, according to Hook, necessitated a Communist revolution to the exclusion of all others, as is made evident by the fact that until ten months prior to the actual revolution no Bolshevik, least of all Lenin, would take seriously a suggestion that revolution was imminent in Russia, of all countries. According to their ideology, the Bolsheviks did not view Russia as a suitable place for a socialist revolution. When Lenin changed his view, he had to work hard to persuade his reluctant colleagues to accept his opinion. Hence, Hook sees Lenin as what he calls an "event-making personality."

I do not, however, find this convincing. Hook agrees that in the six months following the February Revolution a revolutionary situation came into being all over the country. He admits that Lenin in effect gave an after-the-fact affirmation for the rule of the soviets and the seizure of the land. Hence, my contention that Lenin merely jumped on a moving cart. He probably would never have survived in office had he not taken these measures. To ascertain whether Lenin qualifies as an event-making personality in Hook's terms, we must ask whether Lenin could have instituted in October 1917 anything other than a Bolshevik or similar regime. The answer seems to be decidedly no. The range of possibilities open to him was extremely narrow, circumscribed by the wishes of the masses. Lenin was a willing prisoner of the situation, rather than its creator.

What seems to happen in revolutionary situations—and this is an important point—is that the masses are confronted with a kind of supermarket of ideologies and corresponding elites. It is not that a certain elite succeeds in imposing itself on the crowd; rather, the crowd chooses an ideology and elite commensurate with its interests and whims at that particular moment. In the months just prior to the Bolshevik Revolution, the number of its supporters suddenly rose voluntarily and dramatically, although in the preceding years support for the Bolsheviks had been negligible. Why? Because only the Bolsheviks' ideological position allowed them to adopt the popular yearning to end the war. Millions of peasants willingly joined the Red Army (a vital precondition for the survival of the revolution), although for years they had shown no interest in Bolshevik ideology. Why? Because only the Bolsheviks were ideologically sympathetic enough to be able to live (for a while, anyway) with the wholesale seizure of aristocratic lands. Given a different situation in Russia in 1917, the crowd would have brought to power another elite, with a correspondingly different course for Russian history. Thus, there seems to be a close resonance between the needs and wishes of the masses in a revolutionary situation and the outcome.

* * *

I observed above that real social revolutions have been extremely few in the history of the world, and a good many of those were part of a guerrilla war. Why this paucity of social revolutions? This question has rarely, if ever, been squarely tackled. Theories of revolution have typically dealt with revolutions that actually did take place, but one exceptional study that approaches the problem from another angle—why revolutions do *not* occur—is Moore's massive *Injustice: The Social Bases of Obedience and Revolt.* Moore's study shows why avowed radical ideologies have had so little success and also underscores better than any other work some of the essential points that lie at the bases of most of the big social revolutions.

Moore starts by trying to identify some universal factors that create a sense of injustice. This leads him to basic human needs—his reference is mainly to physiological needs, such as food and drink— and failure to satisfy them may result in feelings of anger and betrayal.[31] These needs may be seen as innate in human nature, and their satisfaction a moral code that precedes human society. But part of this innate and universal moral code is also an outcome of social institutions. In most human societies, the social division of labor results in inequality; one aspect of this inequality is the creation of central authority, which exists in all but the most materially undeveloped societies. Moore claims that the relations between central authority and governed populace are also covered by this universal moral code, which delineates in general terms the rights and duties of both ruler and ruled. This means that authority is more than the monopolization of the means of coercion, although it is naturally that, too. The relations between ruler and ruled is governed by an implicit social contract, which defines what makes the rule legitimate—such as the major obligation incumbent on all rulers to maintain law and order. An additional obligation, probably of secondary importance, is to promote the well-being of the governed.

The most basic obligation incumbent on the governed is to obey the ruler's commands.

One-sided violations of this code are bound to create feelings of anger in the other side. Conversely, people in general, and not least in the lower classes, are likely to accept many hardships from a ruler who maintains law and order. In Moore's words:

> It is worthwhile observing that for very many human beings, especially the mass of human beings at the bottom of the pyramid in stratified societies, social order is a good thing in its own right, one for which they will often sacrifice other values. They detest violent and capricious interference with their daily lives whether it comes from brigands, religious and political fanatics, or agents of the powers that be. People will generally support, even if partly frightened into it, a political leader who promises peace and order, especially when he can do so under some color of legitimacy as defined in that time and place.[32]

For a revolution to take place, a prior feeling has to emerge that the ruler does not fulfill his part of the implicit social contract. The legitimacy of the ruler is seen as basic and natural, and for this to change, something drastic must take place at the level of individual psychology.

In principle, people have "moral autonomy"—the human mind is capable of acting independent of external pressures. But Moore marshals a substantial amount of evidence to the effect that in practice this autonomy is extremely fragile and limited; here he cites primarily the famous psychological experiments in which subtle social pressure brought to bear on individuals caused them to cast aside observations of their own senses. Moore is well aware that the incidence of factors that contribute to the promotion of moral autonomy or to the creation of blind submissiveness are anything but evenly distributed. The fact is that governments everywhere possess much more abundant means to influence the minds of the masses than do the potential opponents of authority.[33] Though Moore does not say so specifically, to my mind this analysis amounts to a general explanation for the rarity of revolutions in human history.

Moore goes on to describe the course of the modern German workers' movement in order to find out why no proletarian revolution took place in Germany, despite the presence of many conducive factors. Chief among these factors is the fact that German industry has been one of the fastest growing in Europe. As a background for this history, Moore summarizes the autobiography of an eighteenth-century peasant by the name of Ulrich Braeker.

Braeker had a supposedly benign patron, who sold him as a soldier to the Prussian army. Later in his life he encountered his patron, but could not feel anger toward him: "He could not bring himself to express his anger at a figure of authority who had betrayed him but had also treated him with paternal kindness. In miniature he revealed the classic block against a revolutionary response."[34]

Moore then reviews the activities and demands of the German working classes in the Revolution of 1848; in the Ruhr region in the decades before World War I; and in the major crisis following World War I, when Germany was on the verge of a socialist revolution. In each of these cases, he is surprised to discover that exactly the groups most likely to cherish revolutionary feelings shunned such feelings and demands altogether. What Moore says of the 1848 revolution seems to apply to all these episodes:

> The reader who has followed the argument of this book up to this point hardly needs to be reminded that in the human repertoire of responses to deprivation and injustice an aggressive counterattack is scarcely the one to anticipate as automatic and somehow "natural". Ordinary lower-class German townsmen in the middle nineteenth century had severe obstacles to overcome before they would perform revolutionary acts. In Germany at the time, as well as earlier and later, there was a widespread and deeply rooted tradition of loyalty and submission to constituted authority, especially authority with patriarchal overtones.[35]

In anticipation of Skocpol's theory, Moore is also fully aware that the collapse of the regime's ability to maintain a modicum of order is crucial to the occurrence of a revolution. He makes the importance of this factor especially clear in his analysis of the differences between the abortive German revolution and the Russian Revolution.[36] In Germany, despite the German defeat in World War I, the regime could still draw on the loyalty of many troops; whereas in Russia the revolution broke out when the guards would no longer shoot at the workers, because of the regime's complete loss of legitimacy with the masses. Moore makes it evident that revolution requires an extremely rare combination of circumstances.

* * *

In this book, I investigate one slice out of the broad range of revolutionary theory—the connection between radical revolution and guerrilla warfare. The radical revolutions of Albania and South Yemen each took place as part of a process of guerrilla war for national independence. Was this connection simply chance, or is there a deep-seated logic behind these events? I believe the latter alternative is correct. Guerrilla wars that take place in a certain type of society are likely to result in radical political regimes—that is, a guerrilla campaign carried out amidst a society deeply riven by class antagonism is likely, if successful, to lead to a radical left-wing regime.

The cases of the Albanian and South Yemeni revolutions highlight some weaknesses in the extant theories of revolution, such as in their explanations for revolution's initial eruption. In Albania and South Yemen, the revolutions broke out not in order to replace the ruling regimes, but to do something much more modest—to expel an alien conqueror. (In human motivation, the desire to get rid of a foreign ruler must be ranked with the basic human needs.) Only later, and somewhat unconsciously and unintentionally, was the struggle against the foreign rulers in these countries transformed into something else, which turned out to be a far-reaching social revolution. Nobody involved in the process—certainly not the masses at the social base—planned that transformation. The leaders, of course, had hoped for something of that nature to take place, but what decided the course of events was the special logic of the juncture of circumstances. At first, I thought that my study was of a new type of revolution, a sort of indirect revolution. But, in fact, if we ponder the true courses of the great social revolutions, it becomes clear that something similar happened in all of them. This was certainly true in the case of China's revolution. But even the Bolshevik Revolution did not really begin as the significant event it turned out to be.

What kinds of sociological mechanisms are activated within a society once guerrilla war erupts? This question has been almost totally neglected by scholars, with one notable exception: Ben-Rafael and Lissak's *Social Aspects of Guerrilla and Anti-Guerrilla Warfare*.[37] The authors categorize guerrilla wars in terms of two variables: open versus closed centers (the degree of influence of the periphery on the political center), and the level of "inflation of power" (the degree to which the center has to resort to actual force in ruling, because of deficient legitimacy). They hypothesize that guerrilla wars are especially likely when the center is closed and unresponsive to demands coming from the periphery, and when inflation of power is high.

Although Ben-Rafael and Lissak tackle squarely the connection between guerrilla warfare and political outcomes, I must take exception to their argument. Colonial regimes are, almost by definition, unresponsive to the demands of the periphery, inasmuch as the wishes of the center and the periphery are diametrically opposed. Moreover, I have learned from my study that, contrary to the argument of Ben-Rafael and Lissak, guerrilla wars often erupt in situations in which there is little inflation of power. In Albania and South Yemen, an important part of the explanation for the guerrilla campaigns' success is to be found in the feebleness of the traditional political centers. Moreover, Ben-Rafael and Lissak do not set out to predict (or explain) the actual outcome of guerrilla campaigns in terms of the nature of the resultant regimes. They offer Vietnam as a sole example of situations in which there is a closed center and a high level of inflation of power. Yet, Algeria would also qualify as such, though the outcomes in Algeria and Vietnam were very different. Was this difference a matter of chance and nothing more? As I will show, it was anything but that.

The more general literature on guerrilla warfare contains frequent references to radical implications, but the relevant factors are never systematically weighed. More often than not, experts mention the assumed connection between guerrilla war and radicalism only in order to dismiss this connection as a patent fallacy, citing cases that reveal no signs of social radicalism (Cyprus, Ireland; today, South Lebanon might also be added, especially the anti-Israeli Shiite guerrilla movement). But I propose that there are discernible rules by which to decide when a guerrilla campaign is in fact going to develop radical social aspects.

The theory I suggest starts with the argument that Islam is irrelevant in this regard. Islam as a religion or a worldview was not the crucial factor in deciding the fate of the revolutions in South Yemen and Albania. Comparison of these two cases with others outside the bounds of Islam enhances this impression immeasurably. What I see as crucial is a combination of preexisting social structure and the circumstances surrounding the war of independence. The fundamental rule appears to be that a successful guerrilla war waged in a society torn by deep-seated cleavage between landless peasantry and a ruling, landowning elite is most likely to give rise to a radical regime. Because of its style of life, a landed upper class is unable to take part in a guerrilla campaign. Such participation is extremely exacting physically, and it is also dangerous personally to members of the elite, who may be well known to the foreign ruler and thus easily singled out. So the elite leaves the arduous job of guerrilla war to the lower classes, who no doubt feel resentment.

Moreover, if the guerrilla campaign is an organized movement, it is likely to be led by a counter-elite from the middle or lower class, an elite whose members can and do take part. They cannot be easily detected and, in any case, have little to lose materially. Such an elite is likely to bolster its image and popularity among the people by degrading the ruling class. If the ruling elite's power is based on landownership, or on a similar mode of economic exploitation, the counter-elite is also likely to foster an attitude of delegitimization for that form of exploitation. If the members of this counter-elite are accepted because of their leadership in the guerrilla movement, their messages are likely to carry substantial weight in other matters as well, and the process of delegitimization of the traditional ruling elite becomes a straightforward process. It comes to be seen as a natural thing, something that people of moderate—rather than extreme—psychological disposition would find unobjectionable. The psychological block against revolution is in this way neatly removed.

A number of additional social characteristics facilitate this process. For example, radicalization in a society torn by class antagonism is most likely to take place where the control of the elite allows the lower classes a kind of "tactical autonomy"—day-to-day freedom to organize or be organized by sympathetic outsiders.[38] Because of striking differences between the social structures of the south and north of the country, Albania provides a clear example of this situation.

An additional precondition for radicalization—and for revolution in general—is a severe crisis that cripples the regime, or a far-reaching structural weakness in the regime, or both. It is especially here that the importance of guerrilla warfare in the sociology of revolution is apparent. The literature on revolution often cites as short-term precipitators natural calamities (droughts) and other sudden deteriorations in the position of masses of people, maybe particularly peasants (the French Revolution is a case in point). But the history of guerrilla warfare reveals another factor: It may be an improvement of the *ability to act*, rather than the increasing motivation to revolt, that truly detonates the revolutionary process. In their first stages, guerrilla movements crystallize formidable military power, but no one suspects political appetite or sensitivity, and therefore, no one tries to nip that power in the bud. When the ruling elite finally recognizes the political awareness of the new body, it is already much too late. This is why guerrilla war is a classic example of the birth and growth of an oppositional, contending regime within the womb of the old regime. Of course, the structural weakness of the ruling center is also important, as was the case in both Albania and South Yemen.

Finally, a revolution that comes in the wake of a guerrilla war can happen only under the leadership of intellectuals, an elite that can direct the course of violence and destruction into channels that at a certain point will again become constructive. This point—that all successful revolutions are led by a middle-class elite of intellectuals—has, of course, been noted in the past, but it seems to me that sociological analysis of what lies behind this factor is still curiously lacking. It is clear that, although guerrilla wars (even successful guerrilla wars) are not exclusively a twentieth-century phenomenon, no pre-twentieth-century guerrilla war has ever led to a radical regime. This difference is a result, not of the influence of Karl Marx, but rather of the appearance of a middle-class of intellectuals—people of wide-ranging education, a propertyless class, whose identification with a ruling class based on property is never assured, but which nonetheless might not be too difficult to buy off. Moreover, because of their superior education and lack of property, an incongruence in status is likely to characterize many members of this class. They are also likely to feel—consciously or not—that, in a political context based on strict economic equality, the relative advantage of education is bound to become a decided sociopolitical advantage.

The appearance of such elites around the world (and I consider people like Marx and other radical thinkers to be the outcome of this process rather than its generators) was a precondition for the twentieth-century appearance of radical regimes. I would also suggest that the relatively greater proclivity of such elites for radicalization in the less-developed countries in comparison to those in the West European and North American democracies has to do with the earlier democratization and liberalization of the latter—*before* the rise of the intellectual elite. The earlier bureaucratic governments provided their educated classes with a field for advancement and personal success. In the less-developed states, the legitimate role of this elite within the established government has been much more circumscribed and problematic—hence its tendency for radicalization.

It must be borne in mind, however, that the need for an intellectual elite as a precondition for radicalization is only a theory. And a look at the social history of individual countries reveals that every one—even the most undeveloped—has such an elite. Thus this factor cannot be used to explain differences in radicalization.

CHAPTER TWO

Guerrilla War and
Revolution in Albania

The Communist party came to power in Albania in November 1944, immediately upon the withdrawal of the Nazi occupying forces. This takeover was in effect a Communist revolution, albeit an indirect one, for it did not involve a coup d'état as in "normal" revolutions. The legitimate government, as embodied by King Zog, Albania's ruler, was outside of the country because of the war. Yet, by capturing power, the Communist party in effect (and, of course, before long also formally) deposed the king and totally disestablished the ruling elite, thereby instituting a new political and social order[1]. To understand this process of rise to power we have to go several years back[2].

ALBANIA BEFORE WORLD WAR II

Albania as a sovereign state had come into being in 1912, in the wake of the second Balkan war. The Ottoman Empire was shorn of its remaining European possessions, and fierce competition arose among Albania's neighbors to snatch chunks of territory for themselves. An international conference proceeded to solve the problem by creating an independent Albanian principality. Still, Yugoslav, Italian, and Greek competition to gain influence over and footholds in Albania proceeded vigorously after World War I, and Albania was not likely to be allowed to live its own life.

After World War I, Yugoslavia, Italy, and Greece resolved to bring about a partition of Albania. In April 1920, however, a popular rebellion broke out that thwarted these prospects, driving out an

Italian army of twenty thousand. This rebellion, in fact, won Albania its independence, and the country was accepted into the League of Nations at the end of that year. A National Assembly was convened, and Albania embarked on a seemingly democratic road—but not for long. In 1922 a tribal chieftain, Ahmed Zogu, was elected premier, but his subsequent rule was extremely unpopular and touched off a popular rebellion in 1924.[3] Zogu fled to Yugoslavia, only to return at the end of the year, backed by the Yugoslav army. He instituted a dictatorial government and in 1929 crowned himself King Zog I.

Albania between the two World Wars was considered the poorest country in Europe—so poor in industrial product that virtually everything had to be imported. Albania's poverty was partly a natural consequence of its geographic situation, but it was also partly created by the ruling elite, whose concern for the public interest was less than in other countries. As a British consular summary analysis of Albania's economic situation in 1934 stated,

> [The] situation is very bad and continues to deteriorate rapidly. State officials have not been paid for months. Even if most optimistic anticipations are realized in coming budget, upkeep of the armed forces alone will swallow 50 percent of total revenue. It is probable that before long [the] country will be unable to continue the struggle and Italian penetration will begin anew. . . . There are limits to the endurance of the worst nourished and most patient peasantry in Europe. I hear that the villagers of the Malakastra area have announced that if the tax-collectors make their appearance among them once more it will go ill with them . . . this movement of passive revolt is already spreading to Tepeleni and elsewhere.[4]

But although it is clear that grounds for grievance did exist in Albania at this period, there were no clear signs that a major radical revolution was imminent. Eruptions and insurrections were not lacking, but these were all of minor immediate importance; in none of these events was there a clear Communist involvement. The first of these incidents in the prewar years took place in 1932. In August of that year a hundred people were arrested for allegedly trying to topple the legitimate government. The British consul remarked that much discontent was building up under the soil in Albania, especially among the young.[5]

A second incident took place in August of 1935, when a number of people, led by some public figures, tried to foment public disturbances in the southern town of Fieri.[6] Later that same year, a former minister of the interior, accompanied by supporters, stormed a prison in the south and released three hundred inmates, with whom he started to move toward the capital. However, forces loyal to the government soon intercepted the rebels and dispersed them.[7]

In January 1939, a more significant incident took place. Several scores of students were arrested on charges of carrying out Communist propaganda. A month later seventy-three of them were brought to trial; nine were sentenced to prison terms ranging from five to ten years, and forty-two received shorter sentences.[8]

This was not the first time that communism had been mentioned in the context of sedition—true or alleged—in Albania in the 1930s. Already, in 1936, Communists were alleged to have been involved in workers' protests in the town of Korcha. The British consul described this episode:

> On the 19th February certain shoemakers in Korcha closed their shops as a protest against permission having been given for the opening of a shoe factory at Tirana. This was the prelude to a workmen's demonstration on the 21st February against the high price of bread. A further demonstration was staged later on the same day by students of the high school, which is partly run by French teachers and which is said to breed revolutionary ideas.[9]

The British consul, in remarks that I think are important, offered on this occasion a more general view on the place of communism in Albanian political life:

> There is a tendency in Albania to raise the spectre of Communism on certain occasions. It was mentioned in one responsible quarter as an explanation of the Kortcha business and more than one deputy referred to it as a danger in the last debate in the late Parliament on the 10th November. The suggestion is not entirely new but Albania seems an unfruitful ground for Communist propaganda. It is doubtful whether the alleged menace is spoken of from genuine fear of its existence or merely to supply an excuse for strong government on old-fashioned lines.[10]

Indeed, I believe that this is quite an accurate description of the situation. There is no sign that communism in Albania in the 1930s was any more successful than in other countries at that time. The success it was destined to attain just a few years later is not at all to be sought in the popularity of avowed ideologies but rather in a much more complex combination of factors. Discontent was attributed to malfunction of the system of government rather than to any deep causes calling for extreme and radical measures. Thus, the British consul in the town of Durazzo (Dures) commented in 1936:

> There is a widespread feeling of nervousness in Albania at the present time . . . discontent is almost universal, but no opportunity for legitimate criticism is afforded. The king himself said . . . after the Fieri outbreak that such occurrences must be expected in a country like this, but he does not seem to realize that they would be unnecessary if any legitimate outlet for the expression of public opinion was available. As it is, unless radical changes in the Government are made, which I fear is improbable, the discontent will be bottled up once more.[11]

SOME THEORIES ON THE RISE OF COMMUNISM IN ALBANIA

Several different approaches have been taken to the subject of why communism succeeded in Albania. Possibly the most important study in which an effort is made to come to terms with the historical problem of the Communists' rise to power in Albania is an article by Stephen Peters, in which he gives the following reasons for the takeover:

> The ingredients for the phenomenal success of the Albanian Communist Party were a combination of ineptness and lack of political acumen on the part of the prewar Albanian ruling elite; the tremendous organizational ability and ideological preparation of Tito's emissaries, who founded the Albanian Communist Party and guided it to success during the war; the skill, fighting spirit, and dogged determination of the Albanian Communists in preparing the ground for the eventual seizure of power, irrespective of the cost in human life and destruction to the country; the advent of the Red Army into the Balkans; and the failure of the Anglo Americans to formulate a fixed policy for postwar Albania.[12]

Peters places primary emphasis on the second factor on his list; the organizational skill of two Yugoslav emissaries of Tito. If this explanation is indeed as important as Peters claims it to be, how is it that Tito did not create four or five additional Communist regimes in the Balkans during this period? How is it also that the magic deeds of these mysterious emissaries are not mentioned in a barrage of wartime British reports sent by British liaison officers from inside Albania, many of which eventually found expression in Julian Amery's splendid book.[13] These British officers—probably the only more or less objective observers of the Albanian revolution—were by their own admission hostile to communism and everything that smacks of communism. Yet, they seem unusually dedicated to their task, putting aside their own convictions and reporting facts that often seemed to be painful to them. My intuitive methodological understanding compels me to lay much stock on such a source, if such a source admits that the success of communism in Albania was grounded in more objective factors—such as the gradual appearance of popular support for the Communists where none had existed before the war.[14]

Peters, as a vehement opponent of the Albanian Communist regime, ascribes its appearance to other-worldly factors. Enver Hoxha (pronounced Hoja)—Albania's leader for a generation after the revolution and the leader of the LNC (Front for National Liberation) from its inception—reasoning twenty-five years after the event, uses the same type of logic, only he asserts that it was the extraordinary skill and determination of the Communist leaders that made the difference. Hoxha also bestows some credit on the Albanian people, but only, or mainly, for having the brains to understand whom to follow and whom to recognize:

> The National Liberation War was a real people's war which was waged by the people and in the interest of the people. It ended with our victory over the external and internal enemies, because, from the ranks of the people and at the decisive moment, when the existence and their future were at stake, there came into being the Communist Party of Albania, the revolutionary vanguard of the working class, the reliable and wise leader of all the working masses. The creation of the Party and its emergence at the head of the people in revolt and of their liberation struggle, marked a radical turning-point in the historic destiny of Albania. The party gave the people a clear programme of action and showed them the only correct way to put it into practice.[15]

Such explanations may satisfy the "true believer," but they cannot, and should not, suffice for the historian who takes seriously his or her task of explaining in a causal way what happened in the past. And as long as there is nothing in the historical record to indicate that the Communist leaders of Albania were endowed with some mysterious special gifts, I refuse to believe that in them lies the explanation for the success of that Communist revolution.

ALBANIA'S ROLE IN WORLD WAR II

It may be useful to outline for the reader an important and relevant side issue—Albania's place in the Allies' war strategy.[16] Early in the war—in fact, soon after the German invasion of the Balkans—Great Britain toyed with the possibilities and prospects of general popular insurrections in various countries, Albania included. But this foreign initiative was never successful. Guerrilla warfare, when it began, did so through indigenous initiative and was obviously an answer to local needs. But when it was discovered that local guerrilla bands were active, however meager this activity was at the beginning, Britain strived to establish contact with them and encouraged them by offering supplies of war materials, clothing, and even cash. The only British condition was prior active engagement in actual guerrilla activities. Concerning Albania, it must be borne in mind that until the Allies invaded Italy, the British capacity for aid was severely restricted. First was the factor of distance. Provisions had to be dropped from airplanes, and such operations had to start in distant Cairo. The grave state of the war until at least Stalingrad and El-Alamein also made it very difficult for the British to spare war materials and human effort to a relatively unimportant spot like Albania. But as the war progressed successfully for the Allies, all this changed drastically, and especially so after the surrender of Italy in September 1943. The contact base for Albania was transferred to Bari, across the Otranto Pass, and Britain was then in a vastly better position to provision the resistance movement.

But the one precondition for receiving assistance remained unchanged—actual engagement in guerrilla activities. As we shall see later, in Albania a paradoxical situation had come into being: The Communist movement engaged the Germans and received British support, whereas Britain's avowed allies, the royalist and right-wing groups, failed to do so persistently and got nothing. In the conditions prevailing in World War II, survival came absolutely before ideology. In April of 1944, the British tried to do something about what was obviously an unhappy situation for them by parachuting into Albania a special mission sent to contact the non-Communist groups in order to induce them to join the armed struggle. But the McLean mission, evacuated half a year later, proved a failure, despite unquestionable personal heroism of its members. The leaders of the Right were now more preoccupied by the Communist LNC than by the Germans.

A final note is in order concerning Albania's global role in the war. Albania was one of the countries in Europe whose destiny was decided by its own people rather than by the big powers. Albania was not mentioned on the night Europe was divided by Stalin and Churchill into East and West.[17] Albania was not as important to the West as Greece was, and the West was not willing to take the trouble and send a military expedition there, as it did to Greece. Although such an expedition might have kept Albania for the West, such a landing would no doubt have resulted in a bloodbath. In any case, the impact of Albania's strategic position on its destiny is a classic example of the role of chance in history.

ALBANIAN GUERRILLA WARFARE IN WORLD WAR II

To truly understand why communism succeeded in Albania in 1944, it is necessary to analyze the circumstances surrounding the guerrilla war there during World War II. Albania is the most mountainous country in Europe, and it is not surprising that its inhabitants are ardent freedom lovers. Small wonder, therefore, that active, though initially intermittent and sporadic resistance to the Italians started soon after the occupation of April 1939. Most of the operations in the first years of the occupation were of little military value. An exception is the incident that took place in September 1943, when a partisan unit attacked the town of Leskovik in southern Albania, occupied it, and managed to hold it for fifteen hours in the face of large Italian reinforcements and aerial bombing. The operation ended with 160 Italian dead and substantial loss of military supplies.[18] But this event was unusual.

A new phase in the guerrilla campaign started with the surrender of Italy in September 1943, which was followed by immediate German occupation of the country. It was clear that Albania did not constitute an area of prime importance for the Germans, as only one strategic road, leading from Greece to the Reich, went through Albania. So the Germans were resolved to keep tight strategic control of the country, but their internal, political rule of Albania was quite lenient. For example, they practically left the countryside to its own devices and allowed free reign for indigenous institutions. In retrospect, this autonomy proved essential for the success of the Albanian revolution, although, of course, it would be naive to suggest that after Stalingrad and the entry of the United States into the war the Germans could have acted otherwise.

The Beginnings of the LNC

Within the Albanian resistance, the crucial date to consider was a year earlier, when in September 1942 a group of twenty people convened in the village of Peza, near Tirana, and decided to establish a unified guerrilla movement, which they named the Front for National Liberation (LNC—Levizja Nacional Clirimtare). Although until then the resistance was sporadic and disorganized, initially all political groups in Albania took part in this movement, and the political picture seemed on the whole idyllic. Glimpses of what had taken place first reached the British about nine months later,[19] and they received a first detailed report of events inside Albania only in July 1943.[20] At this stage, the guerrilla movement displayed no revolutionary nature: "Albanian unity is easier of achievement than is Greek or Yugoslav for 2 reasons: the Albanians are not politically minded by nature and they are still guided by the traditional, unwritten law which enjoins the closing of ranks against an outside danger, whether to family, tribe or nation."[21] The second reason supplied for the alleged lack of radical politics in the Albanian resistance was the extremely atomized nature of Albania, borne of the unusually mountainous topography. Nevertheless, the same report also contains the first revelation of the true nature of that movement, when it refers to the partisans' attitude toward the Soviet Union: "The one major surprise which resulted from our finding new sources of information is the pro-Russian sympathies of the guerrillas. In pre-war days the communist influence in Albania was negligible and the cause of the change is far from clear. It is certain only that it has taken place."[22]

However, before long it turned out that below the surface of the resistance movement bitter conflicts were well under way. These were mainly between the Communist party and its rivals on the Right, an organization called Balli Kombetar (National Front). In the middle of 1943 it transpired that the central bodies of the LNC were under Communist control. Moreover, most of the central figures of the LNC were also the leaders of the Albanian Communist party. How did this happen? Was it a result of a putsch, a purge, or some other special device? These are crucial questions to understanding the Albanian revolution. As far as may be ascertained from our sources, nothing of the sort took place. The LNC was initially a democratic body. Moreover, it is known that at the founding meeting in Peza, of the twenty people present only four were Communists.[23] Even later, when it became clear that most leaders in the organization were Communists, the official line was national and no more than national. As late as July 1943 we still hear that the LNC had important leaders of the Right, such as Abbas Kupi, who is reported to have initiated a congress in July 1943 to heal the differences between the Left and Right in the nationalist movement. Abbas Kupi and eight other non-Communists then published a proclamation to the effect that "the L.N.C. was pledged to fight for an independent and democratic Albania; it denied the charge of Communism, declaring that on the contrary it stood for private property and private initiative in industry. It opposed radical social change and wished the people themselves to choose their own regime."[24]

At the same time, the official newspaper of the Albanian Communist party carried a leading article that enhances the view that initially the Albanian Communists were neither seriously planning nor realistically anticipating to be in full control of the country at the end of the war. This article deserves quotation nearly in full:

> True communists and all the Communist Parties of the world are fighting today against Fascist slavery. Their aim is national liberation, and not the setting-up of the dictatorship of the working class. The Soviet Union, the great democracies of Great Britain and America, and all the invaded peoples suffering under the yoke of Hitler and Mussolini, are united wholeheartedly for the complete destruction of the pest of reaction. . . . In the struggle for the destruction of Fascism, our people are united without distinctions of class, religion, party or district. . . . The people, led by the Partisans and the Volunteers, are fighting shoulder to shoulder for the achievement of one single aim, which is the destruction of Fascism and the setting-up of a free and independent Albania.[25]

It is to be recalled that this view was in full agreement with the views expounded at the time both by Moscow and by world communism, the logic being that Communists throughout the world should enable the Soviet Union time to build itself from the inside without arousing the wrath of the capitalist world by fomenting strife everywhere.[26] Albanian Communists were then fully orthodox Marxists, and it was only a special convergence of circumstances that impelled them in the course of the next two years to take a completely different path.

A further indication that the process of disappearance from the LNC of the right-wing leaders was not caused by the machinations of the Albanian Communist party may be found in an episode from late 1943, as told by Brigadier "Trotzky" Davies, head of another British mission, the short-lived and ill-fated one to the LNC partisans.[27] Immediately after the mission was parachuted into Albania in late 1943, Davies conferred with the LNC's council, headed by Hoxha. The atmosphere was tense, and the discussion revolved round the prospects of an Allied invasion of the Balkans. Davies got the surprising impression that the Communists were wholeheartedly in favor of such an invasion. For example, Hoxha asked, "When will the Allies invade the Balkans and particularly Albania? It is important that we should know, we have many arrangements to make."[28] To this, Davies replied that he thought no such invasion would ever take place. The Albanians' response is described thus: "The Council was genuinely taken aback—they evidently thought that the invasion would come to their rescue. . . . My news came to them as a distinct shock."[29] Through hindsight, we now know that had an Allied invasion taken place, the Communist revolution would never have happened. If Hoxha nevertheless hoped for such an eventuality, I take it to mean that he still did not envisage that the guerrilla activities of his movement were going to bring him to power. Apparently he had no interest, therefore, in cleansing his movement of its political opponents. These observations enhance the impression that the process by which the Communists remained the only political factor in the guerrilla movement was a genuine sociological process, to be investigated and analyzed.

Thus, until about the middle of 1943 the LNC comprised all these shades in the political spectrum. It was only later, mainly in the course of 1943, that most or all of the non-Communists broke off with the LNC, accusing it of being a Communist front organization after all. But how could this happen in a country in which prewar communism was well known to have been of marginal importance? Surely the only feasible explanation is that the "nationalist" (that is, non-Communist) leadership remained en masse outside of the LNC. Those few who nevertheless did join consequently found themselves isolated and eventually forced to choose between adopting Communist policies and dropping out. As all of these nationalist leaders had a very strong stake in the ruling socioeconomic formation, there was no question of any of them adopting Communist social policies or even acquiescing to Communist leadership. So the process by which the LNC became a *purely* Communist organization is clear; the fundamental question (which I will address later) is why the nationalist leaders did not join the guerrilla movement from the beginning. But the fundamental fact remains that after about mid-1943 only the Communist-controlled LNC conducted true guerrilla warfare in Albania.

The Balli Kombetar

The Albanian Right did establish a military organization, however— the Balli Kombetar—in January 1943. All the people who were connected with the Balli Kombetar were in some way members of the prewar Albanian ruling elite. Most were big landowners like the organization's initiator, Midhat Frasheri, son of one of the founding families of Albanian nationalism in the late nineteenth century. Many a source defines the Balli Kombetar party as the party of the big landlords, or beys.[30] This body was from the start very reluctant to engage in active guerrilla warfare. Ideological explanations were not lacking: Balli Kombetar "was opposed to the sacrifice of Albanian lives and villages in active struggle against the Axis, and regarded the Greeks and the Yugoslavs as the principal enemy of Albania."[31]

Indeed, in Albania a situation came into being in which the guerrilla movement after about the middle of 1943 was completely under the leadership of the Communist party. One might expect, logically anyway, that if the nationalist leaders broke with the LNC merely because they abhorred taking orders from Communists, they would establish another guerrilla organization. But to the chagrin and dismay of the British liaison officers in Albania, it increasingly became clear that they were failing to do so. Hints of this only start to appear in the British reports late in 1943, the first in a report by Colonel McLean in which he describes the LNC: "Although it was comparatively weak among the backward tribes in Northern Albania, it was the strongest and by far the best organized group in Albania as a whole, had the largest number of both regular and mobile troops, and was the only party which was active against the Axis."[32]

Moreover, with the passage of time, it became clear that the Balli Kombetar was actually siding with the Axis. Suspicion of this was first pronounced in a report of September 1943,[33] and a few months later this suspicion became a certainty, as is made evident in the most important telegram sent out from Albania by Brigadier Davies, head of a British mission parachuted to establish contact with the LNC, in the winter of 1943. The telegram reads:

> I now recommend a change. The situation has developed recently so much that it is imperative now to denounce the Regency Council collectively and by name, also the Balkom [Balli Kombetar] and the Zogists. All are cooperating with the Germans who are exploiting them with arms in large quantities, setting them to guard main roads, police towns and lead patrols, thus freeing German troops. In all recent actions fought by LNC they have met mixed German/Balkom bodies, well armed and German-trained.[34]

A barrage of similar reports in 1944 included the following one from February:

> There is clear evidence that in South and Central Albania members of the Balli Kombetar are fighting with the Germans against the partisans, or, as they would doubtless put it, are availing themselves of German help to rid the country of the foreign communist poison—whether or not this is collaboration in the strict meaning of the term, there is no doubt that the Germans derive considerable assistance from the Balli both in their drives against the partisans and in the policing and administration of cleared areas.[35]

In the course of 1944, the Balli Kombetar further deteriorated and became a byword for "collaboration": "This term [Balli Kombetar] describes a loose organization of conservative landowners. In the south its forces are being used as purely government gendarmeries. In the centre and north it has ceased to exist as a coherent party and its name is apparently notorious throughout Albania for its collaboration."[36] In addition, the Albanian politicians who collaborated with the Germans and agreed to rule Albania in their name were all Balli Kombetar people or from minor groups very close to it. For example, Rexhep Mitrovica, the first German-nominated prime minister, was an active member of Balli Kombetar.[37] The following was observed on the occasion of the nomination of Fiqri Dino as prime minister, in July 1944: "In general the only bounds uniting the members of this cabinet seem to be fear of the L.N.C. and a desire to maintain the existing social order in Albania. The Germans have found their most willing collaborators from among the older politicians, business-men and the Catholics of the Shkodar district."[38]

The problem of collaboration between Albanian leaders and the Germans has to be discussed at some length. What could push such people to commit acts that could so easily be construed as treason of the first order? It might be suggested that we are talking about greediness, or maybe corruption, or possibly uncontrollable lust for power. But none of these explanations holds. These leaders, most of them anyway, were beyond moral reproach in the usual sense. All of them were ardent Albanian patriots who devoted their lives to the Albanian cause—people such as Mehdi Frasheri, a former high-ranking Ottoman official and prime minister in 1935, one of the foremost leaders of Albania in the interwar period and now one of the heads of Balli Kombetar;[39] or Shevket Verlace, also a high-ranking Ottoman official, one of the first prophets of Albanian nationalism, and the first Albanian prime minister after the Italian invasion. The power of both these figures was clearly based on land. In fact, Shevket Verlace was at the time the biggest landlord in Albania; as such, he had "always been hated by progressive elements in the country as a powerful representative of the Bey class."[40] These people were no smaller lovers of Albanian independence and freedom than were the Communist leaders. The road to collaboration with the Nazis was a tragedy imposed on them by the circumstances. These words are not meant, of course, to absolve these people morally or legally, but only to help clarify the sociological situation prevailing in Albania during World War II.

The Success of the LNC Partisans

Political life in Albania during 1943 became intensely divided between Right and Left, with the specter of civil war always in the background. In the long run, such a situation favored the Communists, who had all along been active against the Axis. In numerous activities during the first nine months of 1943 they managed to eliminate most of the Italian presence in the southern countryside. Their success brought them glory and even a growing number of supporters. At the same time, this army was forged by the fire of real battle and became even more skilled. Indeed, a comparison of the views voiced concerning the technical qualities of the partisan army during 1943 and then during 1944 show that a drastic change occurred over that year. In 1943, British officers called the partisan soldiers "a thorough band of rascals of no fighting value whatsoever,"[41] but by May 1944, their estimation was different: "The fighting qualities and skill of the Partisans have greatly increased, and they are now capable of resisting German drives and undertaking co-ordinated offensive action. . . . Partisan strength and numbers are rapidly increasing."[42]

In fact, the LNC partisans had become a serious regular army and, by the middle of 1944, completed their occupation of the south of the country. A short while thereafter the Germans launched what was the biggest military operation in wartime Albania, involving three German divisions, to dislodge the partisans from their positions. The story of that campaign is told in outline in a British intelligence report:

> In the Korçë region the Partisans held their own; the Fourth and First Brigades, and also the Seventh, foiled a German drive southward from Elbasan and westward from Korçë. The Seventh even captured the castle of Berat, but was unable to occupy it for more than one day. The Sixth Brigade fought with particular heroism, and beat off all German attacks on the coastal zone for some five weeks. . . .[43]

This description makes it quite clear that by mid-1944 the partisan army had become a formidable force, far outweighing any other internal force. Long, arduous, but victorious guerrilla warfare had helped forge a strong popular army. The traditional elite, which was unable or unwilling to take the field against the Axis, was unknowingly committing suicide.

In the last four to five months before the end of World War II in Albania, marked by the German pullout in November 1944, the self-confidence and audacity of the LNC partisans grew apace with their popularity. Their numbers and strength increased, and they began to constitute a real threat to the Germans, as is indicated in a British report of September 1944:

> There has recently been a marked increase in the scale and range of operations carried out by the LNC forces throughout Albania indicating a growing confidence in the strength of their arms. The German barracks and posts in Tirana and Elbasan have been assaulted with success; heavy fighting is continuing in Tirana itself and in the immediate vicinity with many desertions to L.N.C. from enemy Turkestani troops and gendarmerie.[44]

And in a report from the same week we hear that "resistance by L.N.C. is steadily reaching its peak. Actions against German garrisons and lines of communications. . . have been sustained. The accumulated effect upon the position of the Germans is appreciable."[45]

Success breeds success, and the victories of the LNC drew to it ever-growing numbers of youths. A cable sent in September 1944 stated, "L.N.C. 12th Brigade who recently liberated coastal area south of Valona are reported to be making a favourable impression on the local populations by their good behaviour. This has resulted in large influx of recruits for service with L.N.C. brigades."[46] This cable gives a clue to the means by which the Communists were attracting Albanian youths: good treatment of the population. There are, in fact, a great many other indications that, contrary to what might have been expected, the Communists did not force themselves on a reluctant population but were rather willingly accepted by a large section of it. This is why the takeover by the Albanian Communist party may properly be called a social revolution. And what is crucial in terms of methodology is that this conclusion is not derived from self-interested sources, but from reporters who viewed the process in dismay, if not with downright disgust. The key factor in the mounting popularity of the Communist party was the fact that it was the only force to raise the banner of popular resistance to the enemy, rather than any sudden conversion of the Albanians to a "true" Communist sociopolitical ideology. An inkling of what was actually taking place may be had from the McLean mission's report:

> Most of the regular partisans are young men, students from the towns or peasants. Many well-known Nationalist leaders have sons or nephews among the partisans. All are full-time soldiers, volunteers, working without pay, and their discipline is very strict. To any young Albanian who hated the Fascist Italians or the Nazi Germans, the L.N.C. was the only organization which offered him the opportunity to fight for his country. Thus, the Communists have become associated in the minds of the Albanians with the struggle for liberation.[47]

Another report makes these points even clearer:

The number of true Communists is almost impossible to estimate. About 10% of the members of the L.N.C. are "Stalinist Communists." . . . About another 15% are probably half conscious of the aims and organization of the Communist Party, but would again blindly obey its orders. The remaining 75%, although calling themselves Communists, have little idea of the aims or organization of Communist Party. Although at the moment they blindly obey its orders, they would probably not be regarded as "politically sound" by the Communist Party. The average Partisan, while admitting with pride he is a Communist, believes he is fighting for an independent, democratic, popular Albania.[48]

Tens of thousands of freedom-fighting youths were attracted to an army forged in the furnace of battle against the Germans; thus, the LNC command was a revolutionary government in the making: "The L.N.C. is militarily by far the strongest party in Albania, politically, and administratively the most highly organized, and at the same time the most active against the Axis. It has by far the largest number of mobile regular troops and its military value is higher than any other group in Albania."[49] Small wonder that the few royalist forces that stood in their way did not constitute a match for the Communists. When the Germans evacuated Tirana in November 1944, the Communist takeover was almost a smooth transition: in October, the LNC had declared itself Albania's government and just waited for the Germans to leave.

Who were the youths who joined the LNC in such massive numbers? And what were their reasons for doing so? One important social group from which youths were drawn was the city intelligentsia. In an early analysis depreciating the military value of the partisans, this was explained as follows:

Since the Albanian has long been noted as a warrior, this suggests that the "young salaried class"—more versed in ideologies than warfare—forms a considerable part of the Partisan forces. This class is inclined, like most of the small-town "intelligentsia" in the Balkans, to rigid doctrinaire politics, an absence of political tact, and a communism based less on understanding of Karl Marx than on a frustration born of the inability of their backward countries to provide the honours and recognition, and with them the salary, to which they feel themselves entitled.[50]

This report—if we discount its obviously racist overtones—may well contain a true and basic reason for the success of the Communist partisans. No doubt, however, groups such as this "intelligentsia" exist everywhere, not just in Albania, so this analysis is a partial explanation at best.

There were other sources of support for the Communists. A report from the beginning of 1944 concerned the difficult position of Albanian government employees. These employees had no land that could nourish them in bad times, but their salaries had not been paid since Italy's surrender in September 1943. As a result, it was judged "small wonder that many of this class should join the Partisans."[51] It is not surprising that a great many people from all classes joined the partisans because of governmental policies, which were notoriously lacking in wisdom. For example,

> Though including a good many peasants, the partisans have also been joined by an "appreciable number" of the young salaried class, such as school teachers and municipal employees. This exodus from their jobs must have assumed large proportions, as the Germans issued a notice that all employees absent from their jobs after 15 December [1943] would be treated as deserters.[52]

Thus, whereas formerly youths would go sporadically to the countryside and engage in one or two actions, government harshness now induced them to connect their lives with the LNC indefinitely. Such severe treatment of the populace by the government contrasted sharply with treatment by the partisans. In July 1943, for example, it was reported that "the Albanian guerrillas now make a feature of attacking government storehouses and distributing to the population the grain which these contain. In South Albania they have also forbidden tax collectors to collect any revenue for the government."[53]

Undoubtedly, the Communists also used intensive methods of propaganda. One British liaison officer made a special report on these. It is clear that the Communists were not losing time in educating their supporters in the "right" direction. Their task was no doubt made easy by the fact that the Albanian ruling class was on the whole collaborating with the enemy, so it was not hard to associate national war of liberation with war against the old ruling elite. It is quite evident that by late 1944 the LNC's supporters were willing to follow their leadership's track on social policies and not only on questions of liberation and independence.[54]

The guerrilla war that had started in the Albanian deep south some years earlier reached its watershed in June 1944. The LNC then completed the liberation of the south and reached the Shkumbi River. North of the Shkumbi the LNC had no influence at all; that area was entirely under the control of the traditional elite. With the crossing of the Shkumbi in June, a civil war ensued and a true revolution started.

NORTH AND SOUTH

At the beginning of 1943, there were three social elites in Albania: One was the new Communist elite; the other two were the constituent parts of the prewar ruling regime—the big landlords, or beys (now organized mainly in the Balli Kombetar), and the leaders of the large tribal confederations in the north. To understand how and why power passed from the old elite to the new, it is necessary to look at the Albanian social structure in geographical and historical terms. The starting point is a somewhat curious geographical fact: Until late in the day—that is, until about the middle of 1944—the partisan movement of Albania was concentrated solely in the southern part of the country.

In Albania, the terms "north" and "south" are a very clear-cut, geographical as well as historical, expression: They mean north and south of the River Shkumbi. This river is the traditional dividing line between the two ancient groups of tribes of which the Albanian nation is composed—the Tosks in the south and the Ghegs in the north. The British liaison officers were aware of the geographical differences between north and south and understood quite well the reasons for them. From a report written in late 1943, we get an inkling of what the British made of the situation:

> The Southern Albanian or Tosk is quicker, more educated, and has had more contact with the outside world. Southern Albania is organized on a feudal basis with a comparatively large number of young students of peasant origin in the towns and villages. Here the Partisan movement under left wing and the Communist intellectuals has made great progress.
>
> In central Albania, in the area of Dibra-Tirana-Mati, the tribal and feudal systems intermingle. The majority of chiefs have joined up with the "Nationalists" in their area, but sometimes they have joined the Partisans or allowed control to pass direct into the hands of the commissars.[55]

There is no doubt that we touch here on the real nub of the argument advanced in this book—that absentee, big landlordism gave the southerners a will to overthrow this regime and the tactical autonomy that enabled them to put it into effect—and must now go into the matter of the Albanian north and south in some detail.

Geography, History, and Sociopolitical Structure

Apart from the Albanian coastal plain—which until the revolution was for the most part swampy, heavily malarial, and hence very sparsely populated—the country is very mountainous, although the northern part is much more so than the south. The major difference between the populations of Ghegs in the north and of Tosks in the south has consisted, in recent centuries, in the fact that for ecological and historical reasons the ancient tribal social structure has been preserved almost intact in the north, whereas in the south this structure has all but disappeared. There is no doubt that one fundamental reason that northern Albania remained tribal until modern times has to do with geographical conditions. Although the south is also mountainous, the northern Albanian Alps are the least accessible mountains in the entire Balkan peninsula— almost idyllic for the preservation of an ancient social order.[56] The effect of this fundamental factor was augmented by historical factors.

Perhaps the most important historical process was the intensive, often violent eradication of indigenous institutions by Ali Pasha of Yanina, the famous ruler of Epirus and southern Albania from 1788 to 1820.[57] Ali Pasha, whose lust for power apparently knew no bounds, exerted tremendous efforts to destroy all vestiges of political power not contingent upon his own authority. He mercilessly dispossessed local chieftains, and the thousand or so estates that he possessed were apparently mostly obtained by doing away with these chieftains. Further, he brutally assaulted the autonomy enjoyed by some towns and villages and, if opposed by force, sometimes reduced such places to ashes. An example is the small town of Nivitza, which he could only occupy by deviously attacking when the inhabitants were in church at Easter time. Leake narrates the fate of this town and two neighboring villages:

> Nivitza and the two villages are now little better than ruins; their lands, divided into portions, are numbered among the Pasha's *tjiftliks* [sic, for *chiftliks*, estates]: and it is for the use of those who cultivate them that the Pasha has built the new village of the Forty Saints, while many of the inhabitants of Nivitza have been sent to labour on his farms near Trikala in Thessaly.[58]

Leake has no doubt that the massive drive of Ali Pasha to destroy all traces of local political autonomy and independence caused southern Albania to become subservient to central Ottoman authority more than at any time previously. Neither Mehmed the Second—the "Conqueror"—nor any of his great successors had achieved in Albania more than superficial control by playing one chieftain against the other, whereas Ali Pasha eradicated all of them.[59] The effects of Ali Pasha's activities on the social structure of southern Albania were understood as early as a mere generation after the event. The traveler Tozer, who was in southern Albania in the middle of the nineteenth century, has this to say about the town of Argyrocastro:

> Many of the houses here are of stone, and strongly built, having been intended to serve as private fortresses, for the system of *vendetta* raged nowhere more furiously than here. Though it has ceased now, it even survived the time of Ali Pasha, who in other places was so successful in putting down the local chieftains, that he may be said to have first brought Albania into subjection to the Porte.[60]

Northern Albania is an entirely different story. In the north the ancient tribal system remained very much alive into the present century and has given rise to quite a few famous ethnographic descriptions. In 1929 Carlton Coon still claimed that the Gheg area was traditionally organized. The population was divided into ten tribes, the most important of which were Dukagin, Luma, Mati, Dibra, and Mirdita. Each tribe was composed of hierarchically ordered sociopolitical organizations, starting with the basic unit—the extended household living together and forming a social and economic unit. Above the household was the village, comprising several households. In contrast to the south, where most villages were nucleated, in the north the rule was dispersion—most households lived quite apart from each other.[61] Above the village came the *bairak*, about which Coon says the following:

> Above the village is the *bairak* (Turkish for banner, standard), a geographical area with some kind of natural unity, so that the people living in it habitually see more of each other than of those without. All of the village councils meet together for the *bairak* council under the *bairaktar* (standard-bearer), or head of the *bairak*. His office is hereditary in certain families. King Zog's father was *bairaktar* of Mat, the principal *bairak* of Mati.[62]

The *bairakdars* were the key figures of the tribe. Coon says of those *bairakdars* who entertained him that they were "great feudal leaders, maintaining large households of armed men, and dispensing lavish hospitality to all comers."[63] Above the *bairakdars* stood the head of the entire tribe; in most tribes, the post was hereditary within one family.

Coon observed the structure of Gheg society within the context of Mirdita, the most important and powerful tribe of northern Albania. Mirdita played a crucial role—although a negative one—in the Albanian civil war that led to the Communist takeover. It may, therefore, be of some use to examine this tribe in some detail. In the nineteenth century, the Mirdita tribe already saw itself as a principality[64] and the traditional term by which the head of the tribe was designated was *capitan*, more than just a chieftain. In the post–World War I period, no sooner had Albania attained its independence than the Mirdita tribe revolted in September 1921 and declared itself an independent republic.[65] On the government of the Mirdita, Coon says,

> The tribal government was in the hands of the prince and his council, which consisted of all of the elders of the tribe. . . . The council met in cases of murder within the tribe, of intertribal warfare, invasion, or other crises involving violence. . . . The strength of the prince as compared to that of the council depended on the former's personality. . . . Jon Markajoni, the incumbent in 1929, [was] a man powerful enough to maintain the tribal system in defiance of the central government, to have his men exempted from military service and taxation, and to exact from Ahmed Zog an annual stipend in return for which he would keep his men quiet.[66]

This prince, Jon Markajoni, well exemplifies the extreme divisiveness of the northern leaders in the face of the formidable Communist power in the final phase of the civil war. Every region and tribe was geographically, hence politically, intensely autonomous and independent, extremely loath to bow its head to external authority. This meant that in a moment of mortal danger the old Albanian elite was unable to unite. Jon Markajoni, who could raise the largest anti-Communist army in Albania, was the most ardent collaborator with the Germans. Abbas Kupi, who tried to establish a united anti-Communist army with the vitally necessary backing of the British, was naturally unable to cooperate with Jon Markajoni. This divisiveness made the Communist takeover easy. In any case, a united front of the old elite would not have fundamentally made a difference; it would only have turned the Communist takeover into a bloodbath. The crucial fact as far as the final outcome is concerned was that the northern "nationalist" leaders had no army worthy of the name because they had not taken part in the actual armed struggle.

A final question in relation to the social position of the northern tribal leaders involves their political and economic position vis-à-vis their tribespeople—that is, to what extent their overlordship was based on class and coercion. What prevented the emergence in the north of full-scale peasant communities was the severe and mountainous nature of the terrain. The region enjoyed an abundance of precipitation, however, so that rich mountain pastures were not lacking, and it seems that this richness gave rise to a much more distinct ruling class than was the case in other, poorer, tribal, or lineage, societies.

Traditional leaders in several areas were losing their traditional positions to new upstarts, whose power was based more on force than on traditional legitimacy. Thus, in a 1944 report from the northeastern area of Prizren, it was observed that

> Outside the towns in this area, such as Prizren and Gjakova, the social organization is on a tribal and patriarchal basis, and leadership is in the hands of local chieftains. These are often, but not always, the Bajraktars. In former times, under Turkish rule, the Bajraktars were always the leaders, but since then many of them have lost their position of leadership through weakness or incompetence, and stronger men have risen up and taken over the power—although the title of Bajraktar remains hereditary. Cen Elesi, for example, is not a Bajraktar, but his father was a strong and able man and raised his family to be the most influential in the district. All members of a family owe allegiance to the head of the family, but when the head of the family dies his position is not necessarily taken over by his oldest son, but by the ablest and most energetic of the family.[67]

No less important was the fact that even in the north there were important feudal enclaves, where the population was ruled by powerful beys. An example was the region of Mati, where "all power, military and otherwise, was concentrated in the hands of four powerful bey families."[68] Thus, a certain amount of class concentration certainly was present in northern Albania. Nevertheless, true classes were obviously lacking, and the artificial effort of some Marxist anthropologists to impose class and exploitation on a segmentary society such as the one in northern Albania seems very dubious.[69] At least one member in the Central Council of the Albanian Communist party in 1944 maintained that there was not much behind the talk of a revolution in the northern part of Albania, as the position of the tribal leaders was not based on a stark and far-reaching exploitation.[70]

Nevertheless, economics were no doubt involved. When Tozer visited Orosh, the seat town of the prince of the Mirdita, in the mid-nineteenth century, he found a ruler living in great wealth; among the prince's possessions were 800 oxen and 1,300 sheep.[71] In the Albanian context, such wealth meant a great deal of political power. Between the full-scale class societies of capitalist countries or of bureaucratic empires and the egalitarian segmentary societies of arid zones in areas such as the Middle East, Albanian highland society occupied a middle point. The deadly terror with which the Albanian tribal leaders viewed the prospects of a Communist takeover was based on rational appreciation of some basic social facts. However, there is no sign in the extant sources that the tribal leaders of the north were losing legitimation amidst their own people.

Agrarian Regimes

The natural regions into which Albania may be divided—the north, the coastal plain, and the south—have had distinct agrarian systems. In the north, the land regime was quite simple and straightforward: Land was owned separately by households, and there must have been very few substantial landlords. The coastal plain was the classic feudal region, a regime that, according to Busch-Zantner, already existed in Albania in the Middle Ages and survived into the twentieth century. One factor in the survival of the medieval Albanian aristocracy was its massive conversion to Islam. Owners of the largest latifundias of this region were the families of Toptani, Vrioni, Vlora, and Frasheri. Along with the great tribal leaders of the north, these families provided most of the leaders of pre-Communist Albania.[72] The usual settlement pattern in the coastal plain was the estate (*chiftlik*). Because of malaria and highway banditry, there were almost no villages in this region,[73] and it has been reported that even in the twentieth century people traveling along the coast have preferred to go by boat rather than take the dangerous land road.[74]

As the coastal plain was so undeveloped and sparsely populated it was the south that was the true peasant area of Albania. Landowners in the south were smaller than those in the coastal plain, but because of the density of its population , the south may be considered the main area of big landlordism. A good early-twentieth-century account is that by Constantine Chekrezi. Concerning central Albania (a transitional area from the north to the south), Chekrezi says:

> Generally speaking, the people of this region enjoy a democratic independence, as a result of the freehold system of land ownership, despite the fact that the largest landed estates, the principal of which are those belonging to the Toptani and Vrioni families, are situated in this region, inasmuch as even on those estates the land is held in the form of perpetual leases, the right of evictement having become obsolete.[75]

It is also worth mentioning that part of the big estates in this region were forcibly seized by small peasants in an agrarian revolt that took place in July 1914.[76]

Chekrezi goes on to speak about the south proper:

The basis of landownership is the freehold, and the class of independent yeomen is very numerous. Most of the land belongs, however, to the great landowners, Beys and Pashas, who have received it as fiefs from the Sultan, especially for meritorious services rendered in war and peace. The land is leased by them to the peasantry, in the form of perpetual leases. The right of eviction has become obsolete, but the exactions of the landowners have proved disastrous to any agricultural development. Usually, the lessee is required to turn over to the landlord one third of the produce.[77]

This picture is corroborated by the account given by Bourcart, who notes that agrarian domination by the Muslim beys in the south became somewhat less onerous when in the nineteenth century these landowners began to receive government positions in Istanbul and elsewhere, thereby becoming absentee landlords. For the traditionally freedom-loving Albanians, this arrangement was particularly suitable.[78] Still, on the eve of the revolution about two-thirds of all agricultural land in the south was owned by a group of only 165 families, who altogether owned 213,000 hectares—an average of 1,290 hectares per family. The biggest of these landed magnates, the Vlora and Vrioni families, each owned 60,000 hectares, and the Toptani owned some 50,000 hectares.[79]

As is evident from Chekrezi's account, the agrarian system in the south was based on *métayage*, or sharecropping.[80] The essential factor in this system that rendered it potentially revolutionary was the combination of, on the one hand, the semblance of security of tenure and, on the other, heavy exactions of rent. Another crucial element in the southern land regime was the fact that the landlords were always absent and were unable to intervene in the life of the peasants on a daily basis. The conditions for revolutionary organization by the peasants were ideal.

Urban Life

Although it seems quite evident that the roots of the Albanian Communist revolution are to be sought in the southern countryside, the urban south also played a role. Despite the nearly total neglect of the south in prerevolutionary ethnographic literature, there are indications that urban life there was more developed than in other parts of the country. Because the entire Communist elite of Albania hails from this sector, the paucity of sources is unfortunate, but

Chekrezi (himself a native of this region) comes to our rescue. His account has a prophetic ring about it:

> Curiously enough, writers on Albania have paid but the scantiest attention to this portion of the country, which is the most progressive, the most educated and civilized, and most likely to exert a high degree of moral influence over the rest of the Albanian people. If it is true, as some are wont to believe and say, that the people of Northern and Central Albania are not as fully developed as the average inhabitants of the Balkans, the people of Southern Albania stand assuredly above that average. . . . Here is to be found also the enlightened bourgeoisie, merchants, businessmen, independent freeholders and landed gentry, as well as the class which will be called upon to govern Albania. The progressive, and thoroughly European, city of Korcha, and the towns of Valona, Arghyrocastro . . . will bear comparison with any city and town of their class in the Balkan. The palatial mansions of Korcha are not to be found except in the Balkan capitals.[81]

Education was certainly more widespread in southern towns. Korcha and Argyrocastro, the two main towns of the south, each had more primary schools than other big towns in Albania even those with larger populations.[82] Enver Hoxha was a high school teacher in Korcha, having completed his higher education in France.[83] What is the explanation for this relatively high state of development of southern urban life in Albania? As there was no exceptional large-scale trade, mining, or industry in the area, the towns must have developed as service spots for the agricultural sector. Once again, the inevitable conclusion appears to be that the revolution's real roots were in the southern countryside.

THE FINAL STAGE OF THE REVOLUTION

We now resume the narrative of the Albanian revolution. As we have seen, an important factor in the success of the Communists was the failure of the nationalist leaders to join the armed struggle against the Germans. This is a complex issue. To what extent was this eventuality dictated by the social structure of the country?

In 1944, a substantial part of the British war effort in Albania was directed specifically at rousing the northern Gheg leaders to raise the banner of revolt. The story of Colonel McLean's mission is told by Julian Amery, one of its members, whose admirable account is, in my view, one of the best books on the sociological aspects of guerrilla warfare.[84] The McLean mission was dropped in the area of control of Abbas Kupi, one of the most important tribal leaders of the north and a well-known supporter of Britain. Kupi was a high-ranking gendarmerie officer at the time of King Zog. In 1943 he broke with the LNC, and as he was an important tribal leader of the Kruja region, it was estimated that he could easily bring in to the field five thousand warriors or more.[85] But nothing of the sort happened, and the McLean mission was dropped specifically to induce Kupi to take the field and convince others to do the same. The mission crisscrossed northern Albania on foot, moving from village to village, trying everywhere to persuade the tribal chieftains to join the armed struggle.

The position of the northern leaders was that they would be ready to do so only on the condition that Great Britain would guarantee in advance the return of King Zog to power after the war. This demand, however, contradicted the British policy of giving support only *after* a group had joined the guerrilla campaign. Also, at this late stage of war the British were quite reluctant to recognize King Zog, for to do so would certainly provoke an all-out war between the Allies and the partisans and, in fact, necessitate an invasion of Albania by the Allies. Thus, the northern leaders remained adamant in not taking the field; they would not go to war just to make life harder for the Germans. This is not a mere interpretation: Nationalist and tribal leaders often said this in plain words. Typical was the large meeting of the beys of Mati that was organized to meet with the mission. The beys' position was very clear: They had learned the lesson of Italian and German reprisals and were not going to expose their properties again to any serious risk. They were willing to revolt only if full success was assured in advance.[86]

The stalemate that was created was suicidal to the northern leaders, for while they were marking time, the LNC was gaining strength daily, numbering by June 1944 some seventy thousand warriors.[87] The partisans held the entire south and crossed the Shkumbi River, thereby declaring a civil war against the nationalist elite. This elite immediately amassed its entire force and hurried to stop the partisans. The northern leaders faced an insoluble dilemma: On the one hand, they could not let the partisans go further and take the whole country. But fighting the partisans would bring on them the enmity of the Allies. The British, however, made strenuous efforts to prevent civil war and went so far as to warn the LNC not to penetrate into the north; they even withheld supply drops to the partisans for two weeks. But the British threats were rebuffed vehemently by the partisans, who relentlessly pushed northward.

Small units of partisans were held back for a short while by a haphazardly organized army, but on the whole the standing ability of the northern armies was poor. They were never able to unite and engage the partisans in a major battle. When the final partisan offensive started on August 10, 1944, it found each northern leader isolated in his own traditional area of domination.[88] Abbas Kupi made defense preparations in Kruja with an army of two thousand men.

A last-minute effort to reverse the tide was made by the nationalists on August 18, when a large delegation of old-regime leaders, headed by the prime minister, Fiqri Dino, came down from Tirana to confer with the McLean mission, in camp with Abbas Kupi. They offered to join immediately the anti-German guerrilla forces in exchange for British arms and aid in stopping the advance of the Communist forces.[89] While these proposals were cabled to Bari, Enver Hoxha did not lose time. It was not as yet clear whether the Allies would land in Albania or not. Therefore the LNC moved to demand the withdrawal of the British liaison mission from Kupi's camp. Hoxha, furthermore, threatened to capture the liaison's members and court-martial them. However, this crisis ended with the partisans' withdrawing their demands.

All the while the partisans were pushing forward. The Kruja region itself was conquered in late September, and Kupi's army was easily dispersed. Kupi and the McLean mission retreated in the direction of Scutari. A few days later Albania's fate was sealed when the Allies finally decided to recognize only the LNC and to cut off relations with all other forces in Albania. In the same month, November, the partisans reached Tirana, and heavy fighting went on between them and the German garrison. In the course of the month the Germans decided to pull out, and Albania's capital and all but scattered areas in the north were in Communist hands. The Albanian revolution was now a final fact.

Some questions remain unanswered. Again, why did the traditional Albanian elite not take part in the anti-German guerrilla activity? An important explanation is found among the documents on which this study is based—important in that it is cast in terms of social structure:

> It is fundamental to the problem that the Nationalist leaders who represent the existing social order can only maintain operation in so far as they can adequately protect their society against enemy reprisals. Failure to provide protection leads either to the rejection of the leader by society or to the radical modification of the social order on which the leader's power is based. Since the road network of Albania leaves very few natural safe harbours where the

supporters of the Nationalists could seek protection with their moveable wealth, it follows that small-scale guerrilla actions by Nationalists are bound to be much inferior to those of L.N.C. Because in contrast to Nationalists, L.N.C. leaders do not base their power on existing social order but rather on its dissolution and lacking the responsibilities of territorial or tribal influence enemy has the advantages of mobility.[90]

This explanation is central to the argument I advance in this book. It is not that the areas under the partisans were not sensitive to terrible reprisals—indeed, they were. A report from Albania, dated February 1944, said in this regard:

> The extent to which South Albania has been devastated during the war is evident from a recent Tirana broadcast enumerating the towns and villages of the Korca prefecture that have been either partially or totally destroyed. Hardly a single village of note appears to have been spared.[91]

Moreover, an intelligence report from the summer of 1944 described the German antipartisan activities in the south as devastating as far as the civil population was concerned and not ineffective: There was large-scale collaboration between villagers and the Germans in reporting partisan movements.[92] But the leaders of the resistance in the south were, for the most part, anonymous people, lacking property and social standing. In contrast, the tribal leaders in the north were much more sensitive in this regard, as the burning of a village belonging to their clan would be devastating to them personally and certainly to their authority. The members of the Albanian landed elite were all living with their families in Tirana, or in other major towns, and were well known; participation in the guerrilla resistance would surely have led to their ruin, personally and economically. Also, these people were used to a very luxurious way of life, and it would have been impossible to them to sustain the hardships of guerrilla war in the mountains.

A good glimpse of the life-style of the Albanian elite, even in the worst days of the war, is provided by Julian Amery's account of his secret visit, in September 1944, to Tirana, where he conferred with two members of the Vlora family. The meeting took place in an atmosphere of luxury, and the host, Nureddin Vlora, "was resplendent in white ducks and a white silk bush shirt."[93] He described to Amery in the darkest possible terms his fears of the partisans, adding that "life in the mountains has made some of these boys rather rough."[94] He went on to speak about "his fears of violent revolution and the destruction of the 'cultured classes.'"[95]

Why were the Communists so successful in enlisting popular

support in the south and so abysmally unsuccessful in the north? The answer lies in the socioagrarian structures of the two regions. We have seen that in terms of daily life, elite control over the peasants in the south was nonexistent. The elite lived in the towns or cities, and peasant communities were virtually free—though they had many grudges against this elite. In the north the opposite was true. Tribal leaders lived among their people, and nobody could so much as raise a finger without their consent. These theoretical considerations find ample support in the sources. When Julian Amery had to pass through the hostile territory of the prince of the Mirdita in 1944, he knew full well he was taking a big risk, and, indeed, he barely escaped with his life. But the situation in the south was much more relaxed. When the cumbersome mission of Brigadier Davies was dropped there in the winter of 1943, its members moved around in the terrain without any hindrance; there was no indigenous leadership to molest them.[96] This tactical freedom allowed the Communists to enlist supporters in the south freely. In addition, they had some ideological "merchandise" to distribute in the south, whereas in the north they could not operate at all.

CHAPTER THREE

Guerrilla War and Revolution in South Yemen

In the last decade or so, the importance of the south Red Sea region in world affairs has markedly increased, as has the interest of the superpowers in the states and regimes there, mainly because of the political destabilization that has plagued the area ever since the revolutions in South Yemen, Ethiopia, and Iran.[1] In this chapter I will analyze the case of South Yemen, which, like Albania proves that under certain circumstances Islam and communism are not incompatible.

South Yemen attained its independence on November 30, 1967, after a rather bloody struggle for independence that lasted for about four years. Britain's last troops were evacuated from the area on that same day. Although Britain had announced its intention of evacuating Aden in February 1966, it did so only on the grim realization that it was not going to be able to retain Aden in the face of mounting nationalist feelings. Moreover, the process of withdrawal was quite disorderly, meaning that effective power was left to whoever was able to capture it. When the smoke lifted, it turned out that power had been seized by the National Liberation Front (NLF), a guerrilla organization of which little was known at the time and not much is known even today. The avowed ideology of this organization was pan-Arabism, with large doses of Marxism. In fact, it was known that during 1965 and 1966 Marxist activists attained majority in several conventions of the NLF, and it is quite possible that in 1965 Marxist ideologies came to predominate within the leadership of that organization, at least in numbers of adherents. In June 1969, this Marxist group, usually referred to as the secondary leadership, overthrew the established leadership of South Yemen. As far as is known, this coup was not a late-night maneuver by a small number of individuals and a small army contingent but was a political struggle that was democratically decided—"democratically" meaning that the majority within the NLF supported the revolutionaries. After June 1969, South Yemen moved rapidly into the fold of the Eastern bloc and became a Marxist country.[2] The South Yemeni revolution thus clearly qualifies as a radical social revolution.

This revolution and its outcome has often led observers to view the region as a wrestling ground for the two superpowers, in which the states in the area are but passive peons. Today, to some extent, such a view may not be entirely erroneous. But the history of the revolution in South Yemen shows that often the truly epoch-making events were an outcome of intersocietal dynamics rather than of the superpower conflict. South Yemen in 1988 is an (almost) integral part of the Communist bloc, and it is possible to receive the impression that this is just another incidence of the domino theory. However, a minute investigation of the making of this revolution will show that the reality was vastly more complicated than this.

To analyze what happened in Aden is to be engaged in a classic case of after-the-fact wisdom. Anyone looking at Aden in 1950 would find it difficult to imagine that this piece of colonial paradise would turn in a matter of a few years into one of the worst colonial traps on earth. Aden looked like a second Hong Kong, a place whose people miraculously forgot the game of politics—certainly the feelings of nationalism. Indeed, Aden really appeared to be the classic case of benevolent domination. British presence brought a large number of jobs in the fueling business and many more thousands of jobs with the transfer to Aden of British Middle East headquarters later in the 1950s. This move of headquarters proves better than anything else that the British saw a bright future in Aden.

But whoever expected Aden to remain like Hong Kong made a terribly wrong calculation. It is true that there are several points of similarity between the histories of the two cities.[3] Both were important nodal points in the vast nineteenth-century British commercial empire. Aden was captured in 1839, and Hong Kong was acquired just two years later, in 1841. And though the two spots filled a somewhat different economic function for the British empire (Hong Kong was an emporium for the trade of China; Aden, a coal bunkering point), the two cities developed in quite similar fashion: Foreign presence brought substantial volumes of business, and the two cities were in an almost incessant state of economic growth. They drew immigration at a pace known in few other places. But there the similarity ends. The crucial difference is that after World War II

Hong Kong became overwhelmingly a place of refuge for those fleeing the Communists in mainland China. A majority of the people of Hong Kong have reasons to fear the date 1998, when the colony is to go back to China, and there is little doubt that they would rather remain under British rule. No such, or similar, logic obtained for Aden. There was no real reason to suppose that South Yemen alone in the Arab world (or in any other part of the world) would accept its political captivity. However, even if projecting that South Yemen would not remain quiescent forever was not particularly difficult, projecting the rise of a Marxist regime there was another matter altogether.

THE MODERN HISTORY OF SOUTH YEMEN

To understand what made such a development possible, it is necessary first of all to acquaint ourselves with an outline of the history of South Yemen in modern times,[4] beginning with the conquest of Aden by the Ottoman Turks in 1538. The Turks occupied Aden for a century. Their interest in Aden was purely military; they had no commercial motives and no desire to turn the region into a political part of their empire. So the area was left entirely to its own devices, and there was no change in local institutions as a result of the Ottoman period of domination. South Yemen, as part of Yemen, gained its independence from the Ottomans in 1640. In 1729, Aden became independent of Yemen when the prince of Lahj rebelled and broke loose from the imam's domination. The rest of the area of South Yemen was effectively a large desert, intercepted here and there by oases, where human habitation was possible because of the water source. There were many such oases, but they were thinly scattered over a large country, with vast stretches of desert in between, so that no one before the nineteenth century even thought of uniting this culturally homogeneous area into one state.

The crucial date in the making of modern South Yemen is 1839, the year Great Britain captured Aden by force. The introduction of steam navigation in the 1820s had made it urgent for Britain to find a convenient halting point between England and India, where coal might be loaded onto ships. Aden was a natural choice, as it was situated about midway and had an unrivaled natural harbor. In light of the international balance of power obtaining in the early nineteenth century, these advantages were more than enough to seal Aden's fate.

Aden's transformation into a coaling station on the road to India marked the beginning of a very brisk development over the next century. At several points, the pace of this development was further boosted by international technological advances, such as the opening in 1869 of the Suez Canal, which resulted in a great increase in the volume of navigation passing through the Red Sea and the Indian Ocean. The consequent growth of business in Aden was enormous. During this time, Britain showed no interest in Aden's hinterland, as it was very sparsely populated and held no promise as a market for British industrial goods or as a source of raw materials for the British economy. This situation changed somewhat in the 1870s, with the beginning of renewed Ottoman interest in Yemen.

The Ottomans, in fact, had shown new interest in Yemen in the first part of the nineteenth century. In 1849, they took Hudaida, Yemen's important port city, and continued to strive to expand their possessions in the country. In 1873, they managed to overcome Dhali', a principality usually considered to be part of South Yemen. This development alerted the British to the importance of the hinterland as a buffer zone against any threat from the north and induced them to reconsider their relations with the twenty-odd principalities, or sheikhdoms, of which the South Arabian hinterland was composed. In the ensuing years, the British signed a series of protection treaties with these principalities, whereby Britain undertook to guarantee external defense in exchange for which the principalities were to refrain from ceding any part of their territories to any foreign power. These treaties, in effect, turned South Arabia's hinterland into a protectorate, without a proper annexation of the territory.[5]

With the conclusion of World War I, the Ottoman Empire was no more, but its place in the north was now taken by a no less aggressive opponent—the imam of Yemen, who viewed South Yemen as an integral part of Yemen and made no secret of his resolution to repossess it, by force if necessary. So the interwar period in Aden was politically a matter of British efforts to keep the imam at arm's length from Aden—if possible, without Britain being dragged into a land war, which it could hardly afford at the time. Incessant diplomatic negotiations yielded no fruit: The disagreement was very deep. The imam insisted on negotiating the fate of the entire area— anathema to the British, who wished to discuss only the question of borders between North and South Yemen.[6]

As these negotiations dragged on, the British developed means to make their arguments more persuasive. They introduced the Royal Air Force into the area as an effective arm of policy,[7] actually part of a broader policy to transform South Arabia from an area ruled only nominally to one under real control. No authorized body decided on this policy, which was enacted by Bernard Reilly, Aden's governor (1931–1940) in the interwar period. Deployment of the Royal Air Force, after its first use during World War I, was a key factor. In the past, opposition forces (such as bedouins) had been able to adopt most technological devices used by ruling governments, but in this case the British had a decisive advantage. So, after lengthy deliberations, Aden's security responsibility was transferred to the Royal Air Force in 1927.

Expansion into the hinterland was a natural consequence. Proper deployment of an air force meant that targets could be bombed that were situated a long distance from Aden; thus, the principalities of the hinterland became vital areas—for example, for purposes of intelligence. Also, planes in those days could fly only short distances without refueling, so that landing strips had to be built in many places and friendly government assured in the areas of the landing strips. The first test of the new weapon came in 1928, when the imam sent his officials to collect taxes in the principality of Dhali', a bone of contention between Yemen and great Britain since World War I. A few bombings of North Yemeni forces in the area were entirely effective in driving the imam out of Dhali' for good.

At the same time, Aden's place in the British empire was enhanced as its commercial importance grew and as India—from which Aden had been governed since 1839—approached its independence. In 1937, the final step was taken in making Aden independent of India, and Aden became a crown colony, providing further incentive to augment the ties with the hinterland. Beginning in 1937, a series of "advisory treaties" were signed between Great Britain and the principalities of the hinterland. These treaties were intended to introduce the "resident advisers," officials who would live in the principalities and represent the British government on the spot in a tangible way. But aside from the advisers, the complete autonomy of the various principalities remained unaffected. This was not, however, the case in Aden itself, where self-rule was almost nonexistent, and everything was decided by the high commissioner and his staff.

After World War II and India's independence, the original reason for Aden's conquest may be said to have disappeared, but there were still excellent reasons for continued British occupation of the area. Ever since the turn of the twentieth century, oil increasingly had replaced coal as ships' fuel. And as the major source of oil in this period was the Gulf, Aden was again favored, by its proximity to the source of oil, and became a major port for refueling. Moreover, in the rapidly shrinking British empire, Aden was still a place strangely uninfected by the germs of nationalism, and as the British were expelled from Kenya in 1954, Aden was their sole surviving colony in the area. The British Middle East Command was hurriedly transferred to Aden, a veritable colonial pearl: Its economy was booming because of its bunkering facilities, and in 1958 it was second only to New York in the number of ships calling for services; Aden's airport became the busiest in the British empire. But just as the situation looked rosy as it never had before, the entire edifice began to crumble.

Trouble may be said to have started with the establishment of the Federation of South Yemeni Princedoms in 1959 and the joining of Aden to it—contrary to the wishes of most of Aden's inhabitants—in 1962. The idea of turning the twenty-odd principalities of the hinterland into one federal state originated in the 1940s and was picked up again in a more rigorous way in 1954. After 1954, a real effort was made to put the idea into effect, as British officials sensed the mounting demands for independence and self-rule throughout South Yemeni society. The logic was, no doubt, that if Great Britain was going to relinquish tight control of the area—at some unforeseen time in the future—control would best be left to a viable and strong state, a friendly regime, rather than to a series of weak and defenseless princedoms unable to stand on their own feet. The monarchical nature of the regimes of these principalities must have commended themselves particularly to Great Britain—not least, perhaps, because for all its social conservativeness, the rule of the shaykhs seemed to be rather mild and to enjoy a wide measure of legitimacy. Time was to prove that this last assumption was quite unfounded. From Britain's point of view, the federation was also the best solution to the question of what to do with Aden itself. Aden in a federal state ruled by royal regimes and effectively controlled as to defense and foreign relations by Great Britain would ensure Aden's important position in Britain's global interests.

The idea of the federation met with strong opposition from most political groups in Aden city, who viewed Adenese society as much more "progressive" and developed than that of the "backward" principalities. The subordination of Aden to the conservative regimes in the hinterland threatened to take Aden back in several respects, not least by sharing its relative economic prosperity with the wretchedly poor principalities. Many of the princes themselves were initially not very keen on the federation, considering the fact that they stood to lose some of their autonomy. But eventually most of them understood that such a structure would profit them in the long run, and in 1959 the federation was at last inaugurated, at first with six participant princedoms, most of the rest joining in later.

The issue of Aden's joining the federation was then tackled. There was fierce pressure from the British government and fierce opposition from, especially, the new political groups that had emerged in Aden after World War II—a salaried middle class of officials, teachers, trade union activists, and the like. However, the political power of these groups was still limited. To the British, they were nonexistent, as the British recognized only the traditional elite of the Adenese business community. This elite eventually yielded to pressure, and Aden officially joined the federation in 1962. But the tranquil and innocent days of the past were definitely over. Aden's streets were hotly nationalist, and in the eyes of this nationalist group, the virtual forcing of Aden into the federation was a blow of major proportions. It cannot be fortuitous that the actual anti-British armed struggle started about a year later.

SOUTH YEMENI SOCIAL STRUCTURE BEFORE INDEPENDENCE

Detailed examination of the process leading to independence and radical revolution has led me to the conclusion that this chain of events remains entirely unintelligible without fully taking into account the preexisting social structure—in this case, South Yemen was actually two separate entities: the port city of Aden with its immediate hinterland; and the countryside, consisting of vast areas of half-desert, inhabited mainly by tribes, with some peasant and town populations. Although all the area was culturally homogeneous, Aden and the countryside developed in completely different ways, and it is necessary to separate the discussion accordingly.

The various components of this social structure were intimately interconnected, so that the functioning of one institution hinged on what happened to all the others. Ideally, I should describe all of them at once, which is, of course, impossible. To overcome this hurdle, I shall briefly set forth a short outline of the whole picture and then pass to a more detailed account of the constituent parts.

There were three main social and political elements— tribespeople, townpeople, and government. Quantitatively, the tribespeople predominated. Ecological conditions were of primary importance in explaining the functioning of social institutions. Rainfall in the entire area was so meager as to allow only the most marginal sown agriculture, except in several oases dispersed over the area, which allowed patches of intensive agriculture and the existence of small towns. The tribes lived between and on the outskirts of the oases, in austere subsistence that did not allow anything more than tribal social organization involving tribal law, feuds, complete political and military independence for the individual tribe, and frequent intertribal warfare. All these institutions look like indiscriminate violence to the uninitiated observer and may have appeared to be a state of anarchy to the distant government, but these are obviously an outsider's view. To the tribes, all this was normal functioning of their institutional traditions.

The extremely warlike social structure of the tribes, coupled with their near-subsistence economy, meant first of all that the state in South Yemen had to be an extremely feeble creature. This was so because the tax base was exceedingly small and those from whom it had to be extracted possessed the physical means to resist that extraction. Only the rudiments of a centralized state appeared in South Yemen. What we find is a series of twenty-odd principalities, each an exemplary type of lilliputian state.

In a situation such as this, in which a centralized state barely appeared, the small towns that could exist in the oases had a severe problem of adaptation—in fact, of survival—in the face of the hostile and violent nature of the tribes. How were they to cope with this problem? It seems to me that the answer is provided by the most characteristic social institution that appeared in South Yemeni urban society—living saints.[8] Saints appealed to tribal members' innermost fears of the supernatural and the irrational and deterred the tribes from storming the towns, even though the towns did not possess the physical force to keep the tribes from doing so. These saints are the "sayyids," descendents of the Prophet Muhammad, who emerged as the ruling caste in South Yemeni society. This was the general political structure in traditional South Yemen, and the mutual expectations of the various groups were appropriately structured. When, in the 1930s, the activities of the British government worked in the direction of undermining the position of the sayyids, this soon led to the weakening and eventual collapse of the entire structure.

South Yemen is a semiarid zone stretching from the Indian Ocean in the south to North Yemen and the terrible desert of Rub al-Khali in the north. Precipitation in this region is meager—50 millimeters per year, which does not allow for the existence of permanent settlements. Permanent habitation is possible only in the few oases where a reliable water supply is to be found. Hadramawt, part of eastern South Yemen, is somewhat exceptional, as Wadi Hadramawt is, in effect, one elongated oasis of some 500 kilometers.

The wadi receives floods originating from the monsoon rains in the mountains of North Yemen; these floods also create underground reservoirs, and, in addition, the wadi receives any rainfall that passes through the area. Consequently, Wadi Hadramawt allows for intensive agriculture and is strewn with a substantial number of villages and towns—all encapsulated within its narrow, wall-like edges. Because of intensive exploitation of water resources upstream, the last 100-kilometer stretch before the wadi reaches the sea is totally barren and devoid of habitation. This magnificent and unique oasis is completely detached from the outer world—with important consequences for its sociopolitical development. Because of the special geographic and ecological circumstances prevailing in the wadi, a full-scale civilization of high material culture was able to develop there—but only in miniature. In the 1930s, the population density in the wadi, which supported about a quarter of a million inhabitants, was already considered much too great for comfort.[9]

In relation to the ecology in this region, people lived in tribes and in towns. Towns grew up in the oases, and in the 1930s three or four had ten to twenty thousand inhabitants (Shibam, Tarim, Sey'un). Most of the tribes lived in villages, on subsistence agriculture, augmented by stock breeding and camel transportation.

The Tribes

Segmentarism. The social structure of the tribes in South Yemen was based on what is called in the anthropological jargon "segmentarism." This is a type of organization in which a central government is missing. Order is maintained through a division of each social unit in half; each half opposes, contains, and balances the other. The first discussion of this type of organization is that by Evans Pritchard in his Nuer study. In another study, he lucidly defines such a system:

> The tribal system, typical of segmentary structures everywhere, is a system of balanced opposition between tribes and tribal sections from the largest to the smallest divisions, and there cannot therefore be any single authority in a tribe. Authority is distributed at every point of the tribal structure and political leadership is limited to situations in which a tribe or a segment of it acts corporately. With a tribe this only happens in war or in dealings with outside authority. . . . There cannot, obviously, be any absolute authority vested in a single Shaikh of a tribe when the fundamental principle of tribal structure is opposition between its segments, and in such segmentary systems there is no state and no government as we understand these institutions.[10]

More recently, the system has become publicized through the studies of Ernest Gellner on the High Atlas in Morocco. Gellner claims he found segmentarism to be the most important political institution permeating the tribal society of the High Atlas. To critics (such as Clifford Geertz) who claim that segmentarism is a construct imposed by the scholar on real life,[11] Gellner retorts that although it is possible that in other places the reality was much too complex to be dubbed simply segmentarism, the Moroccan High Atlas was special:

> The general features of such segmentary societies, with their diffusion of power and the maintenance of order by the opposition of groups to one another at all levels, are well known. The only remarkable thing about the Berbers of the central High Atlas is the degree of perfection to which they have brought the system. They approximate more closely to an ideal type of segmentary society than do most other societies of this kind.[12]

What then, were the main characteristics of this nearly-ideal type of segmentary society. I have already mentioned one such characteristic—balanced opposition between tribal segments. This characteristic finds practical expression in the position of the chief. In the High Atlas his position was characterized by extreme weakness; he was a "lame duck," to use Gellner's expression.[13] The chieftainship was elective, annual, and rotating, which meant that if a tribe were subdivided into three clans, the chieftainship went every year to another clan, and the particular chief was elected by members of the remaining two clans only.[14] It is indeed easy to envisage that under such conditions chiefs were bound to be very weak.

In South Yemen in general and Hadramawt in particular, the situation was substantially different. Hartley, who studied the Nahid (sometimes called the Nahd) in the early 1960s, expressly says that the basic structure of this tribe was segmentarism, albeit incomplete segmentarism. Moreover, he claims that this was true for the entire Hadramawt.[15] Each group of the Nahid, at every level of tribal hierarchy, was subdivided into two opposing groups, but this neat structure existed more in theory than in fact. In reality, conflict and opposition permeated the relations between all types of groups, irrespective of their tribal positions.[16] Feud, the key institution in every segmentary system, operated differently in Hadramawt than in more-perfect segmentary societies, in which feud can take place only between groups that are on the same level of segmentation within the same tribe. Hartley found a completely different situation: Violence, counterviolence, and blood revenge occurred without any reference to segmentation. Likewise, rapprochement was always possible through the intervention of some external force, such as the government.[17]

In fact, the segmentarism of the Nahid was of a special nature. As Hartley shows, the most important political characteristic of that tribe in the 1960s was the split of tribal leadership. The opposing figures were two clan heads who actually competed for the leadership of the entire tribe, each claiming that the other was an imposter and usurper. Signs indicated, however, that this was a ritual rather than a real struggle. In other words, the competition was carried out for its own sake rather than to get to a point of final showdown and decision.

The Nahid tribe at the beginning of the 1960s was composed of four main clans, of which the Rowdan was the biggest and most important. A clan consisted of several dispersed villages, the usual mode of settlement. Each village was also consonant with a particular lineage, the most basic kinship group within the tribe, and was also the vengeance unit of the tribe.[18] Despite the division of the tribe into four clans, the two main political figures of the Nahid came from the Rowdan.[19] These were Hakim Bin 'Ajjaj and Hakim Bin Thabit. In fact, they were not formal, or even substantial, chiefs; the Nahid lacked chiefs entirely. They were judges, and they fulfilled mainly judicial functions. There were other minor judges, but these two were approached in really important issues, such as matters involving 'ayb (shame), which usually meant the murder of someone. These judges also possessed political influence, but this was much more limited than their judicial authority and was direct and evident only in relation to their lineages, beyond which their political authority was weak and blurred.[20]

The competition between the Hakim Bin 'Ajjaj and the Hakim Bin Thabit was the most important political issue within the Nahid. Their positions and their rivalry seemed to fulfill some social function. In daily life, animosity and conflicts of authority existed between them; they refrained from talking to each other and avoided any contact: they constantly tried to wrestle adherents from one another, because a basic feature of this structure was shifting boundaries: Apart from a core of adherents surrounding each of these figures, most Rowdan and Nahid were uncommitted to either and would change loyalty at will. Tribespeople had to keep open lines of communication with both judges, because there was a dimension of specialization in their work: One judge was considered expert in intratribal affairs, whereas the other specialized in intertribal affairs. Too strong a commitment to one of them could obviously be dangerous in some contingencies.

The two judges devoted a large part of their time to attracting followers, mainly by securing more judicial cases. A starting point in this struggle was the judge's house, which is always open to the public, but they were also actively engaged in looking out for cases in the open. Especially in the high agricultural season, they were constantly on the road, visiting people everywhere, taking an interest but also looking for judicial cases.

It may thus be said that leadership among the Nahid was divided institutionally. The competition between the two heads, though intense, was ritual and could not be resolved. Among several proofs of this is the mode of election of a judge. A decision is made by the heads of the important subgroups of the tribe. This decision is usually just a formality, as an heir generally establishes himself years before the death of a judge. However, the formal process of election is important, and in it the rival judge plays an important role: He heads the group of people asking the elected *hakim* to accept the post.[21] Thus, the institution of leadership among the Nahid appears to be a sort of imperfect segmentarism.

Many of the points made by Hartley are borne out by other, more generalized descriptions of tribal society in Hadramawt. R.A.B. Hamilton, a British officer and keen observer on tribal affairs in South Yemen in the 1940s, in his study of the South Arabian tribes, makes an important point concerning the position of the tribal chief.[22] Chieftainship was hereditary within one family, but the chief was not supposed to rule sternly or despotically. Hamilton discerned three patterns of tribal leadership in the protectorate.[23] The first was that of the "appointed suzerain," as in the case of the Qu'aytis; the ruling house had come from outside the principality and exercised firm control over it. A second pattern was the "accepted suzerain," of which the *sharifs* (descendants of the Prophet) of the Beyhan principality were the only example. All the other principalities had "elected hereditary tribal chiefs." It is clear from Hamilton's analysis that, on the whole, a principality ruler was tantamount to a tribal chief, and principality was, in effect, a confederation of tribes headed by one tribal chief. On the mode of election of this chief, Hamilton says:

> In each tribal confederation there is a central tribe. Of this central tribe one family only provides chiefs to the confederation. Normally the election of a chief is the concern, not of his family only, but of the central tribe, while powerful petty chiefs of other tribes within the confderation have a considerable say in it. Such chiefs are, by virtue of the conditions of their election, truly democratic.[24]

Hamilton's study is full of examples relating to the weak authority of
the tribal chiefs over their tribes—for example:

> It must not be supposed that this Sultan of the Beni Qasid is a ruler
> in our sense of the word. In fact, even within his family, his powers
> are very small. A certain aura of holiness attaches to him as a
> hereditary tribal head. . . but the influence he wields within his own
> small tribe dwindles outside that tribe almost to nothing.[25]

Thus, it is clear that although the segmentary structure did exist
in South Yemen, it was distinctly different than the same institution
in Morocco. Some South Yemeni tribes had no formal headship,
and what actual leadership they possessed was divided in two (the
case of the Nahid); in other (probably most) cases, real leadership
existed, but it was weak in the extreme, as befits an acephalous,
segmentary system.[26]

What might be the reason for the difference between Morocco
and South Yemen in this respect? I suggest that it has to be sought in
ecological factors: The seats of principalities in South Yemen were
substantial oases, spots where relatively high material culture was
possible and, hence, also more tangible political concentrations.
This pattern of oases was lacking in the High Atlas of Morocco. It is
also probably relevant that whereas in Morocco the dissident tribal
area was physically cut off from the center-controlled area in the
plains, in South Yemen no such separation existed: The tribal area
was enmeshed with oases and was often contiguous with them. In the
Hadramawt, for example, many tribes found their main livelihood in
camel breeding, camels being still in the 1930s the major mode of
transport and commerce in the country. Also indicative of urban
influence over the tribes in Hadramawt is the fact that, somewhat
astonishingly, tribespeople in Hadramawt used to emigrate into the
East Indies along with urbanites. Particularly relevant is the fact that,
whereas in Morocco the segmentary system purportedly excluded
any possibility of a ruling class, one of the most important features
of the social structure in preindependence South Yemen was the
coexistence side by side of the segmentary system and a ruling
class.

The Pacification of the Tribes. The 1930s constituted a key
period in the history of the tribes in South Yemen. The policy of
penetration into the hinterland that took place in these years
included an effort to introduce a greater measure of law, order, and
road security. Nowhere did this policy have more dramatic
consequences than in the Hadramawt, where formerly control of the
roads was one of the most important weapons in the hands of
warring tribes and roads were frequently impassable. Small wonder

that foreign travelers who ventured into the Hadramawt in the 1930s saw themselves almost as the first explorers of Africa.[27]

Much of this change was the fruit of the work of Harold Ingrams, who was sent by the British government to try and arrange truces between the warring tribes—the Ingrams Peace of 1937–1940. When he reached the Hadramawt, he immediately entered into intensive negotiations with the tribal chieftains, with the express aim of suspending all outstanding feuds and such claims for three years. These negotiations were accompanied by occasional bombing forays by the Royal Air Force on the strongholds of adamant tribes. Such persuasive measures eventually succeeded, and in 1937 a total of one thousand cease-fire agreements were signed with Hadramawt tribes, followed by a large-scale collection of arms from the tribes, which must have greatly reduced their physical strength. But this was not a once-and-for-all operation; British archival documents from the 1940s show that meticulous work continued for years after the signing of the cease-fire agreements. These documents contain, for example, many references to the Nahid tribe, and these allow several insights to be gained. A comparison of the Nahid in the 1940s and in the 1960s shows that the tribe's basic social structure remained fundamentally the same, although its power vis-à-vis the government declined drastically.

In the early 1940s, the basic division of power between the Hakim Bin 'Ajjaj and the Hakim Bin Thabit was already extant, and the tribe was quite intensely involved with the government. The origin of this involvement probably has to do with the fact that the Rowdan clan of the Nahid controlled the western approaches of the Hadramawt and hence had much to do with various issues vitally important to the British, such as millet imports from North Yemen and the smuggling of arms and ammunition from the same direction. The British tried to establish cordial relations with Hakim Mubarak Bin 'Ajjaj, and an opportunity to do this presented itself in 1941, when this chieftain found himself in a severe confrontation with the Hakim Bin Thabit over the ownership of a large tract of land. When the confrontation threatened to deteriorate into an armed struggle, the British and the local Qu'ayti government intervened and transferred the matter to Mukalla, the seat of Qu'ayti government. The decision of the British was finally cast in favor of Hakim Bin 'Ajjaj, who, in exchange, offered to agree to the construction in his area of three border forts to guard the western approaches to the Hadramawt. There is almost no doubt that the decision was political and was intended to buy the friendship of Bin 'Ajjaj. This is made clear by the fact that at a certain point it became known that Bin 'Ajjaj and

Bin Thabit were working toward a compromise. This possibility alarmed the British. To cite the document relating these events,

> The only disquieting news of the affair is that Bin Ajjaj, failing to have confidence in Mukalla support and because the land is rapidly drying, is rumored to have made or be about to make an agreement with Bin Thabit which probably would exclude the Mukalla Government from interference in the land and which would be most unfortunate from a Government point of view.[28]

Soon afterwards, the Mukalla government actually sent troops to the aid of Bin 'Ajjaj, only to discover that he had, indeed, reached an agreement with Bin Thabit. On the arrival of the troops, however, he revoked that agreement and promptly proceeded to take hold of the disputed land, disregarding the Bin Thabit subclan altogether.[29] This interference of government soldiers in intertribal affairs almost brought the Bin 'Ajjaj and Bin Thabit subclans to the brink of open war, as various rebellious elements were trying to instigate action by the aggrieved party by supplying arms and fighters.[30] Eventually, however, the tension subsided. Hakim Mubarak Bin 'Ajjaj became one of Britain's main pillars of support in the Hadramawt. This found expression in the fact that in 1942 he received from the Qu'ayti government a special medal of honor for his service in helping maintain the public peace.[31]

The available documents show that after this incident the interference of the Qu'ayti government in Nahid affairs was quite frequent. In the first place, Bin 'Ajjaj maintained regular correspondence with the government or its supporters in the area, chief among whom was Abu Bakr al-Kaf, the famous sayyid of Sey'n. According to one such document, Bin 'Ajjaj notified al-Kaf that sometime earlier someone alien to the Nahid had attacked two Nahid tribesmen, killed them, and plundered their camels and women.[32] The government also intervened in important issues, thereby severely restricting Nahid independence. For example, in 1943, a tribesman, who several years earlier had killed his uncle and run away, now came back, killed another relative, and found refuge in the house. The objection of the entire tribe was of no avail, and the tribespeople approached the government to send gendarmes.[33]

In what way does this early information on the Nahid affect Hartley's conclusions of the 1960s? In the first place, one gets the impression that the Nahid chiefs in the 1940s were much more powerful than in the later period. The idea to build forts in western Hadramawt was Bin 'Ajjaj's; without his consent, the idea had no chance of success, as Harold Ingrams himself acknowledged: "Without his agreement there would be no possible means of Government building, as the influence of Al Hakim is very great and he has a large tribal following not only of Nahd."[34] By the same token, after 1941 Mubarak Bin 'Ajjaj is sometimes treated on a par with the great Abu Bakr al-Kaf as the chief leader of Hadrami society.[35]

It seems, therefore, that there are grounds to conclude that the power of the Nahid leaders declined from real and powerful chieftainship to something much less powerful. At the same time, the structure of the tribe remained more or less unchanged. The tribe was and remained only theoretically incorporated into the Qu'ayti state. In the 1960s, the Nahid were debarred from freely using firearms, but this change was forced on the tribe, not voluntarily accepted, and there was no change in social structure and political values.

The general picture of the Nahid tribe can also be drawn for the Ja'da, the neighboring tribe to the town of Hurayda in Hadramawt, the subject of a monograph by Abdallah Bujra. A comparison of archival documents from the 1930s and 1940s with the work of the anthropologist, dating from the early 1960s, yields interesting insights. In the early 1960s, the Ja'da were completely pacified. Tribesmen did not carry arms, did not engage in much violence, and did not even consider themselves tribal members in the traditional caste system. Rather, their social status had declined so much that they saw themselves now as forming part of the *masakin* caste ("miserable ones"). A crystal-clear expression of this change was the fact that whereas in the 1930s residence in the town was strictly forbidden to the Ja'da—as the town was a sacred enclave (and therefore tribally neutral)—in the 1960s this prohibition became somewhat superfluous and Ja'da tribespeople began to settle there.[36] A comparison of this state of affairs with the situation in the 1940s is quite striking. Bujra does tell us that the Ja'da of the 1930s were much more warlike than in the 1960s; but only recourse to the actual documents can show just how much more warlike and what this really meant in terms of institution building in traditional South Yemen. Hurayda and its region, the Wadi 'Amd, was described in a British intelligence report from 1941:

> *Wadi 'Amd.* This locality is a centre of tribal dissensions. Two main tribes occupy the wadi, the Ja'ada and Madhi, and both comprise many sections all of which are at feud. The capital of the wadi is 'Amd where the Qaim and Qadhi vainly try to maintain some form of government control, but Huraidha with its influential inhabitants, mainly seiyids of the Al 'Attas family, plays an important part in the inter-sectional quarrels. Throughout the wadi there is a demand for orderly government but the requests are always conditional on the

petitioner having his claims settled regardless, of course, of the claims against him. It is curious that so little attempt at cooperation in settling disputes and establishing order is to be found because many of the inhabitants are acquainted with proper government in Java and in Hyderabad. The Ja'adis in particular are great travellers, but no matter how many years they spend abroad, making money and living a civilized life, they return to their indigo and rifles with the greatest ease and with them to a life of savagery. They are also great slave traders and have been known to bring boys from India for sale in Hadhramaut, persuading the parents to part with them on the pretext of giving them a good religious education. One even brought an Indian wife home and sold her to his brother to pay a debt. The wadi could be a source of much agricultural prosperity and during the three years peace there was a great increase in cultivation but continual warfare soon lays waste the most promising land. The Mukalla Government is unable to maintain sufficient garrison to keep the peace and up to the present the wadi has had to be left in its state of disorder.[37]

Another visitor that year reported again that feuds were under way between all clans of the Ja'da and the Madhi and concluded that "it is difficult to see how the wadi could be pacified without the use of force." The same official also said that "curiously the Wadi 'Amd with all its strife does not affect the rest of the country in any way and for this reason it has been possible to avoid drastic action such as has had to be taken in the case of Bin 'Abdat and the Hamumis."[38] As Bin 'Abdat was the quintessential rebel in this period in Hadramawt, this statement would seem to indicate that the Hurayda area was then considered one of the worst spots in the country from the point of view of the government.

Hierarchy in the Towns

Towns in South Yemen grew up characteristically and necessarily in places where sufficient quantities of water were to be found—that is, in substantial oases. In several such oases in the decades before independence, towns sprang up of ten to twenty thousand people, living mainly on intensive date agriculture supplemented by some millet. However, surrounded by tribes and lacking the protection of a central government in any real sense of the term, such small towns and smaller settlements could not easily survive without some outer defense: They would be overrun by the tribes in no time. Consequently, the town in South Yemen had to be a special kind of institution, designed to withhold tribal violence without recourse to physical means of coercion.

Typically in South Yemen and especially in Hadramawt, the town was originally a *hawta*, a sacred enclave, site of a holy shrine and at the same time a neutral zone between warring or potentially warring tribes.[39] Most of these *hawtas* went on filling this particular function long after they grew up to be substantial towns, and in the decades before independence the *hawta* was a lively institution. Thus, in 1941, leaders of the Hamum tribe living near the town of Einat, in Hadramawt, sent threatening letters to the *mansab* (chief sayyid) and sayyids of the town in connection with an increase in the size of the army contingent stationed there to fifty soldiers, "reminding them that Inat [sic] is a 'Hauta' (place of tribal refuge) and that they have no right to have so strong a garrison posted there."[40]

In a society in which the veneration of saints and pilgrimages to their tombs were such essential parts of human existence, one such sacred tomb towered above the rest, to become the most sacred and central sanctuary tomb in the whole of Hadramawt. This was the tomb of Hud, not just another saint, but actually a prophet from the pre-Islamic period. Every year a mass pilgrimage—of as many as twenty thousand people—used to take place to this tomb, located in eastern Hadramawt in an uninhabited area.[41] Over the years, a veritable town was built just to lodge the pilgrims, and during the month of the pilgrimage a general truce over all of Hadramawt was the rule.

The pilgrimage of Hud was an occasion par excellence for the reenactment of rituals that demonstrated the superiority of the sayyids in South Arabian society. The ceremonies both en route and at the site were headed by the sayyids and centered around them. Prayers said at these ceremonies often referred to the sultans derogatorily, an attitude that could only originate with the sayyids.[42]

In every town in Hadramawt and the rest of South Arabia, holy men formed an inseparable part of the sanctity of the *hawta*. Some of them may have been descendants of the ancient holy man who was buried in the *hawta*; all of them were extremely revered by the rest of the population. In effect, they constituted the cornerstone of the South Arabian stratification system—a rigid system much resembling the Indian caste system and entirely unique in Islam. This hierarchy consisted of the following strata:[43]

1. Sayyids, real or avowed descendants of the Prophet.
2. *Mashaikh* (shaykhs) and *qabail*, tribespeople, two completely separate groups that are usually treated as one category only because their status in the hierarchy is similar. The nature and origin of the group called *mashaikh* is quite unclear. The

accepted version has it that they are descendants of ancient holy men and scholars.

3. *Masakin* and *du'afa*, the miserable and weak ones, the really lowest caste, sometimes grouped together as *reaya*, subjects, and sometimes further subdivided to shades of gradation—*hirthan, akhdan*, and *subyan* (respectively: plowmen, servants, and youngsters). On the whole, the *masakin* were respectable merchants and artisans; the *du'afa* were low-status artisans, such as masons and potters; and the *akhdan*, the lowest group, were descendants of blacks from Africa who formerly had been brought to South Yemen as slaves. The position of this last group was especially degraded.

The gaps between these various groups were complete and insurmountable. A person was born into a group and died in it. There was no way to ascend the ladder.

The differences found expression in outer appearance. The sayyids and shaykhs were as a rule unarmed, whereas the tribesmen always carried arms. This was the customary law as well as the usual actual practice in the area. Further, every caste had its own separate quarter, entirely exclusive to itself. Wherever this was possible, the sayyids occupied the higher elevation. It is thus quite feasible to speak of these groups as castelike classes. Although the harsher aspects of the Indian caste system were missing (there was no untouchable caste), the hierarchy did reflect an attitude of more pure versus less pure. Although the lower classes were not considered ritually impure, they were seen as intensely despicable, were engaged in the dirtiest and most unwanted occupations (such as leather processing or water lifting),[44] and were the subject of unrestrained ridicule and were despised by members of the higher castes.[45]

The superiority of the sayyids found ritual expressions. Thus, in Hurayda the peak times of the year were those of the two Muslim holidays. The beginning of the religious activity was a ceremony held in the mosque, where the lower castes passed in procession between two lines of the sayyids, and each member of the lower castes kissed the hands of each sayyid.[46] The surprising and remarkable aspect of this ceremony is that it used to be held in the mosque, but it should also be noted that a non-sayyid had to kiss the hands of a sayyid in every chance encounter between them on the street.

As a rule, the sayyids were not only the supreme social elite; they also constituted the supreme political elite. In fact, most places in the hinterland lacked government almost entirely, and the sayyids were either the sole representatives of such governments or the only expression of any political power whatsoever. Although this was

particularly true of Hadramawt—aptly called sometimes the land of
the sayyids—it seems to have been true of South Yemeni society in
general. One other example is the case of the town of Habban in
Wahidi Sultanate.[47] Most of the sayyids of Habban belonged to the
clan of Mihdhar, who controlled the town socially and politically,
insolently denying every higher authority. The sultan was powerless
to control them, a fact that led among other things to complete
chaos in the legitimate judicial system—nearly total breakdown, each
caste resorting to an intracaste judicial system. Some time before the
report giving this detail (that is, in 1933), the Mihdhar sayyids of
Habban even took part in an antigovernment tribal insurrection
there.

This extremely inegalitarian status system also had a definite
economic side—although it is clear that a purely Marxist
interpretation of its structure will not do. The sayyids became a
ruling caste because their sanctity was a sine qua non for survival in
the face of the tribes. But economic factors are not to be excluded
from this picture, and Hadramawt cities were bywords for places
where huge differences in levels of consumption were constantly
displayed. Thus, the sayyids of Tarim in the 1930s lived in sumptuous
palaces surrounded by beautiful gardens. Inside these villas, some
families enjoyed a level of living probably comparable to that of the
high classes of contemporary Western Europe. At the same time, the
poverty of the lower classes in this overpopulated country was often
appalling. To cite just one bit of evidence from Van Der Meulen and
von Wissmann: "Manual labour is very cheap in this desperately
poor and overpopulated country. Even first-rate professional men,
architects included, do not earn more than a very moderate daily
wage."[48]

An important issue that has to be raised in relation to such a
stratification system (especially in a study that seeks the roots of a
social revolution) is that of the consent or objection of the
governed. The overwhelming bulk of the material from the 1930s (the
decade of the opening of Hadramawt and thus the one in which
most of the best accounts were written) makes it quite clear that this
extremely inegalitarian social regime enjoyed a far-reaching measure
of consent—at least, acquiescence—with very little physical coercion.
Although this tacit impression is created by the several extant
descriptions, the issue is rarely tackled squarely, with one exception,
which I quote both because it is rare and because I do not wish to
suppress evidence with which I ultimately do not wholly agree:

> The contrast between the great wealth of many sayyids and the
> poverty of the great mass of the people does not seem to be

poignantly felt here. The palaces of the rich stand right in the midst of dying towns. . . . The rich return of their own accord from lands of culture and prosperity to their own land of appalling poverty, to enjoy within its borders the wealth they have accumulated . . . we have noticed little jealousy or class conflict in Hadramaut. This is certainly due partly to the democratic way of living. The privileges of the sayyid class have a religious and not a money basis. Soldiers, household slaves and the free citizens of the village meet in the *madjlis* of the rich and all eat there in company, drink from the same bowl and join in the same converse.[49]

It seems to me that although this description probably reflects the overall situation, there is evidence that this consent was far from complete, that here and there the sayyids' superiority was, in the 1930s (if not earlier), already being challenged—and was increasingly so in subsequent decades. I shall return to this issue later in this chapter.

Landownership and Agrarian Regimes

One aspect of the sayyids' superiority that is of particular importance is their connection to landownership. Although there is a dearth of material on the subject, there are enough indications showing that the great bulk of the cultivated land in South Yemen in the decades before independence was effectively owned by the elite, either sayyids or members of the ruling families. To judge by the information supplied by Bujra, it would seem that the town of Hurayda was exceptional in this respect. There the structure of landownership was quite egalitarian, an average sayyid family owning about 1/2 hectare of land—only slightly more than the average owned by families of lower classes.[50] But other available sources relating to other places leave no doubt that the sayyids predominated in landownership. Unfortunately, none of these sources gives detailed enough statistics or accounts of the means by which sayyids acquired land and operated their estates. But some parts of the picture are clear. Thus, the British *Handbook of Arabia*, published just after World War I, says that "for the most part the land in the settled centers is in the hands of the Seyyids or of other influential members of the tribe."[51] Moreover, it has been estimated that before the revolution, as much as two-thirds of all agricultural land in South Yemen was worked by sharecroppers.[52] This information, culled from secondary sources, is corroborated by information from the British archives.

Land in South Yemen could be owned in one of three ways: collectively by tribes; complete freehold; and religious endowment (*waqf*).[53] The last category seems to have been of minor importance, so we will deal mainly with the other two. Concerning tribes, it is to be noted that despite theoretical collective ownership, land was actually possessed by individual tribesmen. The tribal law of *shifaʻa* gave the tribal head the right of priority to buy tribal land offered for sale.[54] With the Ingrams Peace, this rule became of great importance. A report from 1939 pointed out that one of the major problems plaguing Hadramawt was the rise in land values following the peace and the consequent rush on land by all sorts of actual or would-be large landlords.[55] In spite of this, however, tribal land still seems to have been one of the largest categories of landownership until independence. It must be emphasized right from the beginning that most of those who owned land did not work it, even when—for example, as tribesmen—they owned only small parcels. In one official annual government report on South Yemen we find a section on the prevailing land law, which expressly says that "the system of renting, which is almost universal, is some form of sharecropping or payment in kind."[56] B. J. Hartley, a British official in the Hadramawt who tried, in a 1946 report, to account for the severity of the drought and hunger that had prevailed there for the preceding three years, says that "food supplies in the Wadi ran short and the moneylenders foreclosed on the serf-like Dhafa [*duʻafa*], who are accustomed to take advances from crop to crop, working as debt slaves for moneylenders, merchants and landowners."[57] The important point is that Hartley expressly indicates this to be the general situation in extensive areas of the Hadramawt, which enhances the impression that sharecropping was certainly the most widespread mode of working the land in South Yemen at the time.

Interesting information on patterns of landownership in the important area of Abyan may be obtained from the reports that were the groundwork for the famous Abyan project of the late 1940s, the most important agricultural amelioration project carried out by the British in the Aden protectorate. Abyan constituted a big oasis, some 65 kilometers northeast of Aden. For lack of proper control of the flow of the Bana River, the profusion of waters there created swamps, which did not allow prosperous agriculture. As is well known, after the project was eventually carried through, the oasis became one of the best agricultural areas of South Yemen.

A report from the early 1940s points out that at that time the area was used only for extensive grazing, and the land was therefore treated as tribal land.[58] In truth, however, it was the private property of the emirs of the Fadhli and Yafiʻi principalities, who were expected to claim it as soon as it became of real value. Moreover, the Bana River passed through the principalities of Lower Yafi'i and Fadhli, and an ancient law of the land had it that the rulers of these principalities were each entitled to a third of the produce raised by these waters for half a year.

The reports on the Abyan project enhance the impression, gained from a variety of sources, that whoever owned the land in South Yemen did not work it. For example:

> Share tenancy is commonly followed by farmers who take up the land owned by the larger land owners. In this share farming the landowner supplies the land and improvements in the form of bunds and furrows while the tenant is responsible for his share— pertaining to the acreage he farms—for the upkeep of the irrigation system. Expenses for cultivation, seed and all other costs up to the time of harvesting and threshing are paid by the tenants, costs for harvesting and threshing are equally borne between landlord and tenant after which the crop is divided half and half between them.[59]

A report on land problems in Hadramawt (dated 1939) also took it for granted that the near-universal mode of working the land was share tenancy. This report points out that one of the worst aspects of this agrarian structure is the meager share allowed to the actual tiller.[60] The lot of these sharecroppers was especially difficult in the last three years of World War II, when Hadramawt was hit by one of the worst droughts of the twentieth century. The resultant widespread hunger was worsened immeasurably by the fact that the rich sayyids were cut off by the war from their sources of riches in the East Indies. The state of the sharecroppers was described in an official report: "The impoverishment of the capitalists, whose income from the East Indies used to total £600,000, seriously affected their serfs and dependents whose labour produces the meagre supplies of food grown in the Wadi Hadhramaut."[61]

A short but decisive account of landownership patterns is also available for the area of Lahj, which is not only the hinterland of Aden but was also one of the most important agricultural areas in South Yemen. Maktari, who wrote a study of irrigation laws in this region, had first-hand acquaintance with the land law, the gist of which he describes:

> Most of the cultivated land is owned by the umara', members of the 'Abdali ruling family. Some is owned by the mashayikh, heads of tribes, and by wealthy families. Little, and certainly no rawad land, is owned by the peasant. The term rawad indicates land situated near the wadi next to the watercourse. This is considered valuable land, not only because it is near to the water, but also because its soil is rich and constantly moist.

Mullak (landlords) seldom till the land themselves; instead the land is rented to cultivators on the basis of share-cropping contracts. This is a payment in kind which varies between two-thirds of the crop to four-fifths or, occasionally, three-fifths. . . . Cultivators and tenants are known as ra'aya. . . . These form the bulk of the population of Lahj and their major occupation is tillage of the land, either as tenants or as farm labourers who are bound to the land they till for their lifetime. They live in villages of mud huts and straw tents next to the *atyan* (the cultivated land), and the landlords have great influence with the *'aqils* (the heads of the villages). Originally the landlords were the masters of their fiefs, and today, although they are no longer regarded as such, they retain a great influence both in the villages as well as in the government. *Ra'wis* alone pay the taxes, and they alone repair the irrigation channels and build deflectors in the flood season.[62]

Emigration to the East Indies

One of the most peculiar characteristics of Hadrami society before independence, which explains something of the unusual predominance of the sayyids, was the widespread phenomenon of emigration, chiefly to the East Indies (today's Indonesia).[63] This emigration was easily the largest wave of emigration from the Middle East before modern times. It was also remarkable in that the émigré community kept closer contact with its country of origin than did any other such community, in or outside of the Middle East. Because of the special, even unique, nature of this emigration , an attempt to find an explanation for it would be worthwhile, particularly in view of the strong contact this community maintained with Hadramawt.

The little that is known about the history of this emigration gives the impression that only a small number of individuals were involved until the sixteenth century, when people began to leave the region in substantial waves. These waves became a stream in the nineteenth century and reached a peak in the decades before World War II. Ingrams estimated in the 1930s that the number of Hadramis in the East Indies was 71,000—about 20 percent of all Hadramis.[64]

The main historical importance of this emigration consisted in the fact that the immigrants were unusually successful economically and that—because of the intimate contacts preserved with Hadramawt—large quantities of the riches thus created found their way from the East Indies to Hadramawt. Ingrams estimated that about £630,000 were remitted in this way each year to Hadramawt—easily the most important source of foreign cash to the country.[65] In addition to these remittances of money, those who returned home often did so with substantial riches, which are probably not included in Ingrams' estimate. The imprint of these remittances and of returned emigrants was everywhere in Hadramawt before independence. Thus, Van Der Meulen and von Wissmann remark, in the 1930s: "There are in Ba Surra's province nearly 200 mosques, some among them very fine ones, which are often the property of rich sayyids and connected with their houses. The fortunes of these rich men are always made in foreign lands."[66] Such bits of information are strewn throughout their book, as well as a more general observation:

> Everything that is fine and prosperous owes its existence to money that is earned abroad. The tie between a Hadrami and his birth-place is very close, and if he is doing well, he returns from time to time, and when he sees the evening of his life approaching he longs to spend it in the little mud town where he was born, and, finally, to await the Day of Resurrection in Hadrami soil, which for him is consecrated ground. This is why there are here palaces and country-seats of sayyids and mighty castles of sultans, whilst the Bedouin live in rock-caves or lean-to shelters, always on the verge of starvation, and the home-staying town-dweller does not rise beyond a very poverty-stricken existence.[67]

The only objectionable piece of information in this quotation is that it was not at all the fact that only old and dying people came back to Hadramawt. Everywhere in the country Van Der Meulen and von Wissmann went, no matter how isolated a corner, they found many people who had done well in the East Indies and had come back to turn these riches into positions of power and prestige. Such people included the rulers of the principalities in Hadramawt, who were living from the proceeds of their businesses in the East Indies.[68] They also included the most important political figures of the country, such as Abu Bakr al-Kaf, the richest and most powerful man in Hadramawt in the 1930s and for a generation thereafter, whose family built an amazingly thriving business in Singapore; but its political and social fruits were reaped in Hadramawt.

What is the explanation for this unique pattern of emigration? This question has to be posed as a number of smaller questions: What brought this emigration about? What caused the exceptional economic success of the migrants? These are connected to a more basic question: Who were the immigrants? It seems that the main body of migrants were overwhelmingly sayyids, and most of the success stories that so abound in the literature relate to sayyids.[69]

This emigration occurred in part because Hadramawt sayyids, as Muslim saints, enjoyed in the East Indies an unusual natural social advantage of tremendous potential. This was connected with the fact that from the sixteenth century onwards Islam was on the rise in Indonesia, not through war or the sword but through cultural struggle. Indonesian Muslims felt themselves somewhat detached from the main currents of Islam and were in constant search of ways and means to enhance their connection. Hence, by the late nineteenth century, the pilgrimage to the holy cities became more popular among Indonesians than among any other Muslim populace. And hence, no doubt, the unusual respect accorded to sayyids, descendants of the Prophet.

A final question concerning the emigration is: What propelled the sayyids to keep such close contact with their home country? It seems clear that by preserving ties with Hadramawt the sayyids kept alive their main social quality—they were holy men. Only in Hadramawt did sayyids become living saints.

The Rule and Decline of the Sayyids

The strength of the tribes in South Yemen and the enormous influence of the sayyids over them, in combination with other factors, gave rise in South Yemen to a developed urban society that enjoyed a large measure of political autonomy and self-consciousness, almost unique in the history of Islam. Often this autonomy was tantamount to de facto independence.

It is not to be thought for a minute that this autonomy meant democratic self-rule of the inhabitants. In each and every case it was rule by a kind of aristocracy, composed solely of the sayyids. The lower castes had no say in this political pattern, and real power often could not even be said to reside in the sayyids as a body. The sayyids in every town were headed by an officeholder called the *mansab*, who was both a temporal and religious leader. The case of the village of Thile, near Mukalla, seems to have been typical. Freya Stark found in Thile in the 1930s three good buildings towering above the village; these belonged to the *mansab*, the village's undisputed leader and a saint venerated all over the Hadramawt.[70]

On the other hand, the overlordship of these saints was widely described as benign. Thus, Stark presents a typical incident that exemplifies this, a trial before the *mansab* of Hurayda in the 1930s: "The Mansab's decisions are final and personal, but the Qadhi [sic] is there to see that they accord with the Law. As everything is done in public there is a strong control of opinion, and the listening Elders do not hesitate to say what they think. The feeling was pleasant, democratic and friendly."[71] In another place, Stark dwells on the rule of the brothers Ba Surra in the village of Masna'a and again emphasizes in no ambiguous terms its benevolence.[72] This combination of extremely inegalitarian social hierarchy with an extremely lenient rule is striking and calls for an explanation. Apparently the saintliness of the sayyids, *mansabs*, and holy men in general ensured obedience and quiescence much more (or no less) efficiently than sheer force. There is no doubt in my mind that this extreme reverence bestowed on the saints was a result of an unconscious feeling that they fulfilled an indispensable function for the survival of the inhabitants in a hostile world.

There were good reasons for this deep-seated belief to be seriously shaken and, in the long run, even shattered after the 1930s; the objective social status of the sayyids had to follow suit. The change was connected to the large measures of pacification brought to the area, starting with the Ingrams Peace. In a nutshell, undermining the traditional position of the tribes necessarily meant undermining the position of the sayyids as well. Nobody would accept for long an extremely inegalitarian social regime whose vital function was no longer necessary. The decline of the sayyids was gradual—first, because the decline of the tribes was gradual and, second, because sayyids had tools that helped them stay on top, such as their great advantages in education, wealth, and connections.

If the first big step toward the decline of the sayyids was taken by the subjugation of the tribes in the late 1930s, the termination of World War II saw a new phase. At this time the British government made an effort to further strengthen the central powers of the hinterland at the expense of all sorts of centrifugal forces—such as the sayyids. Among other things, the British targeted a number of independent towns that still defied any central authority. Bujra's study of the town of Hurayda gives a good account of this period in the political development of South Yemen. Until World War II, Hurayda was a completely independent town, ruled by a council of the heads of the main families, headed by the *mansab* of the town. All these people were members of the 'Attas clan, which comprised the entire sayyid population of the town. After the war the British annexed Hurayda to the Qu'ayti principality, and the 'Attases lost their supremacy for a time. However, this new arrangement lasted only for a short while. The 'Attases soon adapted themselves to the requirements of the new era, penetrated the higher echelons of the local Qu'ayti administration, and before long monopolized them. They thus managed to preserve their total supremacy in the town until the revolution.[73]

Before 1945, the tribes neighboring to Hurayda had an important social and political role to play in the life of that town.

They were employed by the sayyids to guard the *hawta* as local police; the sayyids served as mediators in tribal conflicts. The sanctity of the *hawta* ensured for the tribes a safe place of refuge and a safe marketplace. This symbiotic relationship came to an end with the annexation of the town to the Qu'ayti state, when the functioning of several traditional institutions was abruptly terminated. Thus, the tribes had to give up their arms, thereby becoming powerless to threaten anybody or to guard and protect anything. Concomitantly, the sayyids ceased fulfilling judicial and mediatory functions for the tribes, a function monopolized after 1945 by regular state courts.[74]

Modernization in South Yemen thus worked in such a way that the sayyids, who formerly were leaders who fulfilled a real and positive function for the lower classes and tribes, became rulers who no longer fulfilled that function, and whose rule therefore came more and more to be based on sheer power.

The Weakness of the State

The area of South Yemen before independence was divided into twenty principalities. No one central power ever tried to unite the entire area. Most of these principalities were small and contained one or two small towns and several thousand inhabitants (mostly tribespeople); three exceptional principalities were much larger— Lahj, in the western protectorate, and Kathiri and Qu'ayti, the two biggest, in the eastern protectorate. Kathiri and Qu'ayti actually captured the main extent of the Hadramawt.

Most of the smaller principalities were really no more than tribal confederations.[75] Here and there were villages or small towns that were completely independent of any government.[76] Even some of the central towns in the main principalities were entirely autonomous. Information about late nineteenth-century Tarim indicated that the town was ruled by the sayyids and was entirely independent of the Kathiri prince, its nominal ruler.[77] The case of the Qu'ayti Sultanate, the one shaykhdom whose claim to the title of state was somewhat justified, is relatively well documented and may allow us to form an idea about the role of the state in South Yemeni society before the revolution. Qu'ayti was different from the other principalities with respect to size and population, which numbered some one-quarter to one-third of a million people in the decades before independence.

A clear idea of the difference between this shaykhdom and the smaller principalities may be gained by comparing the legal mechanisms of transfer of government. In the smaller principalities, this mechanism was quite "democratic," actually tribal. Ingrams describes it aptly:

> In the western part of the Protectorate when there is a vacancy in the chieftainship a new chief is elected by the . . .'aqils of the tribe from among the members of the royal family. . . . The usual tendency is, perhaps, to elect one of the elder and stronger members of the family to be the new chief, but the election of a child and the appointment of a regent is by no means uncommon.[78]

In the Qu'ayti Sultanate this mechanism was quite different. In 1872 the ruler of this state established a constitutional tradition whereby government was supposed to pass from father to son without any say allowed to the populace, tribal or other.[79]

The authority of many rulers was as circumscribed as that of a tribal chief. Thus, a source from the post–World War I period tells us that the tribes appointed sultans and could expel them and that, as befits a segmentary tribal structure, the ruler had authority only on the level of the principality: He could not give orders pertaining to the clan or the individual family.[80] On the other hand, a number of ethnographic details indicate that principality chiefs were a notch above tribal chiefs. Thus, several rulers had beside them a group of "hereditary retainers," who served as police and bazaar watchers.[81] Also, several sources indicate that in many of the principalities the ruler was actually a foreigner to the local tribes, who may have been elected in order to be neutral in relation to the tribes. Although this may not have enhanced his actual power vis-à-vis the tribes, it nevertheless gave his rulership more of a semblance of state headship.[82]

As far back in history as we have knowledge, no one power had ever controlled the entire land of South Yemen. The Qu'ayti state came into being in about 1830. The family was of Hadrami origin and had made a successful career in the army of the Indian principality of Hayderabad when they were invited by local sayyids to provide protection from tribes. The family started a long, drawn-out conflict with the Kathiri principality, which had already existed in the area for several centuries. The two families each captured parts of Hadramawt by various means—buying land, intrigues, and sometimes through bloody conflict—although the wars that took place between them were mainly static wars of siege. In spite of these events, the main structure remained unchanged, characterized by extremely weak central government versus a relatively strong periphery. No one of the states in South Yemen before independence, not even the Qu'ayti state, fitted literally Weber's definition of the term "state": the organization possessing monopoly over the means of coercion. Thus, Ingrams observed in the 1930s: "Along the length of the valley from the east of Shibam to the east of Tarim, which is considered Kathiri, village after village is a small city-state on its own. It is difficult to pass from one to another, even now that the motor-car has come, without the traditional *sijar*, or escort."[83] Before the 1930s, even the authority of the Qu'ayti state over the tribes was shaky in the extreme. It was based on mutual agreements, somewhat reminiscent of relations between two equal polities. The number of these agreements, signed with each tribe individually, was about three hundred.[84]

An important demonstration of the weakness of the state in South Yemen was the degree to which various social elements in the periphery fulfilled functions usually devolving on the state. Noteworthy in particular was the role of certain sayyid families—for example, the family of al-Kaf and, in particular, sayyid Abu Bakr al-Kaf, of Sey'un in the Kathiri Sultanate. The family of al-Kaf was one of the richest in Hadramawt, wealth made especially in trade in Singapore, and Abu Bakr al-Kaf himself was a great philanthropist. His biggest enterprise was building the first motorcar road from Hadramawt to the coast (an investment of $180,000). Less spectacular projects of his were maintaining single-handedly the educational structure of the Kathiri Sultanate, in addition to building several of the schools.[85] This unusual man practiced large-scale charity, of which Van Der Meulen and von Wissmann describe one aspect:

> It is Thursday, the day for the distribution of food to the poor. As we return home, the street and square before our host's house are black with women, children and greybeards, awaiting the portions of rice and flour that are destined for them. The work of distribution lasts for hours. Servants hand out the portions; others check and sign long lists of names.[86]

This seeming dependence of the sultans on the goodwill of the sayyids was not an isolated example and was, in fact, observed by several sources. Thus, Van Der Meulen and von Wissmann remark that "their influence on the government of their land is great: The Sultans are financially dependent on them, the Bedouin tribes are governed by them both by means of money and by religious influence."[87] Similarly, Freya Stark remarks that the sayyids "run the Sultans, the schools, the trade, the army—all, in fact that there is to run,"[88] and also, referring specifically to the two sultans of Hadramawt, "They are philosophic Sultans and leave to the al-Kaf family the toils of government."[89]

Much light on the sort of stalemate that existed between center and periphery in South Yemen is shed by a detailed report on the

Wahidi Sultanate written by E. S. Kennedy, a British official, in 1941.[90] Ten years earlier, the sayyids of Habban, the main town of the state, had brought the sultan to power and would not let him forget it. The position of the ruler was so precarious that he preferred living in another place, to avoid facing daily the sayyids, who were more than an equal match for him:

> They [the sayyids] are expert intriguers owing allegiance but to their purse: although living at Habban and being the richest section of the population, they wish to be considered a separate entity, entitled to respect, but detached from any responsibility, especially financial, towards the Sultan or their brother citizens; they would like little change of the present state of affairs which gives them ample opportunities to intrigue. So long as they maintain their present attitude there is bound to be unrest at Habban.[91]

The sultan was himself powerless to impose his will on this group:

> While he can deal effectively with his subjects, he lacks the subtlety required to inspire fear or even respect from the Habban Sada [sayyids]: they have more than once dragged him into, and subsequently made him responsible for difficulties of their own making. As the Sada helped to set him up as Sultan they are apt to "overlord" him at times: he naturally resents this and there results one continuous campaign of bickerings over small trifles . . . [the Sultan] excuses himself for not spending more time at Habban on the score that the intrigues there make him angry, the more so as he cannot punish the offenders.[92]

A crucial factor that explains the weakness of the state in South Yemen is its natural ecological restrictions. The effects of this factor were apparent even in the Hadramawt, which was, as we have seen, one elongated oasis, extremely overpopulated when the number of its inhabitants was a third of a million; its last 100 kilometers were devoid of water and, therefore, of inhabitants. The Hadramawt became the site of a rather developed civilization, but which was on the whole too small to allow anything beyond a rudimentary political center. What was missing was a robust layer of stable peasants, producing substantial amounts of taxable grain. Precious little could be expropriated from the little agriculture that was carried out, and as all the producers were armed tribes, even the expropriation of such a small amount of taxation was extremely difficult.

This situation was very clearly reflected in the structure of the Qu'ayti state.[93] In the 1930s, the entire income of the state was something in the neighborhood of half a million dollars, almost all of it derived from customs duties. Expenditures, characteristically, were smaller than incomes by a third. Not only was real taxation almost nonexistent, but one major item of expenditure was actually subsidies by the state to the tribes. Rather than expropriating taxation from its citizens, the state actually paid its citizens off to gain their allegiance. The Qu'ayti army neatly reflected these conditions. It was a tiny army, composed of 350 to 400 Yafi'i tribesmen and 250 slaves as well as some 1,200 irregulars. Uniforms were used only on special occasions. The rest of the state administration was likewise of miniature size, headed by a minister—a *wazir*—aided by one more high official, a treasurer. These probably had some assistants.[94] The government was not much different on the eve of independence.[95]

SIGNS OF DISCONTENT

One claim made in this book is that a major reason for revolution in South Yemen—in fact, for every social revolution—is an extremely inegalitarian social structure. A social revolution is partly an expression of deep resentment against the reigning social order. It is important for such a thesis to demonstrate independently the existence of such signs of discontent. And it must be said right away that although the quantity of first hand, minute observations available on South Yemen is quite limited, there is no shortage of evidence of such signs of discontent. Some of these expressions were directed against the British, others against the government, and yet others against the sayyids. There does not seem any point in differentiating these categories.

Early Incidents

It is relevant to mention here the so-called Irshadi conflict that broke out within Hadrami society in the East Indies at the beginning of the twentieth century. The conflict revolved directly on the special privileges of the sayyids in South Yemeni society. More specifically, it started with the wish of a woman of the sayyid class to marry a man from a lower class. According to the customary law current in traditional Hadramawt, such a marriage was, of course, entirely forbidden. (Even though such a restriction had no legal basis in a colony controlled by the Dutch, they did not force Hadrami immigrants to relinquish their own laws of personal status, and the lower castes resented the sayyids' privileges.) Violent riots broke out in 1916. The conflict subsequently became institutionalized into two opposing movements, of which the antisayyid movement was called the Irshadi movement. The importance of this conflict for the history of Islam in Indonesia is undoubted; its role and importance in Hadramawt and South Yemen is another matter.

It is quite clear that on the whole the Irshadi movement did not succeed in transplanting itself into South Yemen and that no fully fledged Irshadi movement ever appeared there. What we do find are feeble efforts in this direction, often probably more fanciful than real. Thus, Freya Stark traces what seemed to her signs for Irshadi influence affecting the position of the sayyids of Hurayda in the 1930s.[96] Even the sayyids were themselves aware of this trend, as the *mansab* of Hurayda remarked; "Our power is threatened now. . . . But who will take our place here in the valley?"[97] But in any event, these signs remained no more than a trickle. It is worth mentioning that 'Ubayd Salih Bin 'Abdat, the great anti-British rebel of the preindependence period, is said by some sources to have been under the sway of Irshadi influence. If this were truly the case, it is strange that Bin 'Abdat himself did not use this excuse as ideological justification for his rebelliousness but kept it a secret.

Freya Stark recorded two rare incidents of tribal displays of insolence toward sayyids. In one such case, in 1938, a tribesman exclaimed to her: "Oh, we tribesmen think nothing of the sayyids."[98] In the other case a tribesman, a camel driver, got mad at a sayyids' request to enhance the pace of the journey and retorted that he would gladly leave him in the desert. At the author's wonder at such treatment of a sayyid, the man remarked; "We are beduin . . . we like people or we don't like them."[99] Although these remarks are only vignettes, it would be rude to dismiss them as meaningless. There were actions, too, but very few of them are mentioned in the extant literature on South Yemen.

There is no doubt that relations between the tribes and the sayyids were complicated and many-faceted. Although the basis of these relations was the tribes' need for the sayyids, hostility toward them seems, nevertheless, to have been rife. Tribes sometimes extracted taxes from towns and were angry when such a privilege was denied them. In a case from 1941, a tribesman tried to take a sack of rice out of the town of Tarim, as a tax due to the tribe. This tax had been abolished in 1937. When the tribesman was intercepted at the town's gate, he kidnapped a sayyid who happened to pass by. The sayyid was released after a while, but all those concerned realized that pursuing the legal procedure against the tribesman might cause a major clash between the town and the tribe.[100] This case, though it in no way shows actual objection to sayyid superiority, does show that tribespeople could act against the sayyids despite their usual veneration of them.

Even more interesting than the signs of discontent among tribespeople is the subject of discontent of the lower castes, of which only a little is known, as the sources are far from complete in their coverage. But what incidents are documented deserve careful attention, because the feelings of resentment expressed in them are so intense that it is not likely that they were isolated instances. One such episode took place in 1933, in the town of Habban. Rich merchants of this town, all from the *du'afa* caste, showed far-reaching independence and insolence toward the upper castes and the government.[101] In 1933, agents of the sultan arrested a *du'afa* merchant by the name of Ahmed Nasir 'Uleima after he had openly defied an order to appear in court to answer charges of various illegal acts. This defiance in itself is quite astonishing, coming as it does from a member of the *du'afa* class. But the aftermath of this incident was even more revealing. Immediately upon the arrest of the merchant, an obviously premeditated plot was activated, and a tribal attack on Habban started.

Within twenty-four hours some two hundred and fifty 'Awlaqi tribesmen had occupied substantial parts of the town. The attack came to an end only after a week, when the sultan was able to assemble enough loyal tribesmen to his flag. It was clear beyond reasonable doubt that several prominent *du'afa* had made common cause with the 'Awlaqi tribesmen. Ahmed Nasir 'Uleima was described as a most ambitious and dangerous person, who had spent some years in Eritrea, where he learned much about English law and especially about possible loopholes therein. The British official who reported these events added that whereas the *reaya* were, on the whole, "peaceful," "exceptions, such as Ahmed Nasir and Mahdi Obad Uleima who provided the excuse for the Aulaqi attack, are few and only to be found among those who are rich enough to subsidise bedus [bedouins] to cause trouble."[102]

This interesting case of a rich merchant whose wealth made him disenchanted with his status is a classic example of what is called in the sociological parlance "status inconsistency"—that is, incongruity between a person's positions in different social ladders—a classic precondition for subversive and revolutionary feelings. Bujra relates the noteworthy story of a *du'afa* merchant in Hurayda who rose to prominence by amassing wealth, whereupon his shop became a focal point for exchange of information and political activity that was not entirely in line with the traditional caste culture.

Another important account relevant to low-caste discontent against the elite appears in a routine report by Harold Ingrams from the Hadramawt in 1942. He gives an account of Sayyid 'Umar Bin

'Abdallah al-Habashi, *mansab* of a town called Hawtat Ahmad Bin Zein, who is described as having been a modern man, one of the first in Hadramawt to buy a car, and a protagonist in efforts to improve the lot of the *masakin* caste vis-à-vis the sayyids. This initiative is said to have brought upon him the wrath of the sayyids.[103] Another item from the same year's report gives further evidence of the *mansab's* activities and their repercussions. This document is so lucid as to deserve extensive quotation:

> For many years the merchants and other townsmen (or "meskin") who settled there lived quite cheerfully under the most rigid restrictions ruled out to them by the seiyids, who considered themselves alone entitled to display and a gay life. While the seiyids could wear whatever they liked the meskin must go about in humble rags. Green shawls and turban were a perquisite of the Seiyids: meskin women must not decorate themselves with henna or attend the sherifas' parties: only small sized drums might be used at a meskin dance: hajir (shrill cries of joy) was the privilege of seiyids only and wedding ceremonies amongst meskin had to be of the simplest kind. About 25 years ago, however, Seiyid 'Umar bin 'Abdulla Al Habshi became mansab and he removed most of the restrictions on the meskin who began to realise what they had missed. The mansab's action was disapproved by most of the seiyids who considered the meskin gaiety and enjoyment an encroachment on their hereditary rights and privileges, so they approached the mansab proposing that four of them would form a council with him, the idea of course being to control his actions, but the mansab refused and in this way an opposition party was formed.
>
> It was well known that the mansab could not protect the meskin, so the opposition began interfering with them in order to exasperate and humiliate the mansab. Unknown persons burnt the gates of meskin houses; rifle bullets would pierce the windows where meskin were holding a party and no one could trace the offenders. In fact the dispute between the seiyids rebounded on to the heads of the meskin. In November 1941 a serious fight took place during a meskin wedding celebration and was only ended with the intervention of a tribesman, one of the Bin Yemani family. Both parties lodged complaints with the Kathiri Sultan but the seiyids failed to appear for the hearing of the case and it was allowed to drop. The state of unrest, however, continued in Hauta. More gates were burnt and two months ago a car belonging to a seiyid of the opposition was burnt. Merchants, with their godowns full of kerosene and other goods, were alarmed and many of them evacuated to Seiyun and Tarim.
>
> In normal times Hautat Ahmed bin Zein has a population of about 1500 and is a second class caravan centre. From most recent

reports it appears that chaos now reigns in what was once a peaceful sanctuary, and the following extract from a censored letter gives recent news: "People are leaving Hautat Ahmed bin Zein. Anarchy is rife in the same manner as prevailed during Al Talib's time in Ghurfa. Al Jaru, Al Bashir, Al Masha'abi (prominent merchants) have evacuated. The seiyids themselves are at daggers drawn. We cannot describe all that is going on there.[104]

Another type of discontent in South Yemen in the decades before independence is exemplified by the activity of Shaykh Salih Bin 'Abdat, ruler of the town of Ghurfa in Hadramawt. For several years before and during World War II, this ruler defied the authority of the Kathiri state and the British government and behaved as an independent ruler. In June 1942, Ingrams reported that Bin 'Abdat blocked all entrances to Ghurfa and placed armed slaves everywhere. When Ingrams wished to pass by with his car, he was intercepted and told: "Government [i.e., Bin 'Abdat] wants you."[105] After an hour, he was released unmolested.

Two years later, Bin 'Abdat levied heavy taxes on the population and showed clear signs of disobedience and rebelliousness.[106] This time he persisted in defying the authority of the British until the beginning of 1945, ignoring many "last warnings." Finally, in March 1945, a military force was sent against him; it overcame some resistance, occupied Ghurfa, and arrested its ruler. Although the force facing them was militarily of no consequence, the British accorded the operation great importance, which found expression in the fact that the officers involved were decorated and a detailed report reached as high as Buckingham Palace.[107] This attitude is important to bear in mind, as it discloses the distinct lack of confidence that plagued the British authorities in South Yemen in dealing with local armed forces. The issue seems to me to be quite closely connected with the war of independence of 1963–67.

An interesting case of anti-British rebellion occurred in the shaykhdom of Dhali' in 1947.[108] A barrage of complaints had reached the British adviser there about the abuses of the acting ruler, prince Haydara. The British government sent him several warnings to desist, but the prince reacted quite unexpectedly: Taking with him a hundred of his supporters, he proceeded to capture a mountain fort north of the Radfan Mountains, from which he tried to start a tribal anti-British rebellion. Sensing the danger, in February 1947 the British sent a substantial ground force, which captured and destroyed the fort. Not the least interesting aspect of this episode was what it forebode the guerilla campaign in that area twenty years later. When Prince Haydara was dislodged from his fort, he managed to escape to Radfan (where the war of independence started in October 1963): "With Haydara at Radfan, further ground operations were useless. The Radfan confederation can muster about nine thousand rifles, and their mountains are a barrier which Government have not yet penetrated."[109]

Also interesting is the popular revolt that occurred in Mukalla, capital of the Qu'ayti Sultanate, on December 27, 1950.[110] The so-called National party was opposed to the expected nomination of one Shaykh Qaddal as state secretary because of his foreign origin. It was alleged that the sultan actually wished to nominate a local but had to yield to British pressure. Because of tension in the town, the sultan, who was at the time in India, was called back by telegraph, and he arrived on December 26. Early the next morning, representatives of the National party demanded an immediate interview with him, which he agreed to grant at 10 a.m. What happened then is best told in the words of the British resident adviser:

> At 10 o'clock on the 27th December . . . a mixed crowd had begun to collect and were reinforced quite suddenly by a stream of hooligans, Somalis, slaves and low fishermen streaming in through the siddah gate from Sharj village to the west . . . in a few minutes the Palace yard was full of a highly unruly shouting band of mixed types.[111]

At the same time, the meeting began between the National party members and the sultan and some of his assistants, including the British adviser, who reports that the session was calm and businesslike. Shaykh Qaddal spoke and convinced everybody that his nomination was worthwhile. But while the meeting was so peacefully conducted, commotion and turmoil were under way downstairs and growing beyond control:

> Whilst this discussion was going on there was already shouting from a crowd growing every minute more unruly. They were no longer in a state to listen to their deputies and the roughest and most undersirable types were banging on the palace doors. Within a few minutes of the deputies disappearing, certain of these, who, armed with sticks and staves, had already broken into the Palace, rushed upstairs on to the North verandah and with a show of violence tried to force their way into the Sultan's presence. . . . Simultaneously those of the mob who had forced an entry on the first story verandah above were beckoning to those below to break in and join them. The Palace guards were overcome; three of their rifles were seized from them, and one soldier was shot with his own rifle and another bayonetted with his.[112]

Reinforcements were immediately called; these first fired in the air and then, when this was of no avail, charged into the crowd. Eight people were killed on the spot, and eight more were said to have died of their wounds later. The crowd was dispersed and the whole affair thus came to its end. The National party was outlawed and all its assets confiscated.

The description clearly shows a revolt that had two levels: the ideological demands of the leadership (which, as we have seen, were actually not at all radical or revolutionary) and an entirely different aspect—collective violence committed by a large group of people, obviously all belonging to the lower castes. Although, unfortunately, we know nothing about the actual demands of the crowd, it may safely be assumed that these had nothing to do with the nomination of the state secretary. The crowd's violence was more likely an expression of some sort of bitterness aimed at the entire political system. The episode, in any event, is a major proof that strong antielite feelings were simmering in South Yemen long before 1967.

It also exemplified in miniature the relations between leadership and crowd in actual revolutions. Although the report of the British official explicitly claimed that the crowd was only slightly associated with the National party, the entire incident was later officially attributed to the party's instigation and machination. Crowd and leaders seemed to be working hand in hand in violent collective action, when in fact this was only appearance, and the two groups had different sets of motivations.

Arab Nationalism in the 1950s and 1960s

These warning signs of discontent become a flood in the 1950s and 1960s. Bujra is an invaluable source for this period, particularly because his book was written before anybody would dare think of the possibility of a radical revolution in this part of the world.

By the end of the 1950s, Arab nationalism had penetrated South Yemen on a really massive scale, facilitated by the spread of the transistor radio, which made the messages sent from Cairo and Damascus available everywhere.[113] The September 1962 revolution in North Yemen—which toppled the imamate there, establishing a republic in its stead—and the bloody civil war that ensued created in South Yemen enormous interest, even "revolution fever." From a theoretical perspective, these developments were bound to create some social revolutionary feelings in South Yemen. There was a vast difference, sociologically speaking, between the appearance of Arab nationalism in Hadramawt and in, for example, early-twentieth-century Syria. In Syria allegiance to the Ottoman sultan made way for allegiance to the nation; in both cases, allegiance was given to something with which the individual had no day-to-day social relationship. The situation was very different in 1960 in South Yemen, where the original objects of allegiance had been the local ruler and the local sayyids. Withdrawal of political allegiance to the local sayyids was tantamount to cessation of the tacit or explicit acceptance of the superior social position of these leaders.

And, indeed, as soon as the revolution broke out in North Yemen, it became the major topic of conversation in the streets, and everyone took sides, soon forming opposing blocs. Whereas the sayyids were naturally for the royal regime, all the nonsayyids were vehemently opposed to this position and were clearly in favor of the republic.

Bujra also found clear signs that after 1962 resentment toward the caste system was mounting.[114] Thus, in 1962 there took place in Hurayda a mass refusal on the part of the lower castes to take part in what was possibly the supreme ceremony reenacting the caste system—the mosque procession in which each member of the lower castes kissed the hands of the sayyids.[115] Some went further than this and exclaimed that "the people will soon revolt against this kind of custom."[116] Bujra, furthermore, claims that after 1962 a new alignment of forces came into being in Hurayda. The low-caste members joined forces and conducted one concerted struggle against the government and the sayyids; they used the language of nationalism, which all of them shared and which divided them from the sayyids.[117]

The sayyids were perfectly aware of the new vulnerable situation in which they suddenly were situated. They would refer half-jokingly to the possibility that the lower castes would launch a revolution against them,[118] but the joking language was probably meant to make the real fear go away. It is not at all exaggerated to say that in 1962 Hurayda appeared to be on the brink of a social revolution. Severe antagonism and interclass animosity were surprisingly close to the surface. Michael Gilsenan tells a story about his stay in South Yemen in 1959. He was walking with two sayyids when a young student passed them and respectfully kissed the sayyids' hands. On meeting Gilsenan the next day, the student alluded to the street scene: "We kiss their hands now, but just wait till tomorrow."[119] This young man was, in fact, only an Arab nationalist, a follower of Nasser. In South Yemen such a stand was almost by definition also social revolutionary.

ADEN CITY

Aden after World War II looked like one of those rare spots on the globe where colonialism seemed to be working smoothly after all. It resembled Hong Kong, and not only because both places had been conquered at nearly the same time. With the passage of time, the similarities between the two cities grew. The most striking common characteristics were a booming economy and a quiet political atmosphere, devoid of persistent and vociferous demands for independence. But, although the economy continued to boom, in the political sphere Aden after the war became just as unpleasant a place for the colonial power as had the rest of the Middle East. Aden revolted in the midst of continuing economic success—a very strong case against the notion of a universal association between revolution and short-term economic crisis following an extended period of boom.

Economic Growth

When Aden was conquered in 1839, it was a small village of some five hundred inhabitants, with hardly any commerce or artisanship. As a coaling station on the British road to India, however, its development started to pick up speed immediately, and Aden attracted business and new settlers. The opening of the Suez Canal in 1869, an event that gave tremendous impetus to an increased volume of navigation in the Red Sea, particularly boosted its economy. The discovery of oil and its value as the major source of energy in the first decades of the twentieth century also favored Aden greatly. Aden's advantage was that it was one of the nearest good harbors to the first major area of oil production, the Gulf.

Aden's growth was fast and continuous. By 1869, its population had reached 30,000; in 1963 it was 250,000. Economic growth was particularly intense after World War II. First in importance to Aden's economy was the bunkering business. The volume of this trade expanded so much that by 1958 Aden was the second busiest port in the world, after New York. In 1952 the British Petroleum Company began building a £60-million oil refinery in Aden; it commenced production in 1954, employing 2,500 workers.[120] The nature of the work in this business had undergone a radical change. Before the war the employees had been large gangs of muscle workers; in 1954, the workers were professionals, with tenure and other benefits.[121]

Another area of employment opportunities that grew by leaps and bounds after the war was servicing for the British army.[122] In

1960, the British government made Aden the headquarters of the Middle East Command, moved there after Kenya received its independence. Aden was flooded with thousands of British service personnel and their families. Aden's airport, Khormaksar, became "the biggest and busiest R.A.F. station in the world."[123] It is only natural that this sector, which in 1963 employed 20,000 Adenis grew to become the most important in the Aden economy. This growth in employment and population also brought large-scale growth in the building industry, which became one of the largest fields of employment in the city.[124]

For a city so dependent for its economic well-being on its continued link with Britain to revolt is somewhat astonishing to every believer in the materialist interpretation of history. Such an event is also probably proof that nationalism touches an unusually deep chord in human psychology; or, if this is too sweeping a generalization, it certainly did for the people of Aden and South Yemen. Arab nationalism arrived late to South Yemen. But when it did arrive in the 1950s, no foreign power could rule the country for long without paying a heavy price.

Trade Unions

Nationalism in Aden was closely connected with the most important feature of the city's social history at this period—the emergence of organized and strong trade unions.[125] These might, somewhat superficially, be construed as a possible reason for Aden's Marxist regime, but a closer look belies that suggestion.

Trade unions were first founded in 1952 by the European employees of Aden port. By 1960, the Aden Trade Union Congress (ATUC) was the biggest and most lively trade union in the Arab world. It constituted one of the best examples of institution export from Europe to the Third World. As in other British colonies, in Aden the unions were established with help from the British Trade Union Congress (TUC), whose tradition of giving help harks back to the end of the 1920s. Such help tallied quite well with the interest of the Colonial Office in potentially reducing the expenses involved in ruling the colonies. The paradigm of the British TUC was particularly auspicious in the colonies, as the British unions were characterized by their anticommunism and their abhorrence of using unions for anything other than improving the conditions of the workers in the narrow sense. The British unions also formed a loose confederation, which prevented the emergence of strong and potentially dangerous leadership. But although the Aden TUC was modeled after the British TUC, it soon surprised everyone by exposing teeth that could bite.

Starting in 1956, the ATUC discovered the political strike and used it with fewer and fewer qualms. The political nature of ATUC became clearer in 1958 and 1959 with a long series of strikes on purely political issues connected with Arab nationalism and Aden's independence.

Before the war of independence, Aden had become a modern Arab city composed of immigrants from various directions, notably North Yemen and the South Arabian hinterland. These people were all uprooted from their natural social origins and in Aden led lives that were completely detached from traditional ties. Pan-Arab nationalism was thus a natural cement for these people, especially at a time when pan-Arab nationalism was at its peak, reverberating the tremors created by 'Abd al-Nasser. There were, however, few legal ways to express nationalistic feeling in Aden in the 1950s. The political strike was, in effect, the only available channel that was legal and effective at the same time. Small wonder that ATUC activity consisted to such a degree of political strikes.

At the same time, I find it of the utmost significance that the only slogans presented in these strikes were nationalistic. There were no calls to seize plants in Aden or demands to augment substantially the workers' share in profits or any other class-struggle rhetoric. If the radicalization of the guerrilla movement were to be sought in the "proletarian" crystallization in Aden, we should find clear signs of this in workers' demand concerning their own lives.

THE GUERRILLA WAR AND REVOLUTION

The war of independence of South Yemen started in 1963 and lasted until November 1967, when the British left and the country attained it independence.[126] It was a bloody struggle, in fact, a classic example of guerrilla war, albeit not on a scale comparable to that of China or of Yugoslavia.

In many respects, the outbreak of the revolt in October 1963 was anticipated by incidents that had taken place in the 1950s and 1960s. Antigovernment rebellion, especially tribal rebellion, was epidemic. Thus, in 1960 there took place in Hadramawt a tribal uprising against the Qu'ayti state that was only put down by the deployment of the British Royal Air Force. The background of this rebellion was a restriction put on the tribes in the use of their traditional grazing land. Six of the ringleaders were put to death.[127]

Rebellions took place in the western protectorate as well. Thus, tribal rebellions broke out in 1953, 1955, 1957, and 1959. In some of these cases guerrilla-type operations against road traffic took place.[128] The most serious rebellion in the preindependence period occurred from 1957 to 1960. It was led by Muhammad Ibn 'Aydarus, the son of the prince of Lower Yafi'i. In the early 1950s, this man had been the governor of the area of Abyan, the most important agricultural improvement project carried out by the British in South Yemen and a source of considerable revenue to the British government. Ibn 'Aydarus had harassed the British administration of the project, and his hostility toward the British grew with the passage of time.

In 1957 he finally openly rebelled, took to the mountains, and gathered supporters from all over the country. He was successful in attracting a considerable number of tribespeople and conducted guerrilla-type warfare. Only at the end of 1960 did the British take major action against the rebels: They bombed the rebel camp from the air and sent a ground force against them. Ibn 'Aydarus was forced to flee to North Yemen. It seems clear that the rebellion of Ibn 'Aydarus was, for the first time, a nationalist rebellion in the real sense.[129] But it was limited in scope and its leadership was still traditional, with little vision and resources to conduct a major rebellion. All this was soon to be radically changed.

The NLF and the Early Campaign

The crucial phase in the struggle for independence in South Yemen started at the end of 1963, with an armed struggle that the British were unable to quell. It all started with the establishment—very little publicized at the time—of the National Liberation Front (NLF) in Ta'izz (North Yemen) in June 1963. The founders were members of about ten little-known, minor organizations in Aden and in the hinterland of South Yemen; these organization convened in Ta'izz under the aegis of the Egyptians. The avowed aim of the founders in establishing the new organization was to launch an armed struggle. But their major immediate aim was more modest: to harass the British and thereby detract from British ability to help the royalist side in the civil war in North Yemen. This was no doubt in the main an Egyptian initiative, intended to alleviate the pressure upon themselves. Any possible benefit for South Yemen was probably only a secondary consideration at the time.

What did the members of these organizations have in common? One characteristic they shared was complete obscurity. With the partial exception of Qahtan al-Sha'bi, no one of the NLF's founders had been known before as a political figure. Had any of Aden's known public figures joined the guerrilla movement—an unlikely event, as all of them were by now used to a high standard of living—they would likely have been soon detected by the British and arrested or expelled. The absence from the guerrilla movement at its inception of all but lower-class and obscure figures is the key factor to its radicalization.

The obscurity of the guerrilla leaders was to remain the most important characteristic of the NLF, possibly the most crucial precondition for their success; this precondition was superbly fulfilled. 'Abd al-Qawwi Makkawi, a known political figure, the last chief minister before independence, was expelled from Aden merely for declining to condemn terrorism.[130] But the faces of the NLF were unknown; as Stephen Harper, a British newsman who covered the guerrilla war, put it, "The NLF was led by faceless men. It had no known leadership, and British intelligence, often accused of sponsoring it as a secret arm against FLOSY [Front for the Liberation of Occupied South Yemen], seemed to have little idea about it. . . . NLF prisoners provided little information. They knew only their immediate associates."[131] Harper reported on the first news conference held by the NLF during the war, as late as November 1967, in Zinjibar. (Until then, announcements from the NLF were made through leaflets.) Harper was present at the press conference, and his description supplies us with an important insight. Two men were seated at a table. One revealed his name only under pressure from the reporters (this was Sayf al-Dhali'i, an important leader of the NLF). The other declined to reveal his name and was not recognized by this group of (probably) shrewd journalists, who passed the war of independence in Aden. Yet, a mere fortnight later, this anonymous man was revealed to have been none other than Qahtan al-Sha'bi, the first president of independent South Yemen.[132]

Absent from the list of founding organizations of the NLF is the Aden Communist party, a small and unimportant body, but nevertheless an extant one. Why was the Communist party not among these, whereas in Albania it had been one of the most important groups from the beginning of the guerrilla activity? Two main factors are involved. In the first place, Aden was a city of big and militant trade unions, and it may well be that these unions were preoccupied with immediate workers' problems and with ways and means to improve their lot rather than with wider political issues. But probably no less important was the fact that the NLF initially appeared as a protégé organization of Nasser's Egypt, an umbrella not particularly auspicious to Communist parties. In Albania these two factors were absent, hence the natural connection between the guerrilla movement and the Communists.

However, from the point of view of the theory advanced in this book, it seems that whether or not the Communist party itself took part in the guerrilla movement is a question of minor importance. South Yemen is a classic example documenting the point that one should be suspicious of making connections between radicalization and avowed ideologies. Though a virulent Communist party existed in Aden, it was left aside, and the organization that instituted an extremely Marxist regime had nothing to do with ideological Marxism. When the suitable conditions for radicalization came into being at the level of the rank-and-file members of the NLF, it influenced the elite, either by elevating more radical members to leader-ship or by transforming the opinions held by segments of the leadership.

The actual revolt began in October 1963, as a tribal eruption in the mountains of Radfan in the north of the country. It seemed to be an ordinary tribal rebellion that the NLF took over in circumstances that are not as yet entirely clear. The proximity of the region to the North Yemeni border made it particularly convenient for rebellion as supplies could be brought in and escape was relatively easy. At the time, the NLF involvement in that rebellion was not known, and it was taken to be part of the usual tribal pattern of flare-ups. When guerrilla activity persisted, the British gathered a large force that, in June 1964, was successful in dislodging the rebels from their strongholds. But at that same time, inactive rebel forces were established in various corners of the protectorate, composed mainly of tribesmen and headed by NLF activists. At the right moment, these forces—very little about them is actually known—were destined to play a decisive role in the creating of independent South Yemen.

At the end of 1963 the NLF started a new front—urban terror. Targeted first was the high commissioner, Kennedy Trevaskis, who was only wounded, although two of his aides were killed, and about fifty others were wounded as well. This was the first of what was to become a long list of hit-and-run attacks that started in earnest at the end of 1964; these lasted for three years and made the life of the British in South Yemen very miserable indeed. One high-ranking British official estimates the importance of this urban campaign as follows: "The growing terrorism in the urban areas of Aden State was more serious, and it contributed significantly to the manner of our departure; it was also decisive in determining the political situation in South Arabia after Independence."[133]

Highlights of the Guerrilla War

There is no need in this study to recapitulate the minute history of this guerrilla campaign, beyond mention of some of the highlights. It is important to realize the intense escalation of activity that was involved. Paget assembled complete statistics for the guerrilla operations, and these make the point clear:[134]

Year	Incidents	Casualties
1964	36	36
1965	286	239
1966	510	573
1967	2,900	1,248
Total	3,732	2,096

The black day for the British security forces in Aden was June 20, 1967—the day on which the resistance movement in South Yemen scored its greatest tactical success. On that day the British lost control over Crater, Aden's most important quarter—whether through a premeditated guerrilla action or by a mere combination of tragic mistakes remains unclear. A few days earlier, a protest had been voiced by officers of the South Arabian Army against the nominated chief of the army. Some of these officers were suspended. On the morning of June 20, rumor spread that they had been dismissed, whereupon some soldiers started to shoot, probably into the air. At a nearby camp somebody suggested that the British were shooting at Arab soldiers. A general mutiny immediately broke out there. Unsuspecting, a military vehicle loaded with British soldiers approached the camp and encountered heavy fire; eight soldiers were killed instantaneously and eight others were wounded. However, worse was still to come. The rumor of British shooting at Arabs spread to Crater, where 140 members of the local police immediately broke into the ammunition store and started firing at British patrols passing on the main road. Heavy fire continued all day, with the British unable to evacuate thirteen dead soldiers from the rebellious quarter. Only thirteen days later was a large British force able to capture Crater again. Coming barely a week after the Six Day War, the Crater victory was of enormous significance for morale. Small wonder that Paget calls the loss of Crater "a grim and tragic day for the British Army."[135] Of course, it must be borne in mind that the real significance of Crater was limited at best: The exact day of evacuation had long been fixed, and the incident certainly was not a chapter in the struggle between the NLF and FLOSY. But symbolic victories have their value also.

Symptomatic of the combat situation in Aden was the position of two densely populated lower-class satellite towns, Sheykh Othman and Dar Sa'ad, situated some 15 kilometers to the north of Aden, just outside of Aden colony's territory. These towns played a key role in the urban guerrilla movement. In Paget's words,

> These two towns provided the terrorists with an ideal "forward base," and they were freely used by them for the transit and storage of arms, ammunition and equipment. It was with some justification that Sheikh Othman was recognized as the worst trouble spot of all for the Security Forces, and Dar Saad became known as the terrorist Bulk Breaking Point.[136]

One part of the explanation for the special place of these two towns may be the fact that they were situated just outside of Aden colony proper and were thus normally liable to the authority of the federal government, authority that was nomimal rather than real. This is relevant to a point I will make—that one of the major reasons for the success of the revolution in South Yemen was the weakness of the indigenous political regime.

FLOSY Until 1965, the armed struggle in South Yemen was conducted entirely by the NLF. In that year, it became clear that there were other powers vying for power in the area. In fact, throughout the years of struggle in South Yemen, it was not the NLF that attracted the main share of public attention. The main public figure was Abdallah al-Asnaj, president of ATUC and an uncompromising nationalist of South Yemen. World public opinion and even Arab public opinion viewed him as Aden's natural leader. The comparison some (for example, Trevaskis) drew between al-Asnaj and Makarios of Cyprus was, therefore, true to some extent.

Al-Asnaj, however, was very much a politician and intensely shunned violence and armed struggle. He opposed the NLF from its inception, and as the power of the NLF grew, so al-Asnaj's effort to outbid it intensified. His efforts finally bore fruit, when he succeeded in April 1965 in convening in Ta'izz, North Yemen, a large congress of most of the peaceful political organizations who were working toward South Yemen's independence. The organizational body that resulted, headed by al-Asnaj, was called OLOS (Organization for the Liberation of the Occupied South). It immediately made strong efforts to bring about a merger between itself and the NLF.

At that same time such a merger was also in the best interests of Egyptians in Yemen. It was two years after the beginning of Egyptian intervention in North Yemen, and clear victory was not at all in sight. Nasser was trying to reach a compromise solution with the Saudis, one of the conditions for which was uniting the nationalist forces in South Yemen under moderate leadership. Al-Asnaj seemed to the Egyptians a perfect candidate, and after the creation of OLOS they put immense pressure on the NLF to come to terms with al-

Asnaj. Such pressure necessarily meant much to a nationalist movement in the Arab world of those days. Nasser was the ideological authority of last resort, and to risk a break with Nasserism was almost tantamount to political suicide. Yet, groups within the NLF were willing to take such a risk after the Egyptians abandoned a policy of pressure and tried to force a merger: in January 1966, several moderate leaders of the NLF were flown to Cairo and convinced to sign a merger pact on the spot. The body that was created in this bizarre way was called FLOSY, or Front for the Liberation of Occupied South Yemen.

Much of the political maneuvering within the NLF in 1966 was connected with the consequences of this forced merger. It turned out that a large number—possibly the majority—of activists within the NLF were vehemently opposed to a merger with the established bodies from the pre-guerrilla-war period. Under the pressure of these groups, two congresses took place during the year—the NLF Second Congress in June 1966 and the Third Congress in November. In the Second Congress a new politburo was elected, which was more or less a direct expression of the radical groups. The politburo contained such people as 'Abd al-Fattah Isma'il and Salim Rubay' 'Ali, the first two presidents of Marxist South Yemen after independence. Thus congress only attacked the merger and expelled the people thought to be responsible for it, but the November Third Congress broke with FLOSY officially. This break with FLOSY also meant a total break with Nasser's Egypt, which henceforward ignored the NLF entirely and attributed every action in South Yemen to FLOSY. More important, Egypt severed all ties with the NLF, which meant a complete stoppage of military supplies

That the NLF was not hindered by this break must be attributed to its prior hoarding of extensive stocks of supplies as well as to the fact that no serious force stood in its way. The relatively easy victory of the NLF over FLOSY must not be construed as a chance outcome of a struggle between two equal organizations. Although the exact numbers were not known, it seems safe to assume that FLOSY was much weaker than the NLF. The chronology of events makes it clear that until the end of 1966 FLOSY was not at all a fighting organization. It was hardly engaged in anti-British operations even afterwards, so those who wished to join a guerrilla organization after 1966 would still have had to join the NLF, which gave the NLF great numerical advantage, in addition to its self-evident superiority in fighting experience. The NLF enjoyed a similar advantage in fighting motivation; in fact, it seems entirely dubious that FLOSY fighters had any genuine fighting motivation whatsoever. However, a violent showdown had become inevitable, and, indeed, four armed clashes took place between the two organizations in the course of 1967: in January, June, September and November. The first occurred during a mass demonstration organized by the NLF.

The Hinterland Falls to the NLF. The summer of 1967 began with the NLF's biggest move in the entire guerrilla campaign: In preparing for their final withdrawal, the British had evacuated the hinterland in April. The NLF now moved to action that was to be its moment of truth and launched a struggle to take hold of the twenty princedoms of the South Arabian hinterland. The first to fall, Dhali' was captured by guerrilla bands that had been in hiding in the Radfan mountains since 1963. In the next two months, all the rest were to follow. The tremendous weakness of these princedoms was now exposed in a quite dramatic way. The only forces the bands of the NLF encountered were small units of the federal army, renamed the South Arabian Army in June 1967. Hasty moves at its arabization were now taken in order to turn it into a force that might counterbalance the power of the NLF, but it was obviously too late. The main body of soldiers was recruited from various tribes of the hinterland, and tribal loyalties were and remained paramount.

From the point of view of an observer acquainted only with the events of the 1960s, the tribes and the sultans of the hinterland seemed to forming one coalition, but longer-range study, of course, shows this view to be inadequate: There was deep-seated animosity between the tribes and the sultans and very little common interest between them. The tribes had been stripped of their weapons, but they were never integrated into the structures of the princedoms as citizens. They were never asked to accept the rule of these princedoms as truly legitimate, and it seems obvious that they, in fact, did not hold this rule to be so. This tribal attitude was specially true in the more important sultanates, notably those in Hadramawt. In the smaller princedoms, as we have seen, an element of consent on the part of the tribes may have been involved, but unfortunately for these quasi-states, they were so weak as to hardly constitute a serious threat to the NLF bands. Small wonder, then, that one princedom after another fell to the NLF without a real fight. In Hadramawt, the process was also accompanied in several places by popular rebellions of local clubs and other voluntary organizations. This is far from surprising if we remember Bujra's findings from Hurayda, where in the wake of the revolution in North Yemen the entire body of the lower castes came all out for a republican type of government.

One rare account of such a takeover is supplied by Stephan

Harper, and it provides insight into the relations of the NLF and the federal army. The account concerns the fall of the emirate of Dhali' in the spring of 1967. The British, on evacuating the region, handed it over to the federal army. But "soon afterwards, a tough hill fighter known as Ali Antar [actually one of the heads of the guerrilla bands], respected by British troops and revered by tribesmen as a sort of Robin Hood, moved into the Emir's [of Dhali'] Palace. Federal soldiers in the nearby camp were reported to have been 'magnificently aloof.'"[137]

The significance of this important piece of information is, first of all, that it shows quite clearly that the federal army, probably because of the mode of its tribal recruitment, lacked political aspirations. In fact, this army apparently did not develop a personality of its own. Moreover, this excerpt provides a fine example of the revolutionary process, as analyzed by Charles Tilly:[138] a transfer of allegiance from the "legitimate" government to its challengers. What surely has happened is that, after two very arduous years of life with the tribespeople in the mountains, the NLF's leaders were transformed from mere rebels to established leaders of South Yemeni society— not *the* leaders of that society, but a legitimate section of that leadership. This is an inevitable sociopsychological process, and a price the traditional elite has to pay for not taking part in this process. For it is clear that only members of the lower classes in South Yemen would have been able to endure such long and difficult hardships.[139]

FLOSY tried to stop these seizures of power but managed to put forward real opposition only in one place. In August a FLOSY force of some thousand fighters crossed from Ta'izz and tried to capture Lahj, the important princedom to the north of Aden. They were deterred by an NLF force, whereupon they pushed southward to join other FLOSY forces north of Aden, in Dar Saad, where fighting broke out once again in September. The South Arabian Army stepped in and imposed a truce.

The Fall of Aden. In the next month or so there was not much change in the situation. In South Yemen, only the destiny of Aden town itself, the only place where the British still ruled, remained to be decided. Intensive diplomatic maneuvering was under way, intended, from the British side, to prevent the NLF from capturing power and to leave a more or less friendly government. Heavy pressure was put on the NLF and FLOSY to come to terms, but neither of them would give in. Finally, heavy fighting broke out once more at the beginning of November. After three days of hesitation, the South Arabian Army decided to take sides: It declared its support for the NLF and moved promptly to dismantle FLOSY's positions.

From then on there was little doubt that the NLF would capture power. The British, meanwhile, announced for the last time a final evacuation day—November 30—but were still adamant in refusing to acknowledge the NLF and negotiate a settlement with it. Only ten days before evacuation day, they finally agreed to negotiate. By that time, the two parties had very little to talk about, and they were on the worst of terms. Although it might be claimed that Britain's decision to evacuate the base (made in February 1966) was dictated by global strategy, the timing was certainly forced by the guerrilla movement. The withdrawal was, politically speaking, quite unorderly; The British had no say whatsoever on the shape of the government they were leaving behind—a regime that was the worst possible one from their point of view. It is for this reason that any impartial observer has to conclude that South Yemen presented a classic case, despite its small scale, of a successful guerrilla campaign.

The Success of the Guerrilla Movement

The astounding success of the NLF in South Yemen calls for another type of comment. In very few instances have guerrilla movements attained ultimate success, which is driving out the occupying power. This certainly was not the case in Albania—although it might look that way—as the Germans actually evacuated mainly to reinforce their last defense line. In South Yemen the purely military achievement of the guerrilla movement was even less impressive. There the great success of the NLF consisted in the fact that it managed to stay alive until independence. What modest force it may have constituted vis-à-vis Britain was more than a match for local forces. The gist of the NLF's achievement, therefore, was defying British authority while not being crushed by a superior force. How was this achievement possible? Several earlier rebellions had no chance whatsoever. Why was the campaign mounted by the NLF so exceptional?

The answer has to be sought in a minute reading of the descriptions of prior revolts. For example, the Bin 'Abdat rebellion of the late 1940s had as one of its distinct features the fact that the British had great difficulty conducting a large-scale ground operation. The British took more than half a year to quell even the Radfan rebellion, in the initial stage of the guerrilla war, despite the introduction of a powerful new weapon—the helicopter. It is clear that Britain was distinctly reluctant to commit large forces over long distances in unfamiliar terrain and with poor or nonexistent intelligence on the opponent and the region. What distinguished the war of independence from these abortive rebellions was simultaneous eruptions (some of them, no doubt, rather passive) in several places all over the country. Small wonder that the British were quite unable to eradicate all these forces in a definite manner.

An important connection exists between the chronology of the guerrilla campaign and the South Yemenite social structure. It is evident that there existed an alliance between the British and the South Yemeni elite, which consisted of the sayyids and the rulers of the princedoms. I have shown that this social structure was based on a large measure of inequality, more or less legitimate in the past, but less and less so in the years before the revolution. Moreover, there was a strange lack of relationship between the extreme disparities in the social structure and the small degree of actual force used to back up this structure. Only the British could supply the necessary force needed to shore up the regime in the face of mounting radicalism of all sorts: hence, the total dependence of the traditional elite on the British. Although inherently no great lovers of the British, members of the elite were unable to join the anti-British guerrilla warfare, apart from one or two exceptional cases. In the past, when anti-British resistance had sometimes merged with tribal interests, it was often headed by elite leaders. But when the resistance turned into a class war for survival, it seems that everyone knew their right places.

Thus, like the leadership, the rank and file of the guerrilla movement were all members of the lower castes both in Aden and, particularly, in the Hadramawt. As we have seen, the towns in Hadramawt were already in a state of anti-British frenzy before the start of the guerrilla warfare. It is no surprise, therefore, to find that in 1967 the urban crowd of Mukalla prevented by force the disembarkation of the traditional ruler who was returning from abroad. The anger needed for rebellion was clearly present, and because of the feebleness of the state in South Yemen, action was also relatively easy.

INDEPENDENCE

South Yemen was an independent country in November 1967, but two more years elapsed before the radical groups could take over. The new republic faced enormous problems. Foremost among these was the economic situation. The closure of the Suez Canal in the wake of the Arab-Israeli war of June 1967 affected the port of Aden severely, causing a 75 percent reduction in business, and the evacuation of the British army left twenty thousand people jobless.

Purely political problems were not lacking either. Though the army of the federation had supported the NLF against FLOSY, the regime could not really know just how loyal this army was. Moreover, some of the new state's neighbors viewed it with extreme suspicion and were quite ready to help its opponents.

1967–1969: Qahtan and the Radicals

Soon after independence, Qahtan al-Sha'bi was elected president, prime minister, and commander of the army. His first announcement contained a statement of policy and ideology, basically pan-Arabist and mildly socialist. In this statement, he spoke about "positive neutralism" and "socialist revolution," defined as rapid economic development of the economic potential of the country. Qahtan believed that the new republic should respect the traditional social institutions inherited from the past and proceed moderately from there. The NLF's left wing, however, opposed this view and fiercely advocated a radical transformation, including far-reaching agrarian reform and destroying the groups composing the traditional elite of the country. The Left also advocated smashing the entire administrative and military structures of the sate, building everything from scratch, while assuring, of course, recruitment of loyal elements only.

The mainstay of the NLF's Left throughout this period was in Hadramawt, where the far Left was either actually in control of the government or very near to complete control. In Hadramawt—and more particularly in Mukalla, the main town—the takeover by the NLF was at least partially a popular revolution, involving mainly educated youths and schoolteachers.[140] On the dawn of September 17, 1967, the two princes of Hadramawt came back from Geneva, on board an Italian ship. A mass of people in the town forced the princes back to the sea and into permanent exile. It soon turned out that the NLF local leadership that came to power (capitalizing no doubt on the huge distance and poor communication between Aden and Mukalla) was able without great difficulty to pursue a policy much more radical than that pursued in Aden. This policy was a Trotskyist version of Marxism; that is, a call for unrelenting struggle to export the revolution to neighboring countries—notably, if possible, Saudi Arabia.

In internal matters, the Hadramawt leadership announced a far-reaching land reform policy (which, however, under Aden's pressure, was not put into effect). It also called for a complete cleansing of disloyal elements from the army and for the establishment of local councils of poor peasants and workers to serve as the real locus of power in the country.[141] In the two years between 1967 and 1969 (when the extreme radical line became South Yemen's official ideology), the hard-liners in Hadramawt often catalyzed the adoption of this ultraradical line by the NLF for the entire country, or served as a crucial bulwark against the eradication of this line from the agenda of South Yemen. Thus, Hadramawt is a major key to the radicalization of the country. That Hadramawt should take this position is not entirely surprising. We have seen that town life in Hadramawt was the most developed in South Arabia and that the urban masses there held the most extreme antielitist views in the country. Add to this the fact that the caste system in Hadramawt had been particularly stiff and uncompromising, and this radicalism makes good sense.

The contradictory worldviews held by sections of the NLF came to a head in the NLF Fourth Congress, held in March 1968. In this congress 'Abd al-Fattah Isma'il emerged as the ideological spokesman of the far Left of the party. In a full-fledged Marxist speech, he preached on building the revolution with workers, poor peasants, and partisans, leaving aside the petty bourgeoisie and revolutionary intelligentsia, viewed as legitimate even by the Chinese Communists.

Although Qahtan al-Sha'bi held actual power, his views were heavily defeated in the congress, and the views of the extreme Left were adopted. The government was called on to pass measures such as agrarian reform and nationalization of foreign capital, to establish popular councils in villages and towns, and to purge the army and the administration of suspect elements. The fact that these policy directives were adopted against the views of the government must be taken to mean that they were accepted by some sort of democratic process. The necessary conclusion is that a majority among the active members of the NLF apparently held quite radical social views.

However, the decision to adopt these policies remained a dead letter, as Qahtan did not even try to implement them. Instead, he moved to arrest some of the leaders of the Left. A wave of demonstrations throughout the country induced him to release them, and an open conflict appeared between the central government and the NLF militants in power in Hadramawt. The Hadramawt militants are reported to have cut off relations with the capital.

In May 1968, the NLF's Left tried to topple the government by armed popular insurrection in several places, but the effort failed abysmally, as the army remained loyal to Qahtan. The next year presented many security challenges to the new regime, most coming from tribal forces or other elements connected with the old regime, many of whose leaders were in Saudi Arabia trying to undo the revolutionary government.

The Left, too, was only waiting for another opportunity. This presented itself in June 1969 when Qahtan tried to fire his defense minister because of personal rivalry. The Left made a tactical alliance with other anti-Qahtan elements in the state's governing bodies, and after four days of political intrigues—not yet blood baths in those days—a decision was finally passed, on June 22, to dismiss Qahtan. He was replaced by a presidential council of five members, all from the NLF's far Left, which had finally come to power. Salim Rubay' 'Ali was elected president, and 'Abd al-Fattah Isma'il became secretary-general of the NLF.

After June 1969, the regime of South Yemen became an almost full-fledged Marxist one. As such, its history falls outside of the present study, in which I have tried to pinpoint the social circumstances that give rise to such a regime. The only aspect of the subsequent period that concerns us here is the radical land reform that was carried out beginning in late 1970. This land reform started with a popular uprising (intifada), which took place in October 1970 in the region of Abyan, a typical area of large landowners and sharecroppers. This rural uprising was described to J. Stork two years later by someone who took part in it:

> We worked with those who had emerged as peasant leaders and we formed committees to survey landownership and distinguish the real feudalists from the smallholders. We held extensive meetings on how to solve the land problem for a year and a half. The landlords complained to the government about us subversive elements. They didn't know that the Front was involved. So the Government appointed someone to meet with both parties, as a cover. The main function was to set up a meeting of both sides: to get the landlords and the peasants together in one room and see how courageous the peasants were in speaking out.
>
> The peasants came right out and claimed the land of those landlords, even the ones right there in the room. The landlords said they were all for agrarian reform, but according to the Law. The peasants replied that the land was theirs: they worked it. They said they would just take it. The meeting turned into a large demonstration. The peasants went out and surrounded the homes of the landlords. There was some fighting, but no real bloodshed. The landlords tried to instigate and revive old tribal feuds, but it was too late for any of that. They still didn't comprehend the

involvement of the National Front in the uprising, supporting and encouraging it.[142]

Thus, the popular element may be more important than is usually conceded, as is shown in this incident as well as in the many more that were to come in its wake.

The Corrective Movement, June 1969

The regime that came to power in South Yemen after independence defined itself ideologically as pan-Arabist, but it contained undercurrents of the left-wing social radicalism that had appeared in the course of the guerrilla war. Without proper understanding of this development, the final and decisive turn to the left in the "Corrective Movement" of June 1969 cannot be understood.

The first signs of radicalization appeared in the first half of 1965, and the trend came to fruition in the summer of that year, in the Second Congress of the NLF, in which the main theme was strong criticism aimed at the forced merger with FLOSY. For our study, central to this incident is the fact that the NLF was at the time entirely democratic and decisions seemed to reflect mass attitudes. The organization had no accepted leader, and no one could impose his will on the rest. What we see taking place substantively in this congress is pressure exerted from below—by members of the organizations forming the NLF and actively participating in the guerrilla movement—to call off the merger. The new politburo elected in this congress was, for the first time, one with clear Marxist leanings, in some cases quite explicit. This leadership, which has come to be known as the secondary leadership, included people like 'Abd al-Fattah Isma'il and Salim Rubay' 'Ali, two of the first presidents of South Yemen after the final turn to Marxism. It included also many more radicals who became the main figures of the state after the Corrective Movement.[143] Though the biographical information available on these people is not satisfactory, it seems clear that what they had in common was that none of them belonged to the traditional elite—nor, of course, to the real social elite of the protectorate, the sayyids, nor to the Adenese elite. The low representation of trade unions is also distinct. The secondary leadership were marginal people, either from North Yemen or from the hinterland.

This point may be surprising (from whom could one expect Marxist leanings if not from trade union activists?), yet it does seem to come out of the sources. As a contemporary close observer of the South Arabian drama puts it, [the battle between FLOSY and the NLF] "developed into a battle between town and desert. FLOSY . . . stood for the interests of Aden. The NLF following sprang mainly from the tribal territories, [and] transients of the Town."[144] The same observer further notes that "the NLF did look like an organization coming from the hinterland to take over Aden."[145] There is little doubt, too, that most of the NLF's people belonged to the lower castes, and many had had modern education and occupations based on modern education. These people had for two years been living a self-imposed austere and severe way of life that somewhat "miraculously" seemed to bear fruit, in the sense that the NLF seemed now ineradicable and a body with which every South Yemeni could identify. Small wonder that these devout cadres were not going to let less-dedicated groups share in this hard-won success. This is, I believe, the social-psychological process through which the radical trends appeared within the NLF in the summer of 1965.

What is not entirely clear to me is why the proponents of this ideology waited until June 1969 to come to actual power. The answer might lie in a combination of two factors: first, that Qahtan al-Sha'bi, the oldest, most experienced, and best-known figure in the top leadership, seemed to be the most appropriate representative and, second, that the Marxist trend was, in the beginning, quite unselfconscious. Be that as it may, the Corrective Movement of June 1969—the final step in the establishment of the Marxist regime—was intimately connected with the events of the summer of 1965.

CHAPTER FOUR

The Algerian War
of Independence

The Algerian revolt and war of independence that erupted in 1954 and ended eight years later in complete independence is outwardly the most serious challenge to the theory presented in this book, as Algeria presents the only additional extant case of a Muslim society conducting a successful guerrilla war against a foreign conqueror, and yet the Algerian revolution turned out to be rather moderate in terms of social policy. Algeria is, therefore, an obvious test case for my theory. In fact, the Algerian case has puzzled many scholars, who have frantically been looking for solutions to this enigma. Elbaki Hermassi is probably a good representative of these. He says, for example, "Most analysts who recorded the extent of the massive rural mobilization were convinced they were recording a socialist peasant revolution and were confused when, in the end, the movement culminated in a quasi-military takeover."[1]

As explanation of this fact, Hermassi suggests that "of the maghribi elites, the Algerian elites have been historically the most divided in their orientations, the most heterogeneous in their composition, and the most given to dissensions . . . [T]he revolution . . . in reality only intensified the existing antagonisms and created a new basis for dissension."[2] Hermassi is certainly right in suggesting that the Algerian elites were extremely divided before, during, and after the war of liberation. He is probably right, too, in attributing this fact chiefly to the major counterpressure exerted by the French, who effectively segregated one fighter from another inside Algeria and the fighters inside Algeria from their leadership outside Algeria—the main body of which the French even managed to lock behind bars. But he is probably wrong in holding this divisiveness responsible for the revolution's lack of radicalism. A comparative glimpse at other major revolutions is enough to show that nothing is more characteristic of these than friction and divisiveness. Some of these revolutions (such as in Albania and South Yemen) were accompanied by fierce and bloody internecine struggles that make the Algerian struggle look like a picnic. Even China and the Soviet Union have known much interelite dissension. In no known case did dissension stop the revolution from reaching extremes of radicalism. In fact, one could easily make a strong case for the opposite thesis: Dissension, anarchy, lack of restraining hand in the shape of a strong leader may more plausibly lead to extreme radicalism than when these conditions are absent.

In sum, neither Hermassi nor any other of the scholars who have dealt with Algeria come to my general thesis. It seems clear that the failure of so many scholars to come up with a satisfactory answer to the Algerian riddle is a direct outcome of the nearly total lack of real comparative investigation of Middle Eastern societies and polities. In Algeria's case, such an investigation is particularly called for. Those scholars who see the Algerian revolution as a failed revolution (Hermassi, Humbaraci) because it did not attain a certain level of radicalism in fact compare it implicitly with certain models, probably China and Vietnam. Hence, it would seem imperative to pursue such a comparison to its end in order to find out who or what really failed. There is, thus, nothing artificial in our effort to place Algeria in a comparative framework. On the contrary, any other approach seems to be more problematic and, eventually, sterile.

FRENCH OCCUPATION AND THE
ALGERIAN WAR OF INDEPENDENCE

A chronological summary of Algerian modern history will suffice as a base for this analysis. France embarked upon the conquest of Algeria in 1830, thus bringing to an end three centuries of Ottoman nominal overlordship of the country.[3] Possibly because of the unusual proximity between France and Algeria, the conquest proceeded on somewhat different lines than most colonial occupations. It was accompanied by a massive settlement by the French, mainly, but also of other European nationals, whose settlement was greatly encouraged by the French government. This government, despite its lack of a preconceived plan concerning Algeria, increasingly came to see that country as an integral part of France and treated Algeria accordingly, penetrating into Algeria's traditional life. This penetration and intensifying incorporation did not occur without objection. A long series of violent anti-French revolts throughout the nineteenth century bears solemn witness to the existence of this resistance.[4] To a certain extent, these revolts may be seen as a sign of warning of what was to come in the 1950s.

Most nineteenth-century revolts were strongly religious (even apocalyptic) in nature. But the beginnings of nationalism in the Middle East at the turn of the twentieth century did not fail to spread to North Africa and Algeria, and there were clear signs of increasing animosity toward the French government in the first years of the twentieth century. After World War II, there was underground activity by several groups intent on organizing a general revolt against France, which finally broke out in November 1954.[5] This revolt was planned by a roof organization of various secret groups established earlier that year—the National Liberation Front (FLN).

The Algerian revolt broke out as a series of coordinated terrorist acts in various places throughout the country. Initially, the number of insurgents did not surpass five hundred, of whom no less than three hundred were concentrated in the Aurès Mountains in eastern Algeria, an area settled by Berber tribespeople and a traditional center of resistance to any government. The traditional segmentary structure of the tribes in the region had, in recent decades, come under a great deal of strain because of improvement in the means of communication, transformation of subsistence land into commodity under new French rules concerning landownership, and excessive population growth. That Aurès was one of the first centers of revolt is, therefore, not surprising. But it must be borne in mind that the revolt received very widespread popular support everywhere in Algeria. Thus, Braestrup, a foreign reporter who stayed with the rebels for extensive periods of time, observed:

> Peasants showed up with food, water, and information. Some showed the newly healed scars of French "interrogation". At hamlet after hamlet, some within sight of French outposts, the Moslem peasants provided *couscous*, lamb, milk, and coffee for the commando. They were friendly, hardpressed, and scared to death of French retaliation.[6]

At the beginning of the revolt, the French force in Algeria was small. France did not expect large-scale rebellion, and in any case the French position in Algeria seemed secure, as was the position of only a few colonial forces in their colonies. First in importance was the small distance between the two countries. The deep involvement in and control by France of all aspects of Algerian life were probably so reassuring that no serious erosion in French position was to be feared. Not least in importance was the fact that Algeria was by then settled by about 1 million French nationals, a large element in the population that had a deep interest in the uninterrupted continuation of the French occupation. For these reasons, the actual French force in Algeria at the beginning of the revolt was limited, but as the revolt gathered momentum these forces were reinforced continuously and numbered half a million by 1956. With such an enormous force, the French were able to stamp out FLN activities in the countryside. Realizing this, the FLN changed tactics and started a massive wave of guerrilla operations in the cities. This initiative was in turn dealt with by the French in 1957, and very fierce measures put an end to this spurt of urban guerrilla activity as well. Thus, by the end of 1957, the Algerian guerrilla movement was facing a severe crisis: Militarily, it was getting nowhere—in fact, barely managing to survive—and, politically, the French remained staunch and did not move an inch toward the Algerians.

The failure of the FLN inside Algeria moved the organization's focus of initiative outside of the country. There were, at the time, 60,000 Algerian war refugees in Tunisia and 40,000 in Morocco, and the FLN started a strong propaganda campaign to recruit some of these people. By the end of 1957, the FLN external force numbered 25,000, whereas the internal guerrilla force was estimated to number 15,000. The French retaliated in kind and built a formidable defense line on Algeria's borders with Tunisia and Morocco. Defense devices included forts, electric barbed wire, minefields, and the like. Effective as these measures were, they were not foolproof, and so, in 1958, the French went a step further and started large-scale offensive attacks on guerrilla camps inside Tunisia and Morocco. At the same time, they devised one of the most far-reaching and notorious actions by any army against a guerrilla-supportive population: They moved to relocate about 2 million Algerian peasants living near the borders of Tunisia and Morocco, so as to cut off the external guerrilla movement from its supporting base.

These details already show the Algerian war of independence to be one of the biggest and toughest in the history of guerrilla wars. This no doubt had much to do with the fact that French presence in Algeria was so pervasive and strong that the idea of granting Algeria its independence was psychologically more difficult to accept than in most comparable colonial situations.

On the admission of the French army, the number of dead among French soldiers was 13,000.[7] This is a large number indeed if we compare it to the number of British dead in South Yemen for example. The Algerian death toll reached 1 million.

In the final analysis, French military activity was effective mainly inside Algeria. The French also managed to seal Algeria off from its two neighboring countries but were unable to eliminate the Algerian forces in Tunisia and Morocco. This external army thus became an important political factor as well. In Eric Wolf's words,

> At the same time it [French activity] left untouched the growing "external army" which grew more important for the nationalist leadership as a bargaining point in any final negotiation for peace in direct proportion to the decline of the internal army in both strength and effectiveness. Thus the end of the war was to find the external army intact as the only organized body of Algerians under the leadership of Houari Boumédienne.[8]

Although in 1958 the Algerian guerrilla movement and war of independence were on the verge of collapse, they had brought about the entirely unexpected political conditions that would lead to total success. In the first place, the economic price of putting the revolt down was enormous, and the French public was starting to have second thoughts about whether the war was worth its cost. But more important by far was the fact that the excessive measures taken to quell the rebellion had aroused large-scale indignation in many quarters and created a national cleavage that threatened to wreak havoc within French society itself. As this fracture appeared and snowballed, the French colons started a last-ditch fight to save Algeria for France and did not desist from using intimidation and force in the process. This only served to deepen the wound, and for many in France it now became clear that Algeria's independence had become no less vital for France than for Algeria.

As Algeria finally received its independence in 1962, there was no dominant leader who commanded the respect of the entire resistance movement.[9] Three governments were formed, each claiming legitimacy as Algeria's sole government. After a short, bloodless contest, Ahmed Ben Bella, backed by the external army of Houari Boumediène, won out. Ben Bella's regime, which lasted till 1965, was that of a charismatic and highly controversial leader, who talked a great deal about pan-Arabism and socialism and gave the appearance that the country was radicalizing. In reality, however, the social policy of the regime was quite moderate. Aside from this, Ben Bella's regime seems to have promised more than it actually delivered. This fact and the ups and downs in national mood connected with the leader's highly emotional rhetoric were bound to enrage many people. It was in one of these instances that Boumediène, head of the Algerian army since independence, staged a coup d'état and replaced Ben Bella as head of state. This shift in the locus of power from civilian authority to the army has puzzled many observers. Wolf, for example, finds this phenomenon somewhat hard to accept and points out the difference between Algeria and China or the Soviet Union. But it seems to me that the subservience of the army to the civil authorities in China and in the USSR is an outcome of the radical social revolution that had taken place in those countries, resulting in a total lack of social legitimacy for military rule. In Algeria, no such revolution came to pass; hence, no such social block against army interventionism emerged. So the task of explaining the lack of radical social revolution remains.

Many expected Algeria to institute a very radical social regime, but, in fact, nothing of the sort took place, apart from an agrarian reform of not particularly severe character. In addition, there took place some measures of nationalization of the major means of production, such as oil wells in the Sahara. The regime was quite similar to the Arab socialism of Abd al-Nasser of Egypt—plainly, middle-class socialism. The most important measures of the land reform were those taken to nationalize the properties of the departed French colons. Most of the land in question had been captured by those indigenous Algerians who had been workers or sharecroppers on it. The new government moved to nationalize these lands, although effectively land was left in the hands of those who had captured it.[10]

The extent of this agrarian reform is made evident by the following figures: At the time of independence, the agricultural area of Algeria comprised about 10 million hectares, of which 2.7 million hectares were owned by French colons; the French-owned land was, of course, the best in the country. The number of ownership units belonging to the French was 22,000, and the average area per French estate was 125 hectares, compared to 12 hectares for ownership units of Algerians. The gap in average incomes was even bigger. French colons constituted some 2 percent of the agricultural population of Algeria, but they "produced 60 percent of the total crop production by volume."[11] A short while after independence and the nationalization acts, the Algerian government went one step further and established on these state lands agricultural cooperatives, which the beneficiaries of the land reform were obliged to join. These cooperatives were run through self-management, known by the term "autogestion." In this way there came into being in Algeria something akin to a socialist agricultural sector.

About ten years after independence, that is, in 1971, Algeria began to contemplate further land reform. Although, there were no really big landowners in Algeria, large ownership gaps did exist.

Whereas autogestion peasants were earning on average £55 a year, average yearly peasant income was just £25. Although the new agrarian reform seemed mainly aimed at lands of absentee landlords, land was distributed to a large and growing number of landless peasants.[12] Still, the basic fact remained that the land reform was moderate, basically because Algeria never had a class of truly big landlords. Beyond this kind of land reform, Algeria has refrained from any sort of radicalism. Already in April 1964, Ben Bella called on the national congress of the FLN to adopt more socialistic measures, but his suggestions were rejected. Rather, he was "met with a severe rebuff by the assembled delegates who overwhelmingly voted support for the preservation of traditional Islamic principles as guidelines for 'socialism'. Revolutionary ardor clearly was not the mood of the Congress."[13]

THE SOCIAL ROOTS OF THE ALGERIAN WAR

These are the general lines of the Algerian revolt, guerrilla movement, and war of independence and their main social and political consequences. Our problem is to try to understand why this guerrilla movement did not develop truly radical tendencies. We must, first of all, analyze the social side of the Algerian guerrilla movement. The best general study to engage this issue from a viewpoint similar to mine is by Wolf, who views the Algerian guerrilla war as a typical case of peasant war, one of six cases of peasant war that he traces in the major revolutions of the twentieth century.[14] At the end of his book, he builds a theory (a somewhat rudimentary one, it must be said) to explain what aroused these peasant populations to revolt. The major reason he gives is the capitalization of agriculture and the turning of land into a commercial asset to be bought and sold, whereas in traditional agriculture land had been the chief source of livelihood, a part of nature and the eternal order of things. Although some sort of exploitation was, of course, always present in these societies, the traditional formation was also based on mutual aid and sharing of resources, especially in time of crisis and emergency. The intrusion of capitalism severed individuals from their social matrix and thereby exposed them to fears and anxieties. Paradoxically, the constraint put on peasants' access to traditional land came at a time of population explosion, resulting mainly from reduction in death rates. This situation further worked to disrupt the delicate traditional equilibrium between people and natural resources. In the long run, according to Wolf, it has often been the case that the peasants' reaction to these changes has been revolt. But such a revolt can only take place in certain circumstances; the most important precondition is the tactical autonomy of the peasants—the factor that passes like a thread through all the cases touched on by Wolf.[15]

In Wolf's analysis, this desiderata of tactical autonomy have found expression in the fact that the classical—in fact, almost the only—social sector to be engaged in peasant uprisings has been that of small, or middle, independent peasants. This theory is, however, fundamentally flawed, first of all, in that too much is attributed by Wolf to this magic word "capitalism." But, in fact, neither in Albania nor in South Yemen (nor for that matter in China) can much be shown to hinge on the factor of capitalism. It is my impression that peasant revolts have been pervasive quite independently of capitalist intrusion. The level of taxation and the legal-political status of the land have been frequent causes for revolution, and twentieth-century capitalism has been merely an added factor—wherever it has been of influence, which was not everywhere.

Why did the Algerian guerrilla movement not develop into a radical social revolution? It might be claimed that the army that took control of Algeria after independence was not exactly the guerrilla army but an army that came from°the outside. But this argument does not seem to hold. The external army was a guerrilla army all the same; it just happened not to have been involved in actual fighting. Also, in spite of the fact that there were factional conflicts in the postindependence period, no faction was in effect excluded from sociological influence on the underlying political process in independent Algeria. Finally, and most important, the FLN of the guerrilla period did not show any signs of radical tendencies; as Walter Laqueur says,

> The agrarian issue was far from central to the [Algerian] rebellion and the FLN by no means supported a social revolution. As one of the leaders put it, "The problem is not posed for us as in China. The Chinese carried on both national resistance and social revolution. . . . We have taken up arms for a well defined aim: national liberation." . . . [T]he bedrock of the struggle against the French was nationalistic, with socialist demands, other than seizing foreign property, little more than scatterings of topsoil dressing.[16]

Was this choice of ideology a matter of voluntaristic choice, a caprice, floating, so to speak, in the air, entirely free from social determination? I believe the answer must be no and that a careful comparison between Algeria, on the one hand, and Albania, South Yemen, and China, on the other hand, will yield an adequate social explanation. Put briefly, the main thrust of my argument is that in South Yemen and Albania the National struggle developed into an internal social revolution because (1) there existed in these societies a traditional social elite very much detached from the rest of society, yet holding that society at bay; and (2) that elite was unwilling and/or incapable of leading the guerrilla struggle against the national enemy. In Algeria, the thrust of French colonialism into the fabric of Algerian society was so deep and pervasive that the ruling elite in Algerian society came to consist almost entirely of the French. In this way, the main class struggle was simultaneously also the national struggle. Driving out the French and occupying their lands or positions was, in effect, a national but also a social revolution. Nationalist ideology was enough to sustain such a revolution. To see how this came about, we must go back in time a little and review the evidence in some detail.

The French occupation of Algeria was unusual in the fact that the colonial power's penetration into the occupied society was very deep. This occupation started in 1830, as a minor policing operation. Only in 1840 did the French decide to effect a total occupation and colonization of the country, which required as a prior condition the seizure of lands owned by Algerians. To understand this seizure, and its significance, we must first analyze Algeria's pre-occupation land system.

PATTERNS OF LANDOWNERSHIP

Traditional Agrarian Regimes and Rival Class Structure

A French report estimated that in 1830 the entire agricultural land area in the *tell*, the elevated area of pre-Saharan Algeria, was 14 million hectares. Of this land, about 4.5 million hectares was *milk*, or freehold.[17] As in the Middle East, most of the land was garden land in or on the outskirts of villages and towns. But in Algeria, unlike the Middle East, much freehold land was also under regular sown agriculture, within the popular institution of *haush*, a rural estate owned by a group of families, in which each held an average of 8 to 10 hectares.[18]

A category of land that was of considerable importance was the *habous*, or religious endowment. It was estimated that in 1830 this category comprised some 50,000 to 75,000 hectares.[19] Another important land category in Algeria in 1830 was *beylik*, or land belonging to the ruler of the country. This category comprised about

1 million hectares. Most of the land in this category came from land confiscated from individuals. As the Ottoman rulers departed in 1830, lands in this category became state lands, and grants from this category were the natural start in the process of land acquisition by French colons.[20] In addition, there were 3 million hectares of *mawat*, or dead land, unoccupied and uncultivated, not considered in the ownership of anybody, not even the state—land free for the taking, possibly in intermittent use as grazing land by tribes.[21] The last and most important category was tribal land (*'arsh*), consisting of some 5 million hectares and, thus, the biggest land category. These belonged collectively to the tribes, though they were held permanently by individual families.[22]

The predominance of freehold and tribal land highlights the essential feature of the traditional Algerian land system: It was characterized by small landlordism. Lucette Valensi, who has written a study on pre-French North Africa, dwells on this point at some length. About the mountainous regions of northern Algeria, she says:

> The mountaineers of Kabylia and the Aurès are arboriculturists and gardeners producing a variety of fruits and vegetables and olive oil through intensive exploitation of the soil. . . . Despite the scarcity of arable land, Kabyle farmers still managed to grown grains and vegetables. Kabylia was the area, par excellence, of milk (private, transferable and inheritable property).[23]

More to the south of this relatively rich agricultural region of the Maghreb was the tribal area. The system of land tenure prevailing there, though different in important details from that of the north, was, in the final analysis, quite similar:

> Each tribe traditionally controlled spacious acreage whose boundaries were recognized by both the sovereign and the neighboring tribes. Membership in the tribe automatically provided access to the land, but the land was not, strictly speaking, collective. Each family worked the plots which it was in a position to cultivate. Although no property titles verified the claims of individual families, their possession of the fields was legitimized by cultivating them, and was continuous and hereditary.[24]

Equality among small landowners and rarity of big landlords were the main features of the system: A "trait common to both nomadic and sedentary people was the relatively egalitarian nature of property ownership." "Before the population growth of the 20th century, there was no rural proletariat to speak of in the Maghreb, where small land owners and small family farms predominated."[25]

Not only in the Ottoman period, but also in the nineteenth and twentieth centuries Algeria lacked a tangible group of landed magnates or even big landlords. It is true that there was a group of people who fulfilled some of the functions of big landlords, but this activity was based on tax collection, not on rent or anything having to do with actual production. Peter von Sivers, who makes this important observation, suggest that this absence of big landlords was a result of the fact that Algeria's agriculture was based on dry farming and, hence, was not a particularly lucrative venture. Moreover, frequent droughts made farming too hazardous economically for the chief families of the countryside.[26] Von Sivers further claims that in this absence of big landlordism Algeria was similar to most areas of the Middle East. Although this may be an adequate explanation for the Algerian situation, it is only partially true for the Middle East. Despite the limitations posed by ecology, big landlords did spring up in Syria, Egypt, and Iraq after 1858, and so the ecology is a partial explanation at best. The limitations of the ecology in Algeria and, say, Syria, are somewhat different. In a country such as Syria the predominance of tribes in many low-lying lands during the Ottoman period was a result of the extreme weakness of the government. Imposition of law and order after 1858 were enough to push the nomads back, sown agriculture became regular again, and with it big landlords could appear. In Algeria, the constricting power of the ecology seems to have been greater than in Syria. The absence of big landlords in traditional Algeria appears to be an outcome of the prevalence of nomadism and seminomadism and the resultant tribal society. This prevalence of seminomadism has to do with Algeria's geography and climate. A relevant excerpt from a geographic treatise says, for example:

> Although the contrast between *tell* (northern Algeria) and *sahara* is too simple on morphological and ecological grounds, the broad concept of Mediterranean and steppe domains throws light on many aspects of the social, economic and political evolution of the Maghreb: the close juxtaposition of nomadic and sedentary societies and their interdependence . . . the limited extent of stable cultivation except in mountain massifs . . . the political domination of the Maghreb by nomadic groups; the resulting political instability and lack of unity . . . The persistence of pastoral nomadism owes much to the fact that four-fifths of the Maghreb lie outside the Mediterranean climate zone.[27]

There is no doubt that the chief reason for this is the paucity of rain in a large portion of the Maghreb, such that full-fledged sown agriculture could not exist, but only extensive grazing of sheep and cattle. One clear expression of this situation was the fact that in 1830 tribal land clearly constituted the biggest land category. On the other had, tribal tenure is by its very nature communal rather than individual, so that individual tribal members may not alienate tribal land for any reason whatsoever. In areas where ecology allowed permanent villages to appear, as in the mountainous ranges occupied mainly by Berbers, a much higher level of articulation and individualization of the social system necessarily took place, but even there the ecological conditions did not allow truly big landowners to appear, although signs of landlordism certainly did exist. Fanny Colonna's study on the status of the religious leader in the Aurès Mountains in the nineteenth century may help clarify this point.

Colonna found clear evidence that the position of the tribal elite in certain parts of the Aurès was based, among other things, on some degree of landlordism and other forms of surplus expropriation—that is, economic exploitation.[28] But one gets the impression that this phenomenon was neither far-reaching nor present everywhere. And more important, perhaps, is to recall Barrington Moore's generalization that not every landlord–peasant (sharecropper) situation is potentially explosive. Landlords who were living among their people and landlords who were seen as fulfilling positive functions for these peasants were plainly in less sensitive positions.[29] Undoubtedly, the marabouts, highly revered—in fact, holy—leaders of nineteenth-century Algeria, would have been in that favorable situation.

Another area worth mentioning in this context is the Kabylia Mountains, the main region of settlement of the Berbers in Algeria. These mountains were not very accessible to the French, suffered only a little from land confiscations, yet were the site of intense activity in the war of independence. This is one important situation that led Wolf to identify the small or middle peasant as the classic carrier of peasant revolt. René Dumont, a French expert on Algerian agriculture, reveals interesting details on this region in the early 1950s. In one village, population 1,200, Dumont gives empirical data indicating that there were 150 landownership units, varying in size between 1 acre and 15 acres. The top layer in the village comprised sixteen estates of between 10 to 15 acres (2.5 to 3.75 hectares) each,[30] obviously small holdings; indeed, the population was very poor and found it difficult to make ends meet. One evident problem was population explosion.[31] In another case, described by Dumont in some detail, an estate of 15 acres of sown land and 1.25 acres of fig trees—a rather small estate—was nevertheless worked by a sharecropper, or *khammés*, who was entitled to one-fifth of the revenue.[32] This situation is a far cry from that in prerevolutionary Syria, for example, where city landlords might own whole villages. According to this example, it would seem that class articulation in the Kabylia area was not particularly far-reaching.

Writing on Kabyle society in a more general way in the 1930s, Maunier observed that the area was densely populated and agriculture quite highly developed.[33] On the whole, heads of all families owned land, and the population was hardworking and fragile. Hence there was a large measure of continuity and stability. The society in question was a combination of tribe and village. Sedentarism was complete, but villages still somewhat nominally formed parts of more widespread tribes. Tribes were extremely weak, with villages shifting from one tribe to another at will. After the French occupation the tribe is estimated to have declined even further.

The village formed the higher social framework that was of interest to the individual. Anything beyond the village was of little interest, but even within the village the individual family was of far greater importance. The family was the relevant unit for landownership. Only the pasture area was considered common property of the entire village community.[34] The village also assumed a certain importance in Kabyle customary law, and Maunier refers to certain mutual obligations called *touiza* (corvée), mainly in relation to the help a villager could expect to obtain to build a new house.[35]

Maunier states explicitly that Kabyle society was not hierarchically stratified in any substantial manner.[36] Tribes, villages, and families were all more or less similar in status to their counterparts. Some families may have enjoyed higher prestige in the village council in politics and in law, but such prestige had no permanency and was not institutionalized; rather, it was contested and precarious in the extreme. Nor was there a legal rule of "elders." Instead, rule was by a kind of "rustic democracy."[37] In the economic sphere, too, inequality was quite limited. Most people lived in modesty verging on poverty. There were few opportunities for enrichment, and such enrichment mainly found expression in the jewelry of wives.

Throughout history, a major avenue for the emergence of large estates has been rapid population growth, accompanied by rising levels of income, leading to commercialization and growing pressure on the small peasants. Nothing of the sort took place in pre-French Algeria. The population of the town is known to have been declining, precluding the possibility of the existence of drives for commercialization. The country had been sparsely populated, even with the existing technology. René Dumont estimated that pressure on the land in the Maghreb started only sometime around the middle of the twentieth century.[38]

Alternatively, large-estate regimes emerged in history in situations in which central government had an interest in assisting a would-be landed aristocracy in subjugating the peasantry legally and politically—even when the cash nexus did not exist. Something of that nature probably took place in imperial Russia. In the Middle East the central Ottoman government would never cooperate with a landed aristocracy, because it saw itself as the sole repository of power; the situation was probably similar in Algeria, an autonomous Ottoman province.

Further assistance in understanding the mode of articulation of provincial leadership in nineteenth-century Algeria may be found in another study by von Sivers,[39] in which he analyzes the changes in the structures of traditional leading families in the semiarid zone around Biskra. Leading families constituted one of three leadership patterns that von Sivers observes in nineteenth-century Algeria: nomad families moving with their herds of sheep between the semiarid south and the northern *tell* region; families of heads of virtually sedentarized tribes who were settled in villages in the *tell* region; and heads of villages in the mountainous areas. The first type of leadership, like the other two types, was not characterized by livelihood coming from large-scale absentee landlordism or any other stark expropriation of resources and their transfer from a mass of producers to a tiny ruling class. The three families who constituted the leadership of the Biskra region were large-scale livestock owners who lived there. Throughout the nineteenth century, the French government tried to use these families for their own purposes, initially by trying to turn them into a kind of local aristocracy (an effort that completely failed). Later, the French sought to make these leaders officeholders in the French administration; but this attempt, too, bore little fruit. Von Sivers reaches the conclusion that despite these efforts, and despite violent struggles for power between these three families throughout the latter half of the nineteenth century, a somewhat striking continuity took place, and the same families were still leaders in the area in the twentieth century.[40]

Von Sivers further investigated the question of large landlords in nineteenth-century Algeria and, more precisely, among those who are known to have been the leaders of local society.[41] Really big landlords are conspicuous by their absence—the biggest land category was 100 hectares. and the overwhelming majority of holdings studied were from 20 to 30 hectares. Moreover, holdings and incomes in the top category were on the decline:

> There was a secular decline of certain types of small-to-middle incomes and properties to the level of small ownership. . . . There was a similar long-range decline of large earnings and holdings to the level of middle ownership, although it appears that few landowners managed to stay permanently on this level and many descended further to the plane of small ownership.[42]

Was the reason for this decline in the wealth of the traditional Algerian elite connected in some way with the French penetration? It would be a great surprise if this were not the case. True enough, it is evident that most confiscated land was not confiscated from members of the elite, in addition to the fact the elite did not really have much that could be confiscated. Still, it stands to reason that because of French presence, the general position of the elite must have been somewhat adversely affected, and empirical evidence substantiates this assumption, such as the short account given by Jacques Berque of the social structure of the large village of Frenda on the high Algerian plateau in the interwar period:

> Frenda's noble family, the Bu Medin, although still exercising the function of caïds, had lost its wealth and its prestige. It had been partially dislodged from its authority by the rise of small upstart chiefs. . . . Religious institutions had undergone the same vicissitudes. The marabout suffered the same decadence as the *siyyid* (noble). The once terrifying Derqawas still had a *zawiya* in the district . . . but considerably weakened and grown bourgeois.[43]

By way of contrast, the most powerful figure in Frenda in the 1920s was a rich colon, who overpowered his local adversaries and owned thousands of acres in vineyards and cereals.[44]

It may be useful at this point to look also at the few quantitative data that have been published on Algeria's pattern of landownership such as those from Nouchi and Ageron for the twentieth century. Their data for 1950 are presented in Table 4.1. In relation to the upper group, which is our main interest here, it is noteworthy that the highest category presented in the table is about 100 hectares. Estates ten and twenty times as big were common in Albania before the revolution there. Moreover, average size of land per ownership unit in this highest category was about 200 hectares. The significance of these figures may be clarified by comparing Algeria with Egypt.

The first Egyptian land reform decreed the confiscation of landholdings above 200 *feddans* (about 100 hectares). Two further land reforms reduced the limit to 50 *feddans* (25 hectares). Launay

TABLE 4.1   Landownership Structure of Indigenous Algerians in 1950

Category (hectares)	Units in Category	Percent of Total Units	Land in Category (hectares)	Percent of Total Land
0 - 10	438,483	69.52	1,378,400	18.76
10 - 50	167,170	26.50	3,185,800	43.35
50 - 100	16,580	2.63	1,096,100	14.91
100+	8,499	1.35	1,688,800	22.98
Total	630,732	100	7,349,100	100

Source: Adapted from L. Jönsson, *La Révolution agraire en Algérie* (Uppsala, 1978), p. 16.

cites a professional agronomic study that estimates that a typical Algerian family needs a land area of 7 hectares to subsist at a minimum level.[45] Launay comments that this study was purely agronomic and overlooked the fact that Algerian agriculture is still largely based on a two-year cycle, sowing one year and fallowing one year. This means that an Algerian family actually needs 14 hectares to make ends meet. Concerning Egypt, obviously a vastly more fertile country, there is a debate whether the minimal land area needed to nourish a family is 2.5 *feddans* (1.25 hectares) or 5 *feddans*.[46] For the sake of simplicity let us assume the latter, as such an assumption weakens my argument. If we render Algerian landownership statistics in Egyptian terms, we find that the 200 hectares that is the average Algerian landholding in the highest ownership group is equivalent to only 71 Egyptian *feddans*, just slightly above the 50-*feddan* limit in the last and most severe Egyptian land reform. It is evident that a comparison with Egypt enhances my claim that even the top landowners in Algeria should properly be considered middle-sized farmers and no more. Thus, the Algerian provincial elite was not a true land elite in the first place.

French Seizure of Lands

In addition, during the French period there occurred the extremely important process of large-scale seizure of indigenous lands by the government for the use of the French settlers. The French began by capturing the *beylik* lands, legally Algeria's sovereign lands. Uncovering and confiscating these lands occupied the French during the first years of their rule. Almost simultaneously, they tried to lay their hands on the *habous* as well, and soon after the French occupation the new government issued orders that amounted to confiscation and nationalization of all *habous* land in Algeria. These orders were extremely difficult to implement, but eventually they were and caused resentment among Algerians as few other land seizures did, for the *habous* was one of the most important popular institutions in traditional Algeria.[47]

The outbreak of the 'Abd al-Qadir revolt in 1839 provided the French with an excellent pretext to carry out massive land seizures termed "sequestration." The sequestration act of December 1840 provided that all properties of persons fighting against France or even abandoning their land and going over to the enemy's side should be annexed to the public domain.[48] Another French practice was seizure of tribal lands—one of the most important categories in Ottoman Algeria. Much of the extensive agriculture that these tribes carried out was connected with the rhythm of sheepherding and tied to transhumance. The French authorities began a process called *cantonnement*—fixation of the tribe to only a fraction of its former land, confiscating the rest for the use of French colons. In 1861, the French government imposed on Algeria a European land code, which meant individual ownership rights were granted over lands.

In practice, land could now be bought and sold with much greater ease than previously. Soon thereafter, Algerian lands started to pass into French hands on a massive scale. The pace of the whole process greatly quickened in the wake of the al-Moqrani revolt of 1871. A full-fledged, formal, assimilationist policy was put into effect for the first time, a policy that included measures such as abolition of autochthonous institutions (justice, for example); further land laws intended to break up tribal holdings; and extension of the French administration—as well as a massive gallicization of place-names in Algeria, as if to obliterate the traditional Algerian culture.[49] Although this policy was mainly effected in the 1870s, it was never afterwards reversed or even relaxed, either ideologically or in practical terms. Wolf estimates the overall effect of this process on Algerian society:

> The native population thus saw itself increasingly deprived of land and pushed back by the advancing colonists upon ever more unproductive terrain. Its traditional mechanisms of ensuring economic security had been abrogated, lineages and tribes had been scattered, the familiar political structure dismantled. The response to such deprivation was in part wholesale migration, in part open revolt.[50]

The Vineyards

The agrarian situation in Algeria that was basic to the Algerian revolution and war of independence involved another major factor: wine.[51] Wine was, after all, the real driving force behind the massive emigration of the French colons to Algeria. It goes without saying that these people did not come to Algeria to be involved in the extremely poor and semiarid agriculture that most of Algeria allowed. They came because at an early stage of the occupation it had become clear that parts of northern Algeria were rich enough to sustain vineyard growing. It is not surprising that a large part of French efforts at confiscation were aimed at these best of Algerian lands. Of the 400,000 hectares that were under viticulture in 1962, no less than nine-tenths were French-owned.

The vineyards were a symbol for a lot that went on in Algeria in these years and were also, to my mind, the cause for a great deal of it. First of all, wine counts for much more than the land area given to its production would indicate. Though this land area was relatively small, vineyards accounted for 35 percent of Algerian agricultural revenue, compared to 35 percent for wheat and 25 percent for stock raising; wine-producing land brought a revenue ten times that of wheat-growing land.[52] Moreover, wine accounted for 50 percent of Algerian exports. These facts must have had a substantial psychological effect on poor Algerian peasants who had to make do with much poorer and smaller pieces of land. The most sophisticated wine-producing region in all of Algeria was Ain Temouchent, a valley near the city of Oran, near the Moroccan border. French wine producers in this region were particularly wealthy. The capital of this wine-growing region was a European village flanked on one side by something resembling a "concentration camp" (Launay's term), an extremely densely populated barracks area inhabited by some fifteen thousand "native" Algerians—needless to say, the work force of the vineyards.

Such pairs of a small European village and a nearby "black village" (Launay's term) inhabited by a multitude of Algerians were scattered throughout this area. The Algerians were hired laborers: A very small minority were permanent workers on the estate; most were seasonal laborers, working under extremely poor conditions and for little pay. Most of the French owners, even those whose estates were of medium size, did not work on the farm, not even as overseers—a whole class of non-French Europeans did this job. During the war of independence, overseeing became so dangerous that one Spanish overseer told Launay that his pay rose from 15,000 francs in 1954 to 70,000 francs in 1961.[53] The pay of these seasonal workers was so low as to allow them nothing beyond their portion of food. Small wonder that these workers' settlements became the most popular recruitment centers for the FLN.[54] Understanding this, the French in 1958 raised the pay of seasonal workers appreciably, which enabled them to purchase meat once or twice a week.[55] It is quite plain that for these workers the war of independence was at the same time also an agrarian liberation.

MIDDLE PEASANTRY AND REVOLUTION IN ALGERIA

The substantial amount of extant information showing the salience of small and middle peasants in Algeria before the war of independence raises the question of the connection between the middle peasantry and peasant revolutions. Eric Wolf, after showing the prevalence of middle and small peasants in the Aurès and Kabylia mountains, also points out the fact that this was the central area of the Algerian revolt. From these (and some similar cases in other countries), he draws the conclusion that middle peasants, rather than landless peasants, are the classic carriers of peasant revolt.

This theory did not go unchallenged. Once critic was Jeffrey Paige, and the thrust of his theory is that middle peasantry has every reason to be conservative rather than revolutionary; concomitantly, radicalism emanates from the landless peasants. It appears that Paige treats Wolf's theory mildly and without open criticism,[56] but more careful reading shows that he, in fact, refutes Wolf's theory quite totally. Whereas Wolf claims that in Vietnam, Mexico, Russia, and China small peasants spearheaded the agrarian revolution,[57] Paige devotes a large section to a detailed refutation of this argument and comes back to his conclusion that it is peasants with no land who initiate agrarian revolutions.[58] Although following the arguments of these authors in relation to at least part of the evidence would seem to bear Paige out, certainly in so far as Algeria is concerned, Wolf is correct in pointing out the coincidence between rebellion and middle and small peasantry. Must we conclude that there is no solution to the discussion?

Not at all. It seems that the two authors are talking about two different types of rebelliousness. The sociopsychological motivations for a rebellion against a foreign occupier need not be the same as those for rebellion again a ruling social elite that is resented and disliked. The first kind of revolt, if successful, becomes a nationalist war of independence; the second, if successful, is a social revolution. If the two converge, we get a radical guerrilla movement. The case of Algeria raises the possibility that the connection between independent peasantry and national rebellion is especially strong. In the first place, as I have already argued, the motivation to revolt in such a situation as that of Algeria was in itself explicable: The wish to get rid of alien occupation seems to rank with the basic biological urges.

But beyond that, it does seem that an independent peasantry would be particularly well placed to assist rebellious bands by supplying shelter and all kinds of provisions. What's essential in relation to such an ability is that the villagers are not externally controlled. They may easily get organized to help guerrilla fighters yet have no political reason to opt for socially radical ideas. To my mind, the validity of this explanation in the case of Algeria is doubly enhanced by the fact that not only was an indigenous upper landed class missing, but the alien ruler placed itself in the uncanny position of being something akin to a ruling upper landed class. Was this the reason for the unusually brutal nature of the Algerian war of independence? This is only a speculation, of course.

URBAN MIDDLE-CLASS LEADERSHIP

National or radical, a war of independence had to have an urban middle-class leadership, and Algeria was no exception. Algerian towns were hard-hit by the French occupation; they had already been in a process of decline in the last decades of the Ottoman period. Only several decades after the beginning of the French occupation did this trend reverse itself and urban population start to grow again. Between 1886 and 1960 the proportion of urban population in Algeria rose from 14 percent to 32 percent.[59] In the 1950s, emigration to the large cities became a veritable flood. The city of Algiers, whose population numbered 470,000 in 1948, grew to 870,000 in 1960. Urban growth was a result more of the push of the village than of the pull of the city—an outcome not of any serious economic upsurge in the cities, but of growing poverty caused by land hunger in the countryside. This immigration was accompanied by large-scale unemployment and a shortage of housing. All this was happening under the French and was, at least in part, attributed to their activities—both objectively and, even more so, subjectively. Not only was the situation in the villages caused in part by land seizures by the French, but in the cities French citizens occupied tens of thousands of jobs that the Algerians considered rightfully theirs.

First signs of Algerian awakening and political demands appear in 1910. Such demands came from young Algerians who had been trained in French schools, and who, as Algeria was part of France, demanded to be treated like other French citizens. Only twenty years later, the first organization that expressed real resistance to the occupation appeared—a religious organization, the Association of Reformist Ulama, founded in 1931 by Chiekh Abd al-Hamid Ben Badis. Ben Badis was a religious scholar and teacher of Arabic. His political activity was indirect: In journals that he published and in schools that he opened, Algerian nationalism was openly preached. Ben Badis introduced into Algeria the orthodox version of Islam that is usually called "scripturalism"—that is, the Islam of the Book, as against the Islam of saint veneration that had reigned in Algeria. As Ernest Gellner puts it, before the appearance of Ben Badis "no one [in Algeria] supposed that Islam could be anything other than the cult of holy men."[60]

In a context of foreign occupation, such purely religious and politically unassuming teaching was nevertheless quite revolutionary. The neighborhood saint was no longer the focal point of identification and the central symbol of the faith; a wider framework of identification appeared. But to attain unison (even theoretical) with this larger body, it would be necessary to get rid of French rule.

The appearance of Ben Badis and reformist Islam in Algeria is to be interpreted, among other things, as a symptom of the growth of the urban middle class in Algeria. This is so because, as we have seen, popular Islam as a predominant cultural expression was a major characteristic of the previous era, and such Islam was no doubt an expression of a society lacking broad-based education, whether Muslim or not. The growth of relatively more educated groups in the cities allowed these new groups to broaden their horizons and enabled them to feel identified with more regular forms of Islam.

In the 1930s there also appeared secular organizations that expressed genuine protest against the French occupation. The most famous figure in this regard was Ferhat Abbas, a son of a middle-class family, so completely immersed in French culture as to claim that no Algerian culture existed at all—only French culture counted. So identified were people such as Abbas with French culture that they wished to see Algeria not only as a formal part of France but as a real, integrated part of it. This would mean giving the Algerians full voting and other political rights, something the French were entirely unprepared to grant. Disappointed of achieving these aims, Ferhat Abbas was soon to become one of the main spokesmen for the new Algerian nationalism.

The figure who captured the most interest in Algerian public opinion in the formative, interwar period was Messali Hadj, a leader of a left-wing organization named North African Star (ENA,

Étoile Nord Africaine), founded in 1928. The ENA originated, sociologically speaking, in the community of some hundred thousand Algerians who emigrated to France as workers during World War I. It was a French-based organization that originated in a proletarian context in French cities, and it was the first political organization that demanded full and unconditional independence for Algeria. The organization was illegal, and Messali Hadj spent many years in jail, but the message had an impact on the Algerian public.

After World War II, two legal political parties were established in Algeria, one by Ferhat Abbas and the other by Messali Hadj. Hadj was, however, deported to France in 1947 and lost control of the party he had founded. Under the facade of Hadj's legal organization, a small, underground, secret organization was formed in the early 1950s, which called itself Special Organization (OS). It was the OS that was in 1954 to raise the banner of revolt against French rule; from the start it included many of the revolution's leaders.

The nationalist elite of Algeria were quite homogeneous as to class of origin. Most of its members came from an urban middle class. This conclusion seems to stand in opposition to William Quandt's interpretation of Algeria's modern political development, in which struggle between elites is the focal point.[61] It was apparently impossible for the postindependence Algerian central government to control the periphery. Ben Bella came to power on the back of a coalition of forces pulling in different directions; part of these people were connected to provincial areas, others to statewide bodies, such as the army. He tried to weaken this amalgam of forces by building something above it—a centralist government, if possible—but in this he was not successful, and the same coalition that brought him to power toppled his government in 1965. His successor, Boumediène, opted, on the contrary, for a sort of collegial decision-making process. This tendency developed in time until some subgroups within the elite attained virtual autonomy, and the ability of the center to make decisions became seriously compromised.[62]

Quandt suggests as explanation that political life in Algeria since 1954 has been characterized by severe conflicts among the members of the political elite and by a series of crises of authority.[63] These crises had to do with different types of political socialization characterizing each of three different political elites.[64] One such elite is that of the "liberals," assimilated Algerians like Ferhat Abbas, people who modestly asked some rights from the French.

The second elite is that of the "radicals," the *ulama* and related groups, who came later, people who demanded independence but without pressing the issue too much, certainly without resorting to force in order to achieve it. Finally, there came the "revolutionary" elite of Ben Bella and his colleagues, who resorted to violence.

But, in fact, placing Algeria in a comparative context would show that, paradoxically, the particular outcome in Algeria is a result not of struggle of different elites but rather of conflicts within the ruling elite. In a country such as Albania, the conflict of interests between the guerrilla movement and the landlords was so severe as to make a life-and-death showdown inevitable. The outcome was rule by a small elite of unusually homogeneous character. The lack of such deep-seated conflict in Algeria allowed, or resulted in, a far wider measure of leniency.

To conclude, it seems possible to say that the Algerian revolution was a middle-class revolution—a Third World middle class, if you wish. If such a use of the term "middle class" seems unwarranted in a society in which there was no upper class in any real sense of the term, we may find some consolation in the fact that the term is also applied to other societies lacking aristocracy (the United States is a notable example). In a very general way, what we mean by middle-class revolution in Algeria is a revolution of the urban educated, who took power from a ruling class composed of a million French nationals, most of whom had occupied urban middle-class positions, and from the traditional rural Algerian elite, centered on the marabouts, or religious holy men.

A fine example of this revolution, and a certain reassurance that we are not imposing on the chaotic reality categories that are more fanciful than real, is the present-day preoccupation of the Algerian elite with reformist Islam as the main cultural manifestation of the revolution. This aspect of the Algerian revolution is brilliantly analyzed by anthropologist Fanny Colonna.[65] She shows how Algeria of the nineteenth century was controlled by an elite of marabouts, living saints, who were focal points of popular and Sufi Islam. The simultaneous feebleness of the towns gave rise to a situation in which the main expression of resistance to occupation was in religious movement and religious symbols. However, this elite was hard hit by the nineteenth-century French assimilationist policy. At the same time, the cities grew and there appeared a new Algerian middle class, which more and more became the real center of Algerian resistance. This elite adhered to orthodox Islam, which in this context was, in effect, reformist Islam. It is thus evident that the swing of the pendulum[66] today in Algeria from popular Islam to reformist Islam is an expression of the rise of a new middle class. But it is also to be emphasized that the very preoccupation with religious themes is a symptom of the ascendancy of this class. The contrast in this regard with Albania and South Yemen is striking and revealing. In these two countries, religion is being swept more or less aside as part of the old cultural world that is being discredited and repudiated.

CHAPTER FIVE

Islam and Revolution in Afghanistan

The examples we have examined have all related to the main theme of this book—the relation between guerrilla movements and radical revolution. But I have also claimed that this material demonstrates that there is no apparent contradiction between Islam and radical revolution. In other words, my argument is that Islam per se is not a bulwark to communism. It is very difficult to document this point empirically and comparatively, because in all the cases in which such a revolution did not take place, just why this did not happen is a matter of conjecture. Nevertheless, recent history provides us with an excellent opportunity to probe a little further into this problem—the case of the anti-Communist and anti-Soviet uprising in Afghanistan.

In April 1978, a Marxist revolution took place in Afghanistan—the so-called Saur Revolution. Soon afterwards, the government began implementing far-reaching reforms in the countryside. After about half a year of wait-and-see reaction, popular rebellions started to crop up in various places; these spread and engulfed the whole country. Up to five million Afghans fled to adjacent countries and from there joined forces with Afghans within Afghanistan to form a truly formidable guerrilla force, which, it may be argued, would have vanquished any occupying force sensitive to public opinion.[1]

Soon after the beginning of the rebellion, the Afghan rebels came to be known as *mujahidin*, warriors of *jihad*, the holy war to defend Islam against its enemies. The major role played in this resistance by religious ideologies and leaders is well known; we seem to have in Afghanistan a case in which Islam is, after all, a bulwark against communism.

Of course, the war in Afghanistan turned into a major theme in a propaganda war between East and West, in which words and truth lose objective meaning. One side's "freedom fighters" are the other side's "reactionaries" and "imperialist stooges." The most naive and seemingly unrelated facts become value-laden political issues. Yet, this interest in the facts as well as the uniqueness of the Afghan case make it imperative to take it into consideration.

GEOGRAPHIC AND TOPOGRAPHIC FACTORS

Afghanistan is governed by factors of geography and topography more than most countries are. Its geopolitical position also has greatly affected its history.[2]

In the first place, the country is landlocked. It is situated between the Mediterranean climate area and the monsoon area and enjoys the climatic advantages of neither of these regions. Rainfall is little throughout most of the land—300 millimeters, on average—which only allows for extensive semiarid agriculture. Afghanistan is dominated by the formidable Hindu Kush mountain range, the westernmost extension of the Himalaya. This means that large portions of the country consist of extremely mountainous and rugged terrain, hardly fit for sown agriculture. If we also bear in mind the fact that Afghanistan lacks port cities and maritime trade—a major source of living for countries with somewhat similar topography, such as Lebanon and Greece—we may begin to understand why human adaptation to nature in Afghanistan has been so arduous.

Geography and climate have dictated in Afghanistan a special pattern of human settlement and organization, in which the nomad and semi-nomad tribe have been of overwhelming importance. Poor agriculture in the plains, combined with relatively rich pastures on the high slopes, made transhumance and semi-nomadism (or semisedentarism) an important way of human adaptation in Afghanistan—despite the negative approach of centralized governments to such modes of life. Although the tribe as a social unit has been under attack at least from the nineteenth century mainly because the central government considers tribes a threat to public security, tribal social organization is not only within memory for most Afghans but is even a reality for many.

HISTORICAL BACKGROUND

This special geographical structure had a major effect on Afghan history; in turn, knowledge of Afghan history is indispensable to understanding the events in Afghanistan since 1978. There had not been an Afghan state until the middle of the eighteenth century.[3] In 1747, Nadir Shah, rule of Persia (of which Afghanistan was a province), was assassinated. Ahmad Khan, a general in his army and a chief of the Pashtu tribal confederation (the biggest ethnic group in the country) rebelled and established an independent princedom in the city of Kandahar, where he ruled until 1773. He named himself Ahmad Shah Dur-i-Duran ("pearl of pearls"), or Durrani, thereby bestowing this name on his whole tribal confederation, which was to give Afghanistan its rulers until 1978. The centralized state created by Ahmad Shah Durrani held for only a short while and disintegrated at the time of his successor, for a reason that was to characterize Afghan history since that time: the intractable nature of the Afghan tribes.

The Sadozai family ruled until 1818, when another Durrani, Dost Muhammad Khan, rebelled. Dost Muhammad, who declared himself emir of Afghanistan in 1835 and ruled until 1863, succeeded in once again uniting the country. During his reign, problems surfaced that were connected with Afghanistan's geopolitical position, destined to be crucial to the country's history: Afghanistan was a buffer state between a southward-expanding Russia and British India. During the time of Dost Muhammad, the Russians became increasingly involved in the intricacies of his court. Afghanistan's position in relation to India began to worry the British, who in 1838 invaded the country, in what was to become the first of three Anglo-Afghan wars. The British hoped to be able to rearrange Afghanistan at will and were initially successful at this, but before long tribal rebellions erupted, eventually leading to a total annihilation of the British expeditionary force in Afghanistan (1842). Later in the century this "Great Game" (as it came to be known) between Britain and Russia completely dominated Afghan history.

After 1842 Dost Muhammad came back to power, and his relations with Great Britain improved, as Russia was drawing ever closer to the Afghan border, and as Iran, too, was showing threatening interest in Afghan affairs. The country's independence was internationally acknowledged in 1855, in the treaty that ended the Crimean War. In the 1860s and 1870s, Russia finally reached the Amn Darya River, the traditional northern border of Afghanistan. British policy meanwhile oscillated between noninterference and strong interference in Afghan affairs—all in order to secure the Indian rear.

British disappointment at Afghanistan's supposed failing to keep an evenhanded policy between Britain and Russia led to a second invasion of Afghanistan in 1878, in what became the second Anglo-Afghan war. On this occasion also, the British were quick to withdraw their forces in the face of mounting tribal rebelliousness. But this time British policy secured some gains: The Afghans agreed to sign a treaty that put the conducting of their foreign relations in British hands. In 1893 the British forced the Afghans to agree to a permanent border line between Afghanistan and India (later Pakistan)—the so-called Durand Line—which left about half of the Pashtu settled area outside of the Pashtuns' natural homeland in Afghanistan.

At this time, Afghanistan was ruled by Abdur Rahman Khan (1880–1901), who carried out one of the biggest pacification drives in Afghan history. He made strenuous efforts to reduce the power of the tribes and showed some activity in establishing an Afghan central administration. Most of all his fame was made in subduing to Islam areas of the Hindu Kush, until then religiously pagan.

In 1919, Amanullah Khan ascended the Afghan throne. Sensing Britain's weakness after World War I, he sent his forces to attack British troops in order to achieve Afghan independence, thereby starting the third Anglo-Afghan war. His drive failed militarily, but politically he was entirely successful, and in June 1919 the British formally recognized Afghan independence. Later in his regime, Amanullah opted to introduce into Afghanistan Western-style reforms such as those adopted at the time by Turkey, Egypt, and Iran. Afghanistan, however, turned out to be not quite as ready, and these reforms touched off a widespread rural revolt, joined by the religious jurists, who designated the rebellion as *jihad*. At the beginning of 1929 Amanullah abdicated. Initially, the throne was captured by a Tajik rebel of low class, but an ex-general and a relative of Amanullah soon organized the Pashtun tribes to revolt, which brought the Durranis, headed by Nadir Khan, back to power. When Nadir Khan was in turn murdered in 1933, his son, Zahir Shah ascended to the throne; he ruled until 1973 when a coup by his uncle, Muhammad Daud, put an end to the monarchy.

The debacle of Amanullah in 1929 proved to be of long-range social importance. For the next fifty years its hard lesson was not lost on all Afghan governments; despairing of subduing the tribes, these governments pursued a policy of avoiding them and the entire rural area as much as possible. This policy meant that very little taxation flowed during this period from the rural region to the central government, and it meant that rural autonomies remained largely intact up to the 1978 revolution. It also meant that Afghanistan witnessed a minimum amount of economic and infrastructural development.

This conscious and far-reaching avoidance by the central government of interfering in the affairs of the countryside was no doubt the root cause for the fact that in 1978 tribalism was still of major importance in Afghanistan. Thus, the 1969 *Area Handbook of Afghanistan* states unequivocally that despite the fact that only some 25 percent of the population was fully nomadic, tribalism and kinship were of overwhelming significance:

> Who an Afghan is, what he does and what he can expect to do, are matters primarily of his membership and position in a particular family, lineage and tribe. . . . The stress on kinship and genealogy reflects the strong tribalism which has been retained to a far greater degree in Afghanistan than in most Middle Eastern countries. More than two-thirds of the population has some tribal connections.[4]

Similarly, as late as 1984 it was said by an anthropologist that Elphinston's 150-year-old account of the Pashtun ethnic group was still largely valid.[5]

What little development that, nevertheless, took place in Afghanistan before the revolution came from foreign assistance, which slowly began to constitute a factor of major importance in Afghan affairs, in particular in relation to the Soviet Union.[6] The relations between these two countries rapidly developed a unique pattern among the Soviet Union's relations with its neighbors. On the one hand, Afghanistan was a country in which the USSR could not avoid being keenly interested: A common border of some 2,300 kilometers assured that. On the other hand, there was no other country with a common border with the Soviet Union in which the West was so little interested—particularly after Britain left India in 1947. Afghanistan was effectively detached from the rest of the world, left alone to cope with a mighty neighbor. It definitely had to be extremely cautious in dealing with USSR.

Thus, Afghanistan could not afford to antagonize the Soviet Union (as Turkey could), and Afghanistan did not have readily available Western sources of assistance (as Turkey had). The Soviets were quite pleased to fill the gap and so became a major source of foreign assistance for Afghanistan. Thus, a unique mode of close friendship began between the USSR and a non-Communist, Third World country.

This pattern intensified particularly after 1953. In that year Stalin died, and with him the Soviet conception whereby the world was conceived as a two-camp affair in which non-Communist countries were mere puppets of the West. A new Soviet conception developed that treated such regimes with much more respect. Also in 1953, Muhammad Daud, the king's uncle, became premier and started a vigorous development drive. As a result of these two eventualities, Afghanistan became the recipient of massive military and civilian aid—slashed prices, gifts, low-interest loans, etc. A particularly noteworthy project made possible by assistance was the construction of a ring-shaped highway connecting Afghanistan's major cities. The diamond for this ring was the Salang Tunnel under the peaks of the Hindu Kush; this impressive engineering feat connected Kabul with the Soviet border. Military assistance was particularly important. The Soviets not only provided the Afghan army with modern weapons; it also trained Afghan officers in the Soviet Union, where at least four thousand such officers stayed for extended periods of time (up to four years).

Meanwhile, Daud was ousted as premier in 1963 and found himself sitting on the fence, waiting for another opportunity. As a prince of the royal family he had excellent connections with every possible influential circle in the country. He had already shown that he was critical of Afghanistan's slow forward movement. In 1973, King Zahir was in Europe and Daud struck. With the consent of most of the army units, he carried out a coup, abrogated the monarchy, and made himself the president of a republic.

This second Daud period saw a partial reversal of his distinctly pro-Soviet policy. Now he tried to implement a much more evenhanded policy. He also was much more cautious than formerly in his relations with Pakistan over the Pashtunistan issue. Nevertheless, Afghan-Soviet relations remained as cordial as ever, with substantial quantities of Soviet assistance continuing to flow in.

Although Daud was not considered particularly popular between 1973 and 1978, there had been no crisis of any sort—economic, political or social—when suddenly the old world was turned upside down. On April 17, 1978, a former police officer and Communist activist was murdered. His funeral turned into a mass demonstration of surprising magnitude. Daud was alarmed and began arresting all known Communist leaders. One of these leaders, Hafizullah Amin, took out of a drawer an emergency plan for a street revolution, which he managed to release via his son minutes before his arrest. Soon afterwards, Communist activists in Kabul proceeded to capture key points in the city, assisted by some army units. These forces encountered only weak resistance, with most of the army remaining aloof, for reasons that are entirely unclear to this day.

Twenty-four hours after this revolution started, the Communists were completely successful. Despite strong insinuations to that effect, no Soviet complicity in the conspiracy was ever revealed, and it does not look as if the Soviets even had any prior notion of what was going to happen. The Afghan revolution seems to have been completely homemade. On the other hand, it does not seem to have been precipitated by any deep sociopolitical factors. But it was aided by part of the army, and that support may well have been connected to the long-range influence of the USSR in the country. Current evidence renders all this no more than speculation; the case of the 1978 Communist revolution in Afghanistan appears to lack a deep-seated social cause.

A few months later the new regime—the Khalq-Parcham regime, as it came to be known (after the two factions of which the People's Democratic party of Afghanistan was composed)—embarked on the inevitable course of social transformation of the country. First and foremost this meant, of course, a far-reaching land reform, as well as reform of some particularly ancient-looking customs that were irritating to some modern minds (for example, the brideprice).[7] As the implementation of these and other reforms got under way, the first signs of resistance appeared.[8] It is completely beside the point to claim that the Communists, at this point, should have reacted in the style of the old Afghan governments,[9] for if they had theirs would not have been a Communist regime. They did the only thing a Communist regime could do, and under the circumstances their policy aroused popular disturbances, which soon engulfed the entire country. The regime reacted with a horrible wave of repression. Again, it misses the point to claim that the Communists overreacted or that they could have conceivably done anything other than what they did: The rebellions were led by the old Afghan rural elite, the quintessential embodiment of the reaction, as far as the Communists were concerned. How could they even think of a compromise with the reaction?

By the end of the 1979, it was clear that the regime was not going to survive on its own, an observation made all the more clear by a mass defection of army units. Thus, the Soviets invaded. It seemed evident that the close association that existed between the Khalq-Parcham regime and Moscow forced Moscow to intervene. Any other approach would have created a major precedent in the collapse of a Moscow-sponsored regime. But the history of the Soviet intervention is really beside our topic. As soon as the invasion happened, the struggle of the Afghan people became a war of independence against a non-Muslin conqueror. It is only natural for a Muslim society to call such a war *jihad*. And indeed, the Afghan rebellion in the 1980s assumed a distinctly religious character.

WAS THE AFGHAN REBELLION AN ISLAMIC ONE?

There is a small step from this observation to the claim that Islam, in fact, constitutes a bulwark against communism and/or Communist revolutions. If such an Islamic mechanism existed, it should have surfaced between April 1978 and December 1979, the date of the Soviet invasion. It is always difficult to find hard facts relating to such an embryonic phenomenon. Luckily, a group of anthropologists conducted field research among Afghan refugees in Pakistan during the first year of the revolt, so that a certain discussion of the problem is possible.[10]

Although the general tendency of this collection of anthropological studies is to claim that the Afghan rebellion was indeed a specifically Islamic rebellion, such a claim is not entirely convincing. The most far-reaching attempt to attribute a specifically Islamic nature to the rebellion is that made by Nazif Shahrani.[11] He sets out to refute one by one the conventional arguments concerning this problem. The strongest such argument is clearly that the Afghan state was an extremely decentralized state in which each village, tribe, and community was a "city-state," an almost totally autonomous entity. The new regime wished to introduce far-reaching reforms it was ill prepared to enforce. Moreover, these reforms were more of an irritant to the population of the countryside than were the Amanullah reforms of the 1920s.

So the argument claims that the countryside revolted against an effort to subdue traditional privileges of all sorts. Shahrani tries to refute the autonomy thesis by claiming that the revolt erupted first in areas such as Nuristan, "where government traditionally had firm control and the people had benefitted from its presence."[12] However, Richard Strand, in his article dealing with Nuristan, says that "the isolation of the Nuristanis from national life has stemmed as much from their aloofness toward the Afghan state as from the rugged fastness of their territory. They have tended to regard themselves as conquered peoples, subjugated by a foreign and corrupt system of government."[13]

A clearly Islamic characteristic of the Afghan rebellion is, of course, its avowed nature as *jihad*, but I belive this is somewhat too simplistic. Anthropologist Ernest Gellner suggests a useful distinction within Islam between scripturalist and folk Islam.[14] Scripturalist Islam is Islam of the jurist, of the *ulama*, consisting mainly of learning and prayers at regular mosques. Folk Islam is more closely connected to local customs and, instead of the world of learned Islam, would place at the center some form of saint veneration. It is quite clear—though far from satisfactorily explicated—that the more a society is nomadic and tribal, the closer will be its version of Islam to the folk version. Maybe the explanation suggested by Brian Spooner is correct: "Religious expression among nomads, even under the aegis of universalistic religions, takes the nomadic relationship between man and an omnipotent, intractable natural environment and reflects it in a stoical, unritualized relationship between man and an intractable supernatural."[15]

Afghan society fits this analysis perfectly. In no other Muslim society was the fusion between *sharia*—Islamic law—and local customs so complete as in Afghanistan. The *pakhtunwali*, the ancient customary law of the Afghan tribes, was considered the quintessential expression of Islam.[16] It is in this light that we have to view *jihad* in an Afghan context: It was first and foremost a folk *jihad*—that is, holy war in a customary sense rather than in the classical Islamic sense. Even in a classical Islamic sense, though, it is naive to view *jihad* as a holy, or religious, war pure and simple. It is inconceivable that undercurrents of complex motivation were not involved. This is admitted even in a scholarly account of the concept that tends usually to emphasize the formalistic aspects:

> [In societies] where ideology is entirely dominated by religion and where there is no separation between the realms of politics and that of religion, wars and revolts, *regardless of their actual causes*, acquire a religious dimension in that their aims, their justifications and their appeals for support are expressed in religious terms. It is precisely the doctrine of *jihad* that provides this dimension in Islamic history.[17]

The proof that the usual Afghan sense of *jihad* is a folk sense rather than a scriptural sense is to be found in Afghan history itself—namely, in the rebellion that toppled Amanullah in 1929. There is no doubt that Amanullah was a perfectly regular Muslim ruler. He tried to introduce into his country some foreign habits, but even if this were blameworthy, it is doubtful whether it was enough reason to dub a rebellion against him *jihad.* Probably no reasonable Muslim jurist would agree to this. But by Afghan customary law, it made sense to view a political opponent in a negative religious light, and *jihad* appeared to be the proper way to express this. It is obviously not enough, therefore, to take the avowed ideology of present-day Afghan resistance at face value and to decide that the rebellion came into being because of reflexive Islamic objection to communism.

To elucidate this point more fully we have to examine in some detail the first appearances of revolt in 1978-1979. One of the accounts—by Bahrain Tavakolian, who studied the Sheikhanzai tribe in southern Afghanistan—agrees fully and explicitly with my argument.[18] The relations of this tribe with the government before 1978 were characterized by deep animosity: "The authority of the Afghan state. . . is conceived as illegitimate, usurped, totalitarian and infidel."[19] Indeed, the state was conceived as "a foreign rule." The author deals explicitly with the relations that developed between the Khalq-Parcham government and the tribe and shows that the tribe resisted efforts to extract from it conscripts, taxes, and various types of valuable data that it was not prepared to give away.[20] For Tavakolian, these considerations were the crux of the explanation for the revolt; the *jihad* was the cultural-ideological vehicle:

> For the Sheikhanzai, religious belief and practice provide ideological and structural reinforcement for their internal solidarity and their collective strength against foreign interference . . . we are witnessing a similar process in the nationwide rebellion of the people of Afghanistan against the DRA. Both in microcosm and in whole, Afghanistan is not experiencing a *jihad* against atheism, but a political struggle against usurped authority. In this struggle Islam serves as a convenient and morally powerful unifying symbol.[21]

However, some other accounts of the initial stages of the anti-Communist revolt show more Islamic contexts. It is my argument that specifically Islamic mechanisms come into play only when the regime resorts to a frontal attack on Islam, such as forbidding prayer or directly subjecting schoolchildren to anti-Islamic propaganda. In such contexts, religious sensitivities would be irritated to the point of unbearability in any society. In other words, there is nothing exclusively Islamic here. In the two cases mentioned, other, conventional factors were also involved—for example, the new and unfamiliar effort by the Khalq-Parcham regime to interfere intensively in the affairs of local communities, thereby destroying the delicate balance of powers in the countryside.[22]

Another version of the problem is presented in two case studies by Hugh Beattie and Jon Anderson. Beattie observed a small town in northern Afghanistan—Nahrin.[23] In Nahrin, we do not find in the first year of the revolution a frontal attack on Islam; rather, the revolution found expression in three basic laws: a land reform law, a law cancelling debts, and a law prohibiting the traditional brideprice.

Local reaction was on the whole extremely negative, though not for specifically Islamic reasons: "Taken together, the Khalq government's reform . . . amounted to a vigorous . . . attempt to change existing economic and political relationships. . . . The overall reaction was one of irritation and anger."[24]

Nevertheless, Beattie insists that local objection to the revolution was also specific to Islam: "Islam it was believed, sanctioned most, if not all, of their cherished customs, particularly those concerning the status of women and marriage. Hence it was felt that in trying to change these, the Khalq government was attacking Islam."[25]

A very similar point is also salient in Jon Anderson's study on the Ghilzai tribes.[26] The Islam practiced by this tribe was quite nonscripturalist: "Ghilzai will freely admit to being in their words, "bad Muslims" and to not following the religion (*din*) for avoiding the sharia courts and disrespecting men of religion."[27] Yet, he claims, "tribalism is for the Afghans a primary manifestation of their identity as Muslims."[28] Thus, by making every social institution Islamic by definition, it is easy to construe the Afghan resistance as Islamic per se.

The argument concerning the specifically Islamic nature of the Afghan resistance is taken furthest in Robert Canfield's study on the importance of saints (*pirs*) in Afghan society.[29] Canfield claims that it is a mistake to look for "real" causation behind the publicly Islamic character of the movement. Looking for such causation makes sense in the West, but is entirely wrong in a Muslim society like Afghanistan because "the moral framework that informs public affairs does not clearly distinguish religious obligations from political ones."[30] Although every student of Islam is familiar with the basic fact, Canfield goes further and claims that "Islam," in fact, subsumes *all* aspects of life as well: "As has often been said, Islam is a way of life. As Muslims see it, it entails an understanding not only of the nature of family obligations, but also of economic and social obligation; and because economic and social relations are the stuff of politics, Islam is inherent in the business of politics."[31]

The argument is, however, untenable, and as is so often the case, its weakness is exposed when it is subjected to the test of comparison.[32] A whole series of Muslim rebellions against foreign occupants was conducted in the last century with no religious salience in them, such as the Turkish war of independence (1919–1921), the Syrian rebellion of 1925, and the Palestinian rebellion 1936–1939. These and many more situations involved Muslims who should have been motivated in accordance with Canfield's analysis. Obviously, his is only a half truth that will work only in certain circumstances, to be detected by comparative research. Nothing here can be taken for granted. It is, therefore, in my view, unjustifiable to see the Afghan rebellion as a specifically Islamic rebellion. Islam is its proper expression but not its explanation. Probably better is my more mundane explanation—that mentioned above.

A major study that deals specifically with the Islamic nature of the Afghan resistance is Oliver Roy's excellent *Islam and Resistance in Afghanistan*.[33] To date, this is apparently the most comprehensive treatment of the internal structure of that movement. Based on Roy's several extended stays with the guerrilla forces since 1980, the book is a superb collection of facts, though it is not clear whether Roy sets out to make a point or just to tell a story. However, it does seem to make at least an implicit point, and this has to do with the fundamentally Islamic nature of the resistance.

It must be emphasized that Roy deals with the period of the Soviet invasion, when formal Islamic ideologies clearly dominated the movement. I have already claimed that the prevalence of these ideologies seems to be adequately explained by the fact that the resistance was being waged against a foreign Communist occupant. However, Roy looks for his explanation to a strong fundamentalist tradition in Afghan society—a theory that must definitely be dealt with.

Roy surveys Afghan history and dwells at length on the religious aspects of that history, to which he ascribes great importance. It seems that he tends to exaggerate in this. An example is his analysis of the short episode in 1929 when the rebel Bacha-i Saqao ruled in the wake of Amanullah's departure.[34] This ruler was brought to power by fundamentalist elements, and, therefore, the event serves the fundamentalist thesis well. It is only natural for Roy to play down the fact that Saqao's reign lasted only a few months, and was ended by rulers who represented the tribal element in Afghan society, and who stayed in power unopposed until 1978. So, the episode merely means that fundamentalist tendencies existed (as they undoubtedly do in every Muslim society); elucidating the special socioeconomic and political circumstances that make them grow is the proper task of the historian and political sociologist.

Roy claims that the explanation for the unusually strong fundamentalist tendencies in Afghan society and history is the influence India/Pakistan has exerted on Afghan Islam.[35] He refers mainly to famous Muslim scholars from Ahmad Sirhindi to Abul Ala Mawdudi. Again, my objection to this reference is that ideas in themselves are no proof of their *social* importance, which should be proven independently of the ideas. Otherwise, we should expect these ideologies to win out in Pakistan itself, as that state was created in 1947 as the only Muslim state in the world established specifically for its "Muslimness." As studies have shown, the enactment in Pakistan in recent years of some ancient Islamic penal law has been shallow and has not been an outcome of a popular success of radical Islam.[36] It is all the more the case that thinkers like Mawdudi do not explain the Afghan resistance, any more than Ibn Taymiyya explains radical Islam in general.

In several places Roy speaks about the future programs of the various Afghan religious parties in the resistance. All surely want some version of "true," scripturalist Islam, cleansed of spurious additions made over the centuries.[37] In Gellner's terms, the dominant Afghan Islam of today is highly scripturalist. It is entirely erroneous to present this form of Islam as a continuation of pre-1978 Afghan Islam. Let us recall once more, in the words of Louis Dupree, what this Islam really looked like: "The Islam practiced in Afghan villages, nomad camps, and most urban areas . . . would be almost unrecognizable to a sophisticated Muslim scholar. Aside from faith in Allah and in Muhammad or the Messenger of Allah, most beliefs related to localized, pre-Muslim customs. Some of the ideals of Afghan tribal society run counter to literate Islamic principles."[38]

THE CONSERVATIVE NATURE OF
THE AFGHAN PEASANTS' REVOLT

Beyond the problem of the role of Islam, the Afghan rebellion poses another major puzzle. On the one hand, it is evident that peasants and semisedentarized peasants constituted the bulk of the fighting force of the rebellion. On the other hand, the political direction of the rebellion was basically conservative. One scholar has even mentioned in this context Skocpol's and Moore's theories and suggests that the Afghan rebellion does not fit these.[39] On inspection, however, the Afghan rebellion is superbly explained by these theories. To see this let us examine the Afghan land regime in some detail.

The Afghan land regime before 1978 was characterized by a great deal of complexity and diversity. As Donald Wilber noted in 1962, "Ownership of property cannot be discussed in one word; it is both concentrated and diffused. A relatively small group of *khans* hold vast amounts of land, yet a host of small individual farmers own plots in many areas. Nomads rarely have any real estate."[40] In fact, formally there were two forms of ownership: private (*melk*) and common-tribal (*khaliseh*).[41] Truly private property could come into being only in the nontribal areas, which is one good reason why the problem of big landownership was not as acute in Afghanistan as in many other countries. To cite Wilber once more, "The typical evil of most Middle Eastern countries, oppressive landlordism, has not been a characteristic feature of Afghan rural life. The farms consist primarily of a large number of small holdings of individual proprietors, with the most frequent size ranging between five and fifty acres."[42]

Dupree substantiates these points with quantitative figures, to the effect that in 1963, 60.5 percent of the country's cultivated land was actually cultivated by owners, whereas 13.8 percent was worked by tenants and 27 percent by other means.[43] This data would seem to indicate a prevalence of small owners. Dupree further notes that only thirty people in Afghanistan at that time owned estates of 250 acres (62 hectares) or more.[44] But large landlordism did exist and may, in fact, have been more important than is made clear by the data— even if we view with disbelief Halliday's figures, according to which less than 12 percent of farmers in Afghanistan were in possession of enough land to ensure their bare subsistence.[45]

When one talks about big landlordism in Afghanistan one is actually talking about the khan, the key figure in the traditional Afghan rural elite. Basically, he is the tribal chieftain, and by extension, because of the predominance of the tribes in Afghan society, "khan" has become the term by which all powerful leaders in Afghan rural (and even urban) society may be designated. A good starting point in analyzing the place of the khan is Wilber's 1962 introduction to Afghan affairs:

> The leader in tribal society is the *khan*, who is usually a member of the most aristocratic family group in the tribe, the *khan khel*. In most cases the *khan khels* have over the years increased their wealth as well as their prestige and collectively form a powerful sector of the Afghan upper class. Even within the settled areas and the towns it is generally these same families which have the highest position in the social scale. To them belong also the descendants of those who were rewarded by the nation's rulers with chief's title and tribal lands in reward for loyal service or for political and personal reasons. To some degree comparable distinctions prevail among the village communities.[46]

Indeed, it is doubtful whether khans became less powerful as Afghan society passed from being fully nomadic to being half-nomadic and half-sedentarized. Wilber claims that in actuality the opposite was more likely—that, often, as tribes settled, the khan became more a landlord than a tribal leader.[47]

In some places, khans seem to have been pretty much like feudal landlords in medieval Europe. An excellent example of this pattern was in the Kunar Valley, south of the city of Jalalabad, an area studied by Lincoln Keiser.[48] This was the rice-producing area of Afghanistan, blessed with a relative abundance of water that allowed extensive and lucrative production for the city market. In this valley, land was the issue rather than tribal affiliation; and it is not surprising that land was tightly controlled by khans. Much as in medieval Europe, khans lived in fortresses (*qala*), with their extended families, retainers, servants, guards, and lackeys, while their tenants inhabited tiny hamlets surrounding the fortresses or occupied scattered houses.

In the last generation, the institution of khanship has undergone a great many changes, at least in parts of Afghanistan, as described in an excellent study by Jon Anderson.[49] The essence of these changes was transformation of the relationship between the khan and his followers from a patron-client one to a relationship based more on class exploitation. Anderson's study deals specifically with the phenomenal rise in the use of tractors in the dry-farming area around the city of Ghazni. These tractors, enormously expensive in Afghan terms in the 1970s, were sold (official policy notwithstanding) only to the khans. In order to recoup such substantial investments, the khans had to turn themselves into cool, maximizing entrepreneurs, caring for profits, whereas formerly they had cared more for the social uses of their reaches. Formerly, social etiquette had obliged them to plow for their clients even before they plowed for themselves, but this type of benevolent khan now rapidly became a thing of the past, and farming became more commercial in nature.

That khans had once plowed for their followers before plowing for themselves is also interesting because it shows that big landlords enjoyed massive political influence in their communities even beyond their direct control of land and tenants. This significant fact is what I had in mind when I mentioned the possibility that large landlords may have been more important in Afghan rural society than is apparent from the figures.

The introduction of tractors also made the ever-increasing number of tribespeople who had practiced part-time agriculture redundant, and some of these people had to emigrate to the towns. Among those who stayed in the rural areas, fewer were employed as sharecroppers and more as wage laborers. The old pattern of social relations was clearly passing, but it is equally true that the change was slow and that everyone involved was tenaciously clinging to the old pattern, which was definitely still valid. The prospects of change were universally viewed with alarm and anxiety—particularly germane to the argument I shall try to construct in this chapter.

A final glimpse of the pre-1978 Afghan rural class structure is provided by a 1951 study by Dupree, which depicts harsh, feudal-like conditions; these conditions seem not to have been very widespread, but they nevertheless deserve mention.[50] Dupree studied the village of Badwan, near Kandahar, where about half of the villagers had pieces of land of their own, and the other half worked the land of absentee landlords. It is not made clear in the study whether these landlords were actually khans. In any case, the land of these landlords was worked by tenants who were brought from other villages and very frequently transferred to other places. Dupree condemns the system harshly:

> This *split-farming* system . . . keeps the individual villages and groups of villages in a constant state of social upheaval. Any efforts to organize for clan or village projects is difficult under such conditions. . . . From dawn to dusk, half of the Badwanis work fields miles away from their villages, side by side with farmers from other villages. In few instances is there any opportunity for any organized activity or friendly intercourse.[51]

Another seemingly exceptional—though still pertinent—case, is one studied by Richard Tapper in Saripul, in north-central Afghanistan.[52] This study reveals a network of relations based on open and naked, even bitter, class relations exacerbated by ethnic conflicts. These conflicts harked back to the 1950s, when the rulers of Afghanistan wished to enhance Pashtun settlement of this area and tried to achieve this by large-scale distribution of lands to Pashtu khans, at the expense not only of tenants of different ethnic groups but also of members of the elite of these other ethnic groups. It is no surprise that this was fertile ground to the appearance of relatively extreme classlike attitudes, such as the adoption by one aggrieved non-Pashtun social leader of Maoist ideology.[53] On the whole, however, it is clear that the situation depicted by Tapper was exceptional in Afghanistan, and nothing remotely reminiscent of it was detected in any other study on the pre-1978 land regime of the country.

To sum up, although no less than half of Afghan farmers were living off their own land, a great many of the other half were living off land that they did not own, under conditions that probably allowed them only bare subsistence. However, a crucial factor in the land regime, which has been left out of this picture, is the fact that khans in Afghanistan were, on the whole, not absentee landlords but organic leaders of their communities, sharing with their clients whatever was happening to them in their daily lives. Thus, as Wilber observed in 1962, "a *khan* assembles his farmers in the morning to give orders; to those who need help on their own farms he sends his own employees. During the day, he makes the rounds of his property, inspecting and instructing. In the evening, he eats with his men in his own courtyard, where, after the meal, they all sit and talk and listen to the *khan's* radio."[54]

This relationship has also been clear in the various accounts of the khans I have mentioned. They lived with their men in a most symbiotic way, and their role in the social fabric of the community was important. Even their main way of using the surplus expropriated from tenants was through recycling it by entertaining and feeding.[55] Barrington Moore has shown in 1966 that societies in which the landed elite lives in the midst of its dependent population are not sensitive to rural revolts and ultimately to agrarian revolution.[56] This is so because this elite is seen as performing a certain positive function for the rural population. These observations are unquestionably borne out by the material relating to the Afghan khans. Moreover, even disregarding Moore's theory, the rural poor are extremely unlikely to engage in rebellion against their landlords even if they wish to do so, because—as the sociology of revolution teaches us—to revolt they need tactical autonomy.[57] The presence in the countryside of the rural elite rules out such tactical autonomy.

I believe that all this explains quite effectively what has taken place in Afghanistan. The revolution was originally a Kabul business; nobody in the countryside even took notice of it, let alone became involved in it. Immediately, however, the new regime targeted the khans and tried to destroy them, hoping to attract to its side the rest of the rural community with, among other things, offers of land to be confiscated from the khans. For the Saur Revolution to succeed, the rural poor had to revolt. It is perfectly in line with the sociology of revolution that they preferred the side of the khans. This, rather than the supposed erroneous execution of the agrarian reform in Afghanistan,[58] is the explanation for the seemingly surprising fact that even the beneficiaries of the land reform joined the anti-Saur rebellion.

CHAPTER SIX

Guerrilla War
and Revolution:
Comparative Perspectives

HISTORICAL SOCIOLOGY AND
COMPARATIVE SOCIAL HISTORY

This book contributes to a relatively neglected branch of history, one whose renovation and development are long overdue—comparative social history ("social" here meaning total—economic, social, and political). Contrary to the situation in the field of history, there has been an astonishing upsurge of interest in this renewed discipline in sociology, in which it constitutes part of what is called, in general, historical sociology. This new scholarly field was recently "canonized" in a book edited by Theda Skocpol.[1] Skocpol wrote an introductory chapter and conclusion, in which she documents and analyzes the expanding popularity and influence of this new field as well as its logical and methodological structure. In sociology, interest in this field looks like a small-scale scientific revolution.

What is true of sociology should be all the more so of history (and particularly Islamic history, because of its unity and variety). Why do I say that comparative social history should develop in history even more than in sociology? Because the logical structure of historical development (change over time) is not *the* major interest of sociology, as it is of social history. Typical in this regard is Neil Smelser, a sociologist who is hailed as one of the founders of historical sociology. Smelser, who studied social change in the English Industrial Revolution, claims he was not really interested in the Industrial Revolution as such:

> The thing that set my research off most from what many historians do is that I approached the Industrial Revolution as a case

147

illustration of an explicit, formal conceptual model drawn from the general tradition of sociological thought. . . . It was this abstract, analytical model . . .that generated problems for me, not the period of the Industrial Revolution as such. I might well have chosen industrial change in another country and another period, or even an instance of rapid social change in which industrialization did not occupy a significant place.[2]

For the sociologist, history may thus be a mere pool of information, more accessible sometimes than contemporary populations. The sociologist, typically, remains committed to the overarching, preconceived theory even when he or she is engaged in archival research. Thus, Victoria Bonnell, one of the foremost practitioners of this kind of research, observes:

It is striking that historical sociologists, while shifting to new sources and evidence, have continued to employ specific types of explicit, abstract generalizing concepts and theories in historical analysis. . . . For the foreseeable future, a preoccupation with theories and concepts will continue to dominate and shape research strategies in the sociological study of history.[3]

Indeed, we have here a sort of mirror image of what Darrett Rutman has observed about the relation of historians to anthropology. History is likened by him to Clio, the muse of history, a seductive young lady who lures her lovers, in this case anthropology, to her bed only to dump them soon thereafter, not knowing even their names. Thus, historians take from anthropology one or two convenient ideas that they need, paying no heed to the main thing, which is the logical structure of the argument—that is, the theory.[4] It does look as if sociologists are doing the same to history. Too often they use history as a data pool, selecting what fits preconceived theories. In so doing, they ignore the main pillar of historical research: sticking to the truth wherever it may lead, disregarding any theory whatsoever.

Social historians are much more lonely creatures than historical sociologists. They do not enjoy the company of theories in their re-search. They may know a great deal about Max Weber or Karl Marx. But when they come to the archives, they soon find that what is there is next to impossible to reconcile with these theories. Very soon they must decide whether their commitment is to facts or theories. If the social historian choses the former, the problem to be faced is how to make sense of the masses of seemingly loosely related facts: In particular the historian's biggest task is to explain phenomena causally.

It is at this stage that the methodology of comparative social history may provide a new paradigm to help solve the problem. The historian is not required to abandon traditional methods but only to add a new dimension to them, a powerful tool for the enhancement of historical understanding. For example, I have shown in Chapter 2 the weakness of the argument claiming that the Albanian revolution succeeded because the people were convinced by the logic of the Communist ideology and its appropriateness to Albanian needs; when we ask why this did not happen in other contexts, the patent inadequacy of this explanation is made clear.

Even in cases in which causal explanation does not seem to be a crucial component of the study, comparison may still fulfill an important function. An example is Donald Quataert's study on the Western economic penetration into Turkey in the late Ottoman period, a clear case of dependency theory with very little of the theory.[5] A comparison with, for example, contemporary Egypt might put this study in a wider perspective and greatly enhance its scientific value. Human experience in other contexts is the laboratory of the historian and it is hard to visualize anything else that so closely approximates such a laboratory. One characteristic of the study of Islam as an area study is that the temporal border between history and the social sciences is blurred—so much so, indeed, that people sometimes speak about "contemporary history." In that sense every branch of the human sciences is in some way history, and it may be be superfluous to say that the comparative approach is badly needed in all of them. Anthropology is a case in point. Judging by what is published, one gets the impression that anthropologists, like historians, tend to be bogged down too much in fact gathering. Although anthropologists try, at least, to connect these facts by some kind of meaningful thread, they do so only on the level of the minute; we are expected to be interested in, for example, each of Turkey's forty thousand villages individually. Anthropology must design a mode of transition from the concrete case study to the whole that it purports to explain (such as, in this case, Turkish village society).

It is easy to see that the root cause of the difficulty with anthropology is the sacredness of the field study—a great accomplishment of that profession, no doubt, but possibly an obsession that has gone too far. Thus, we find in the most important introductory book to the field of Middle Eastern anthropology a fine inventory of facts and observations but little real comparison and, hence, little causal analysis.[6] Marabouts (living saints) are treated only in the context of Morocco.[7] But did not similar phenomena exist elsewhere? Were not the living saints of South Yemen related? And what is the difference between the two cases? Only a real, causal comparison would be able to adequately deal with these questions. The omission is all the more notable as it is in anthropology that we find the only work in Islamic/Middle Eastern studies in which the comparative approach is seriously, and quite successfully, attempted. I refer, of course, to Clifford Geertz's *Islam Observed.*[8]

For the social historian, comparative history is much more than just a voluntary methodology; in a very real sense it is obligatory. This is so, at least, for any historian who sees in tracing causes the main task of history. Every statement that something happened because of *a, b,* and *c* claims, in effect, that the same thing would have happened in any other society—given the existence of the same preconditions. This really amounts to finding the general in the specific, which is, after all, the task of historical sociology or comparative social history.

Geertz's work is usually used these days for a purpose that is opposite to the one I have in mind.[9] Thus, just as I think there are important points of contact between history and the social sciences that should be brought into the open and developed, most of those who cite Geertz wish to see this trend go away. But these scholars cannot rely on *Islam Observed,* as a proper reading of this book will show that it is based on much more than just "thick description." Rather, it is based on comparison grounded in economic causation, the most solid basis for comparative analysis.

The major factors determining the course of development in both Morocco and Indonesia are ecology and geography. In Morocco there is a division between the low-lying coastal plain and the formidable mountain chain of the High Atlas, which ecologically can sustain only a nomad or, at most, a seminomad population. The tension between the area of sown agriculture and the mountain determined the main cyclical pattern of Morocco's history, a phenomenon observable soon after the Islamization of the area. In Geertz's words,

> The combination of the intrusion into the western plain after the thirteenth century of marauding Bedouin Arabs, and the fact that Morocco is located not at the core of the grain-growing world but at its furthest frontiers, prevented the development of a mature peasant culture which would have buffered tribesmen from townsmen and allowed them, milking the peasantry of tribute or taxes, to go more independently along their separate ways. As it was, neither urban nor rural life was ever altogether viable. The cities, under the leadership of their viziers and sultans, tried always to reach out around them to control the tribes. But the latter remained footloose and refractory, as well as unrewarding. The uncertainty of both pastoralism and agriculture in the climatically irregular, physically

ill-endowed, and somewhat despoiled environment impelled tribesmen sometimes into the cities, if not as conquerors then as refugees, sometimes out of their reach in mountain passes or desert wastes, and sometimes toward encircling them and, blocking the trade routes from which they lived, extorting from them.[10]

The typical structure of Moroccan culture over the ages was basically the outcome of this interplay of ecological factors:

> The critical feature of that Morocco so far as we are concerned is that its cultural center of gravity lay not, paradoxical as this may seem, in the great cities, but in the mobile, aggressive, now federated, now fragmented tribes who not only harassed and exploited them but also shaped their growth. It is out of the tribes that the forming impulses of Islamic civilization in Morocco came, and the stamp of their mentality remained on it. . . . Islam in Barbary was—and to a fair extent still is—basically the Islam of saint worship and moral severity, magical power and aggressive piety, and this was for all practical purposes as true in the alleys of Fez and Marrakech as in the expanses of the Atlas or the Sahara.[11]

In Indonesia the basic ecological formula was completely different and, hence, also the resulting institutional structure and culture. To cite Geertz again,

> Indonesia is . . . another matter altogether. Rather than tribal it is, and for the whole of the Christian era has been, basically a peasant society, particularly in its overpowering heartland, Java. Intensive, extremely productive wet rice cultivation has provided the main economic foundations of its culture for about as long as we have record, and rather than the restless, aggressive, extroverted sheikh husbanding his resources, cultivating his reputation, and awaiting his opportunity, the national archetype is the settled, industrious, rather inward plowman of twenty centuries, nursing his terrace, placating his neighbors, and feeding his superiors. In Morocco civilization was built on nerve; in Indonesia, on diligence.[12]

For historians, very few examples of application of the comparative approach exist. There is, of course, the famous case of the French historian Marc Bloch, who has not, however, carried out major research in comparative social history.[13] The most notable case is undoubtedly that of Barrington Moore, in his *Social Origins of Dictatorship and Democracy*. Though formally a sociologist, by conducting his research without prior commitment to any particular theory, this scholar has crossed the thin line that still separates historical sociology from comparative social history.

As far as historians proper are concerned, it seems to me that until a formal, full-fledged introduction to the field is written, Edward

Carr's brilliant little book *What is History* [14] should serve as a make-do manifesto. It is true that Carr does not write specifically about comparative history, but what he does say nevertheless constitutes the main bulk of the theory associated with it. Following Carr, there are two minimum basic tenets of comparative social history:

1. Comparative social history has a dual interest, in the specific and in the more general. Its practitioner is especially interested in the general that is discernible in the specific. In Carr's words,

> No two geological formations, no two animals of the same species, and no two atoms, are identical. Similarly, no two historical events are identical. . . . Embarked on this course, you soon attain a sort of philosophical nirvana, in which nothing that matters can be said about anything. The very use of language commits the historian, like the scientist, to generalization. . . . The historian is not really interested in the unique, but in what is general in the unique. [15]

Moreover, comparative social history holds that there is no good social history that is not interested in the complex and delicate relations between the general and the specific, because the search for the more general is also the search for causative explanation, which is the second basic tenet of comparative social history.

2. The student of comparative social history believes that every historical development or event has a traceable reason and that "the study of history is the study of causes." [16] As in daily life, it is unacceptable that some events are simply causeless or unaccountable. This does not mean that there is no pure chance in history. And Carr rightly disposes of those arguments that, using philosophical devices, try to discard chance from the picture. A good example of chance is Albania's geographical situation in a small and relatively unimportant corner of Europe, which prevented an Allied invasion and the likely destruction of the Communist revolution. So chance exists and there is no justification to overlook its role. What is meant by the mandate to account for every event causally is that it is incumbent upon the historian to explain that part of reality that is accessible to him or her—not necessarily everything. On the other hand, the fact that every historical fact has a cause does not stand in contradiction to the belief in individual responsibility and free choice. These are simply different points of view of the human condition. Thus, from a philosophical and legal standpoint, the individual is responsible for his or her acts. As historians, our task is to find the cause of every event.

Comparative social history, as I have outlined it, is a new mode of thinking for historians and sociologists. Scholars from the respective disciplines may "use" one another's work without taking the thought paradigm seriously, but in comparative social history the situation is somewhat different. The thought pattern of comparative social history may serve as a common meeting ground for scholars from both disciplines, who may remain in their fields while sharing a common scientific paradigm.

THE SCOPE OF GUERRILLA WAR

Walter Laqueur, who has written the most detailed book on the history of guerrilla war,[17] sees it as war by the defeated population of an occupied country against the superior power of the occupier. It is by necessity, small-scale warfare, secretive, carried out by small teams, usually against minor targets. Frontal confrontation is out of the question because of the complete military inferiority of the occupied population. In this form, guerrilla war is an extremely old institution, already found in the Roman Empire and encountered later almost regularly in many contexts. Such warfare was epidemic under Ottoman rule in the Balkans for at least three centuries and rife in nineteenth-century Europe as part of the national wars. All the historic empires suffered guerrilla wars, and no corner of the globe was free from them. What is germane to my analysis is that a distinct feature of pre-twentieth-century guerrilla wars is that their outcomes were never radical.

Guerrilla war in recent decades has been a topic of considerable importance, both in international politics and within states. One expert somewhat daringly suggested that future observers may be surprised to discover that guerrilla war has affected the fate of the world more than nuclear weapons.[18] The important role guerrilla warfare played in the Chinese revolution was later conceptualized and generalized by Mao and turned into a sharp weapon readily available for adoption by any would-be revolutionary. By doing so, Mao may have proven (to me anyway) that he did not grasp the full depth of the sociological nature of the guerrilla movement (including the Chinese guerrilla movement) and may have overemphasized his own role in it. But Mao certainly created a sort of guerrilla theory—and, consequently, some sort of guerrilla-mania in the Third World— which may have affected (marginally, I would guess) some events.

One of the most important processes that the world has been going through in recent decades is the process of decolonization, and this has come to pass pretty much through protracted struggles of the weak against the strong, largely by resorting to indirect, resourceful, and unconventional forms of armed struggle. Similar wars of independence have, of course, been taking place in human history as far back as it exists, but in the last two generations or so the nature of the conflict has been substantially changed: In the past, resurgent populations could be and often were routed and massacred mercilessly by the occupying power, unanswerable as it was either to world public opinion or to internal criticism. Today, this situation is ancient history, and no power—from France in the final stage of the Algerian war of independence to Israel in the Lebanon of 1982—can claim that it was unaffected by the pressure of world public opinion, moved by the suffering of the underdog in a struggle of unequals.

The advent of vociferous internal political democratization has made guerrilla war a doubly more devastating weapon that it used to be in the past. Increasing criticism against unwanted foreign wars mean that casualities have a political price for the occupying power. Such a mounting, and eventually unbearable, price is what cost France the Algerian war, what cost the United States Vietnam, and, most recently, in textbook fashion, what cost Israel southern Lebanon.

There are various types of guerrilla war, and some of these types are not really relevant to the study of the relationship between guerrilla war and political regimes. A major example is the Soviet guerrilla movement during World War II,[19] the classic case of a guerrilla campaign that was not a spontaneous revolt by a subject population against an occupying power. As soon as large parts of the western USSR were conquered by the Germans, Stalin called on Soviet officials in the occupied area to start a guerrilla campaign, and the Soviet government for its part erected a complicated and well-organized state apparatus to oversee and conduct that campaign. The secret services of the Soviet Union were placed in charge of the operations. Party officials in the various provinces were made officially responsible for the movement. Nevertheless, there was also an element of voluntary participation. At first, the warriors numbered about thirty thousand, as most of the population adopted a wait-and-see attitude. But as the German advance was stopped, this number grew ever larger and reached two hundred thousand by the end of 1942. The Soviet territory that was at that time under German control was bigger that Germany's own area, and it is quite clear that German lines of communications were stretched to their limit, making the life of the guerrilla warrior relatively easy. The areas in question were so vast that the partisans actually ran several small "republics" freely. A vast number of guerrilla activities were carried out by this army of partisans, and some of their operations were truly astonishing, such as the mining of the railway line at no less than eight thousand spots in one night, a well-known example. The Soviet guerrilla movement is, thus, clearly a unique case of guerrilla warfare, properly outside the scope of this book.

SPAIN, 1808–1813

The Spanish guerrilla movement between 1808 and 1813 is one of the most famous guerrilla campaigns before the twentieth century and, in fact, the context in which the term "guerrilla" ("little war") was invented.[20] It is relevant because it is the foremost guerrilla campaign before the twentieth century in which signs of radicalism may be easily observed. An examination of the Spanish campaign may thus help clarify certain important points.

The guerrilla war was aimed against Napoleon, whose army attacked Spain in 1808 and easily defeated its regular forces. The Spanish king was captured and deported to France, and Spain disintegrated into independent city-states, each ruled by a committee (junta) of local notables. These juntas organized such a successful popular resistance to the invaders that Napoleon himself led more troops to invade again. The first wave of lower-class resistance occurred in May 1808 and aroused great fears among the upper class, as the historian Raymond Carr notes: "Of the great fear of the men of property our sources leave us in no doubt."[21] The guerrilla war started in 1809 and is characterized by the emergence of small bands of warriors, headed by peasants in entirely local initiatives. The most important leader of the guerrilla movement was a peasant named Espos y Mina, who headed a guerrilla army that contained at its peak some three to four thousand fighters.

This guerrilla army was engaged in attacking supply convoys, isolated small units, and sometimes even regular armies. They showed a great deal of courage and heroism and were never decisively routed in battle. Eventually, as is well known, they won and Napoleon was expelled from Spain. Of course, this victory in itself was not the achievement of the guerrilla army but was rather a result of the invasion by a British army headed by Wellington. But the guerrilla army worked in coordination with the British army and certainly had a share in the final result. Most important for our purposes, this guerrilla movement was victorious—an obvious precondition for it to have significance in any discussion of the political consequences of guerrilla war.

Spain was at that time one of the most important vestiges of medieval Europe and under the control of a most powerful feudal socioeconomic regime. The guerrilla campaigning entailed years of the most arduous stay in the mountains under very difficult conditions—a life that the Spanish aristocracy would never endure. Small wonder that the aristocracy left the guerrilla movement entirely to the lower classes. One would expect under such circumstances signs of social radicalization, and sure enough, such signs are not lacking. A source of major importance is Marx's detailed account of the Spanish guerrilla campaign.[22] In fact, Marx formed his views on the phenomenon of guerrilla warfare entirely on the basis of the Spanish campaign, which is thus the source of his devastating opinion of the historical role of guerrilla wars, an obviously false prediction. Marx's famous concluding remark on the guerrilla war in Spain deserves quotation:

> As to the guerrillas, it is evident that, having for some years figured upon the theater of sanguinary contests, taken to roving habits, freely indulged all of their passions of hatred, revenge, and love of plunder, they must, in times of peace, form a most dangerous mob, always ready at a nod in the name of any party or principle, to step forward for him who is able to give them good pay or to afford them a pretext for plundering excursion.[23]

Marx's analysis led several twentieth-century leaders (Lenin is the notable example) to cherish the most critical opinions about the radical potential of guerrilla wars. This was, of course, a classic error in judgment on the part of Marx. But his analysis is, nevertheless, important in pointing out the radicalizing mechanisms that the Spanish guerrilla movement evinced—radicalizing mechanisms that appear to have been without an avowed "leftist" ideology.

Spain in the beginning of the nineteenth century lived under a tough feudal regime. When the central government disintegrated in the wake of the French invasion, and everywhere there appeared local committees that tried to seize the opportunity and ameliorate the position of the population, the ruling elite tried to stem this process by undermining these committees. Typical is the case of Galicia, where the representative of the central junta appointed military rulers and dismissed the local committees that sprang up. Why was this done?

> And what had been the shortcomings of the district and provincial juntas of Galicia? They had ordered a general recruitment without

exemption of classes or persons; they levied taxes upon the capitalists and proprietors; they had lowered the salaries of public functionaries . . . in one word, they had taken revolutionary measures.[24]

It is not surprising that the radical signs that were obvious among the middle class in the towns were even more far-reaching among the peasants and other social elements in the guerrilla campaign. It must be emphasized that this radicalism is affirmed by historians who, unlike Marx, are less suspect of seeing the footprint of the revolution in every historical episode. Here is, for example, what Carr has to say about the Spanish guerrilla movement.

> Guerrilla warfare shared many of the characteristics of resistance movements in the Second World War. It was a rural phenomenon . . . an aspect of peasant hatred for urban civilization. . . . Guerrilla warfare "accustomed the Spaniard to live outside the law, to reject the norms of social life and take as his great achievement the maintenance of his own personality."[25]

So far we have seen how signs of radicalism appeared in the Spanish guerrilla campaign of 1809–1813. But why did this radicalism fail to result in any change in the post-Napoleonic Spanish regime? Marx's analysis is revealing. He subdivides the period of the Spanish guerrilla movement in three. During the first period, there took place an uprising of wide-ranging groups; during the second period, guerrilla bands were formed, composed of ex-soldiers, deserters, peasants, and the like; in the third period, these bands were transformed into full-fledged armies, thereby entirely losing their identity. They "were now frequently overtaken, defeated, dispersed, and disabled for a length of time from any further molestation."[26] The shift from one period to another paralleled shifts in the corresponding political history of Spain:

> By comparing the three periods of guerrilla warfare with the political history of Spain, it is found that they represent the respective degrees into which the counter-revolutionary spirit of the Government had succeeded in cooling the spirit of the people. Beginning with the rise of whole populations, the partisan war was next carried on by guerrilla bands, of which whole districts formed the reserve and terminated in *corps francs* continually on the point of dwindling into banditti.[27]

What clearly differentiates the Spanish case from, say, the Albanian one is that in Albania there was a leading elite that directed the revolutionary violence that emanated from below to a specific purpose, which, at least for a while, was resonant with the wishes of the insurgent masses. This leadership prevented the guerrilla campaign from degenerating into indiscriminate looting and killing, and it eventually made something out of it. One senses quite clearly that exactly this element was missing in the Spanish guerrilla movement. The special methodological importance of the case of Spain is that it highlights the place of leadership. But what is evident from the historical record is that the lack of a proper leadership to lead a lower-class social insurrection is a premodern phenomenon. There is, to my mind, no twentieth-century society that could not provide such a leadership. Thus, it seems that in the twentieth century the crucial factor in the incidence of radical guerrilla war is the social environment.

CHINA

China and Vietnam are two major cases that prove not only that often it is not at all by chance that a Communist regime takes over in a certain society but, moreover, that the explanation for what has taken place is not to be sought in any special quality of the leadership, such as its ability to convince and propagate successfully. The similarity between the circumstances surrounding the emergence of the Communist regimes in Albania, South Yemen, China, and Vietnam is so striking as to suggest a major avenue for the development of communism in the Third World. In both China and Vietnam we find a stark, two-class division between landlords and landless peasants.

Traditional Chinese society was based, on the one hand, on a central bureaucracy and, on the other, on a landed upper class that ruled the provinces on behalf of the central government.[28] The economic mainstay of this class was its control over extensive tracts of lands, about half the lands in China; the other half belonged to small peasants. This gentry ruled the countryside by way of decentralized sharecropping. The social gap between the gentry and the peasantry was enormous, and the peasantry was despised and extremely maltreated, such that it is small wonder that the traditional Chinese peasantry was much inclined to rebelliousness.

Internal peace and security from the sixteenth century on led to huge population increases and the appropriation of all free land reserves in China by the nineteenth century—developments that resulted in great deterioration in the economic situation of the peasantry and enormous pressure on the land.

In the nineteenth century, China was subject to European penetration, intended mainly to acquire a piece of the Chinese market for cheap industrial products. This penetration resulted in large-scale political and commercial concessions made to the European powers, which increasingly compromised China's independence and territorial integrity. Tottering under the European pressure, the traditional culture of China, and with it the reigning political formula, came under increasing attack and commanded less and less respect. The result was a liberal revolution that in 1911 swept away the Chinese traditional empire. However, the revolution was unable to establish a viable and stable regime, and the country was soon dragged into a period of near anarchy, which only ended with the Communists' assumption of power in 1949. There was an almost total collapse of central authority, and the country disintegrated into geographical regions run by army warlords. Chinese public opinion objected to the warlords, and a united front of the two main parties, the Kuomintang, or nationalist party, and the Communist party, brought an end to warlordism in 1927. Immediately thereafter, Chiang Kai-shek, leader of the Kuomintang, broke his alliance with the Communists and massacred a large number of them.

The government that Chiang Kai-shek established after 1927 did not, however, solve China's urgent problems. For one thing, this government did not change the basic parameters of the Chinese socioeconomic system. China's powerlessness vis-à-vis the rest of the world did not change either. Given the continued state of anarchy and the extreme weakness of the central Chinese government, the Chinese Communist party broke with orthodox Marxism and forged its own version of communism. At that time, a Chinese proletariat hardly existed; China's vast expanses of area were only nominally controlled by the central government; and no effective, legal political force ruled the provinces. Small wonder that the Chinese Communists hit upon the idea of capturing small rural areas and running them as tiny independent states. They first did this in the region of Shensi, in southern China. The Kuomintang government tried several times to wipe out this base, and was on the verge of finally doing so, in 1934 when the Communists pulled out en masse with one hundred thousand followers.

The Communists had to find another place of refuge, or they would be hunted down and exterminated by government forces. So they looked for an uncherished corner of China, where the nationalist government would not mind their existence. Their march to this new place of refuge in north China, the famous Long March, took a year to complete and cost the lives of about 90 percent of those who had started it. It is clear that the Long March, its story told as a great historical epic in the official version of the history of the Chinese Communist party, was in the short run a retreat for the sake of survival, and those who survived had no reason to be optimistic about the future of communism in China. Indeed, there is no reason to believe that the Communists would have come to power in China without an entirely new development—the Sino-Japanese war that started in 1937 and lasted until 1945. As one scholar puts it, "For those inclined to ponder the role of 'accidents' in history, the Japanese invasion of China is undoubtedly a most intriguing case. Were it not for the Japanese attempt to conquer China in 1937, it can plausibly be argued, the conditions essential to the Communist victory would not have been present."[29]

The war started after Japan conquered Manchuria in 1931 and the Chinese were unable to dislodge the Japanese without recourse to war. Amid loud clamor for organized resistance in Manchuria, Chiang claimed that such resistance was impossible before eliminating the inner danger posed by the Communists. However, he finally gave in to strong public pressure to put internal divisions aside and to form a united front. The Japanese immediately retaliated with an all-out war against China. But, as Lucien Bianco says, the Japanese army "was swallowed up in the vastness of China."[30] What this meant was that the Japanese could not hope to control more than large cities and major roads, and a golden opportunity was thus offered to the Chinese to organize an anti-Japanese guerrilla campaign, an opportunity soon realized. As it turned out, besides the Communists no political power was ready to engage in this activity. The Communists' waging guerrilla war won them more popular support than any socialist slogans or programs did. According to Bianco, "Patriotic propaganda was much more successful in winning over the peasants than agrarian revolution had been several years before."[31]

Moreover, wherever the Communists took over in this period, they were extremely careful to create an image of a very moderate party. The party "all but abandoned its program of social revolution, including the confiscation of large landholdings . . . and was content instead with strict enforcement of the law limiting land rent. This was enough to win over the tenant farmers without jeopardizing the party's official moderate image."[32] In other words, the Communists' breakthrough in their appeal to the Chinese masses came not because the peasants were rationally converted to Marxism-Leninism but because the peasants were ready to follow the leadership of the Communists in the guerrilla campaign. The crucial question is, therefore: Why was the Communist party the only political force that was ready to engage in actual guerrilla warfare?

Bianco suggests that the reason has to do with the social implications of guerrilla warfare, which "are obvious. Mobilizing the rural masses would have required transforming the Chinese countryside and limiting the power of large landowners; hence Chiang's aversion to the idea."[33] This explanation seems dubious to me. Why would it have been necessary to affect the power of the landlords? In fact, had the landlords led the guerrilla movement themselves, their power might have been enhanced. It is more reasonable to suppose that something akin to what took place in Albania during the same period must have taken place in China as well: In the first place, the landlords (absentee even in normal times) would not have been found in the countryside in such a difficult and dangerous time.[34] Moreover, the traditional gap between the gentry and the peasantry would have precluded the possibility of their sharing arduous, austere, and intimate companionship. Only the relatively lower-class Communists were up to the task. What happened in China was a natural consequence of a guerrilla war waged in a society torn by deep-seated class cleavages of agrarian nature.

What happened during the war was the sine qua non for the success of the Communists in China. Although the remaining advance to power was anything but an afternoon stroll, as far as scientific explanations go the main chapter ended with Japan's surrender in 1945. As soon as this happened, it became clear that a life-and-death showdown between the nationalists and the Communists was inevitable. After a short period of wavering, the war started in earnest in 1946 and lasted for two and a half years. On paper the Communists had little chance. Only the nationalists had an air force and tanks; they also outnumbered the Communists in soldiers by four to one. But the position of the nationalists, after initial success, grew continually weaker. There were only two head-on confrontations, and in both of these the nationalists were severely beaten. The rest was really no more than a march southward for the Communists.

The explanation for this somewhat surprising victory is apparently to be sought in the Communists' vastly higher morals. To be precise, whereas the Communists (all volunteers) knew full well what they were fighting for, soldiers of the nationalist army did not. Nationalist soldiers were all peasants, forcibly recruited, maltreated, and despised by their superiors as befits a traditional Chinese social framework. To be recruited into the army was considered a disaster.

As against this, the soldiers of the Red Army were fighting to defend land rights, which the peasants had acquired through the land reform that had been carried out in the Communist-held regions during the war. The soldiers of this army were treated as equals by their superiors. Therefore, they fought willingly and their morale was high. It is fairly obvious that the clear-cut outcome of the civil war was a natural, inevitable consequence of the guerrilla campaign during World War II. Great leader that Mao may have been, the series of events that really explain the rise of the Communists seems to lie in the guerrilla war amid a class-riven society.

VIETNAM

Vietnam supplies us with yet another example of this process. The sociopolitical regime of modern Vietnam is a result of two conquests.[35] The first is the ancient Chinese conquest, which came to an end in the tenth century A.D. The second is the French conquest, which started in the middle of the nineteenth century. By that time the Vietnamese state was in the process of expanding from the north southward. This process involved a bitter struggle by the state against internal opponents, mainly large landlords, and support for small landowners. In the north, strong Chinese influence was always present in all aspects of life. From an agrarian point of view, the north has always been characterized by a regime of small and independent landowners. Large estates were conspicuous by their absence. The village constituted a cohesive social unit. Within the village a tangible degree of stratification was present: The elite were the villagers with more land than the others. Frugality and hard work allowed peasants to acquire land and rise in social esteem. This system was an incentive to political conservatism, and no objective reason was created to lead peasants to ponder a revolution against the social order.

In southern Vietnam the situation was completely different. In 1859, the French conquered Saigon, in the Mekong Delta, thereby intending to facilitate the creation of markets in southern China. In 1867, the French captured further areas in the south of Vietnam and established the province of Kochin China. This region, in the south of the Mekong Delta, was largely swampy and very sparsely populated, and the village community, strong and cohesive in the north of the country, was as yet weak and ephemeral there. Soon afterwards, it occurred to the French that the province could be used to produce and export rice, and they started to award large estates to people for that purpose.

Indeed, within a short period of time this area became one of the world's foremost rice-exporting regions. From an agrarian point of view, these estates were run by decentralized sharecropping—that is, the peasants produced in the traditional ways but with the difference that they had to part with a substantial part of the produce. Peasants in the Mekong Delta were entirely dependent on the big landlords. Within the existing regime they had no legitimate means for social and economic advancement except by sheer luck.

In Vietnam, as in China, the Communist revolution was strictly bound up with a struggle for independence. The Japanese conquered large parts of Vietnam in the wake of the French defeat in 1940, and soon thereafter a guerrilla war was started, originating in the mountainous border area between Vietnam and China, where an ethnic minority, the Tho, mixed anti-Japanese feelings with a desire to regain long-lost autonomy. In 1942, a small guerrilla band was formed there. Its membership consisted of Tho members and some Communists, and it was the first cell of the Vietminh, the Communist underground that was to capture power in the north in 1954.

As World War II ended and the French had not as yet returned, Vietnam was held by China and Great Britain. Britain's rule in the south remained entirely nominal, and the Vietminh's influence became paramount, especially in the Mekong Delta, where their social propaganda struck an extremely sensitive nerve. However, French forces arrived in 1946 and drove the Vietminh out of the plains and into the mountains, from which place the French never really tried to dislodge them. Instead, the French were content to control a few isolated strongholds, a typical one being Dien Bien Fuh, a major symbol in the decline of colonialism. Under this growing pressure from the Vietminh, the French gave up their rule of the north, while an extremely anti-Communist elite took control of the south and, with large-scale Western support, cut it off from the north. This southern regime was unpopular from the start, and its unpopularity increased with time. The heart of this region, the Mekong Delta, was an area where the Vietminh had been particularly popular in 1945–1946, when the peasantry there received free land in lavish quantities. The regime that took hold of the region after 1954 reversed this policy, returned lands to their old owners, and in other cases forced peasants to pay for land they had gotten free from the Vietminh. Most of the population in south Vietnam apparently had reasons to think that they had been better off with the Vietminh than with the Diem regime. The outbreak of the second Vietnam war and the support of most of the population for the Vietminh is, therefore, not at all surprising.

THE PALESTINIAN REVOLT, 1936–1939

An important case study bearing on the connection between guerrilla war and social radicalism in general, and within Islam in particular, is the Palestinian revolt of 1936–1939, aimed at the British mandatory government and the Zionist movement.[36] This revolt was for all intents and purposes a guerrilla war and is therefore an important comparative case, as it holds constant the factor of Islam. It has in recent years been subjected to detailed studies, notably by Yehoshua Porath, so that an examination of its social aspects is made possible for the comparative social historian. Such a study is especially called for, as no scholar has as yet analyzed it from this point of view.

In the middle years of the 1930s, the tension between Arabs and Jews in Palestine grew considerably. Ever since the end of World War I, the Arab community of Palestine had been in a constant state of extreme agitation, and anti-Jewish violence seems to erupt in a cyclical manner. In this period, the exploits of Shaykh 'Iz al-Din al-Qassam, head of a secret band of warriors that killed a number of Jews and was finally wiped out by a British unit at the end of 1935, created a strong impression on the Arab population. The Arab Revolt started in 1936 in spontaneous acts of violence against Jews and the British. All parties concerned—the British, the Jews, and even the Palestinian leadership—were taken by complete surprise. Though tension had been visibly mounting, no one had anticipated such a massive outburst. However, when the Arab leadership realized what was happening, it hastened to direct the movement.

In the first phase of the revolt the main activity was concentrated in the towns, villagers joining much later. It is not at all simple to find a specific explanation for the participation of the peasants in the revolt. Purely economic reasons are problematic: Although in the 1930s there had been some bad drought years, in the year before the revolt crops were abundant. It is also noteworthy that the peasants rose mainly in the mountainous area, where Jewish penetration and land purchases had been minimal. What apparently motivated the peasants was identical to the motivation of the population at large—nationalist feeling and a passion to get rid of an intruding foreign element.

Be that as it may, the Arab Revolt of Palestine, which spanned the period 1936–1939, falls naturally into two parts. The first wave of activity took place in 1936; then there was a lull of about a year. At the end of 1937, there was another eruption, this time much more massive, which lasted until the end of 1939. The main activity that may reasonably be called guerrilla activity was carried out in the second period, and it is this period which I propose to analyze in some detail.

The second part of the Arab Revolt began with the assassination of the acting British governor of the Galilee, an unprecedented murder that shocked the British, who reacted sternly. They tried to capture Hajj Amin al-Husayni, the chief Palestinian leader and other leaders of that movement, but al-Husayni eluded them and after a while escaped to Lebanon. In the middle of October, the revolt broke out in earnest in all corners of the country. Targeted were Jews everywhere, British military installations, telephone lines, and the petroleum pipeline from Iraq to Haifa.

The first intensive wave of activity lasted for about a month and then ebbed—possibly, among other reasons, because of the strong British effort to curb it. But in the spring of 1938 it grew strong again. Toward the summer there appeared the most important expression of the revolt: hundreds of more or less isolated peasant bands who took to the hills and started a small-scale guerrilla campaign against the British and the Jews. During the summer of 1938, these bands managed to attain complete control of several cities and roads. Government offices and police stations in many places were attacked and burned down. The railway line between Jaffa and Jerusalem stopped functioning because of recurrent attacks. In short,

> In summer 1938, the rebels were in control of most of the mountainous parts of the country. They were walking fully armed in the streets of Nablus without any hindrance. The Arab civil servants bought their lives by disclosing all official documents and secrets to the rebels, and their wounded were hospitalized in Government hospitals. By September 1938 the situation was such that civil administration and control of the country was, to all practical purposes, non-existent.[37]

If September was the peak month of the revolt, October signaled the beginning of its decline. In the middle of that month, rebels captured the Old City of Jerusalem. The authorities reacted swiftly, first by declaring Jerusalem a military area and then by extending that emergency status to the entire country. Putting down the revolt received high priority and proceeded in earnest, backed by substantial reinforcements pouring in from Europe. Tough and even oppressive measures were taken, such as the forbidding of any traffic on the roads without special permits. This order spelled ruin for the lucrative export of Jaffa oranges, which dealt a major blow to the whole Palestinian revolt. Such persistent measures caused the revolt to weaken and die out in the course of 1939. At its peak, the number of rebel fighters is estimated to have been between nine and ten thousand, of whom about six thousand were peasants.

There is no doubt that one of the important reasons for the failure of the revolt was the internal rift in the Palestinian movement between the Husayni and the Nashashibi factions, which in the course of the revolt assumed a military dimension. At the rebellion's height, opposing bands fought each other no less than they did the British or the Jews. It must be said right away, however, that from a comparative perspective attribution of the failure to this factor is not entirely convincing. The cleavages that we have seen in the national movements in Albania and South Yemen were no less bitter than in Palestine. The major reason for the failure undoubtedly had to do with the fact that Britain was not in a position to lose its control of a province at such as tense time as the late 1930s—certainly not because of some peasant guerrilla bands. British public opinion would not have been too sensitive at that time to a few casualties. In such circumstances, a guerrilla campaign has no real chance of victory.

But this is not our main interest in the Arab Revolt; rather, it is the social structure of the revolt and its meaning. A distinct characteristic of this guerrilla activity is that it was conducted almost solely by bands composed of peasants and headed by peasants. It is not surprising that most of the activists came from the mountainous regions of central Palestine, where most of the activity also took place—no doubt because this area, rather than the coastal plain, was suitable for a guerrilla campaign.

The most interesting aspect of the revolt for our purposes was the few signs of radicalization during its course; these signs are important, both for what they reveal and for what was missing from them. At the height of the revolt, the bands controlled several cities, and their attitude toward the populace showed some class undertones. Most notable was the case of Jaffa, whose population was subjected to serious tax extortion. Even more interesting, the rebels declared an unlimited moratorium on repayment of debts owed to city moneylenders, pending punishments of death in second offenses. The decree relating to this matter included these prohibitions:

> In view of the economic crisis in the present position of the fellah during this agricultural season and the heavy burden lying on their

shoulders, certain creditors in towns who look after their personal interests only have begun to visit the villages pressing the debtors to settle their accounts. Due to these reasons attention is being drawn to the following points: 1) Creditors are warned not to visit villages or send their agents to ask for settlement of debts. 2) Any person who takes legal steps against his debtor will be held responsible for his actions.[38]

In another decree, the rebels ordered the total abrogation of rents in the town of Jaffa. More symbolic, the bands in Jaffa (and in this they were quickly followed in other towns) ordered the entire city population to use the traditional Palestinian peasant headgear, the *kufiyya* and *'iqal.*

These clear signs of social radicalism did not, however, go beyond these specific acts. There was not, for example, any effort at full-blown social ideology of any sort, and no act of the rebels implied any latent ideology. Porath is quite unequivocal on this:

> Was there any social ideology which the rebels cherished and which might have influenced their action? . . . The reply . . . is very simple: the rebels did not articulate any ideology of their own. . . . Being devoid of any social ideology, the rebels did not attempt, when they reached the peak of their power in summer 1938, to bring about any change in the social structure of those large rural parts of the country which were then under their control.[39]

Why this lack of radical ideology? Let us first analyze carefully what did take place. The rebels had relations with villages and with towns. As they were themselves peasants, their relations with villages were on the whole cordial. They needed resources, and from time to time their extortion of these made them quarrel with the villages, but the important point is that they did not target any one particular group for special treatment; their dealings were always with the village as a body.

In the cities, they exhibited social antagonism. But it is characteristic and important that this was directed at moneylenders and city real-estate owners. In addition, the rebels showed some cultural antagonism to the city population as such. In total, they expressed the cultural resentment of the village against the city and against the money lenders but made no real attack on extant property relations. More specifically, these were peasants let loose on the entire country, who did not, however, evince demands concerning landownership. How can we account for this fact?

We shall not be able to understand this point without briefly examining the preexisting agrarian regime, an outcome of four hundred years of rule and agrarian development.[40] The starting point, the sixteenth-century Ottoman land system, was a centralized regime that abhorred feudal aristocracy and did everything possible to prevent an aristocracy's establishment. The alternative was the independent peasant and village community. This land regime came under attack in the seventeenth and eighteenth centuries, when the central government lost much of its power to local satraps. One outcome was that people deserted much of the plains and low-lying areas, where they were unable to keep the nomads at bay. However, this development had little effect on the mountainous regions, with the consequence that there population remained dense and the sixteenth-century land regime remained more or less intact up to the modern period.

A new phase in the agrarian history of the region started with the 1858 Ottoman Land Code, which enjoined landowners to register their land in the registry books of the government. There was a substantial increase in public security all over the Middle East and, at the same time, in population growth, which also created a demand for grain. The outcome of these eventualities was a rush on the empty lands in the plains and coastal areas—a rush in which, no doubt, big landowners won out. However, it has been shown that this development entirely bypassed the already densely populated areas, among these the central mountainous region of Palestine. This situation was clearly reflected in the history of the two national movements that fought over Palestine during 1918–1948. The agrarian situation that came into being in the wake of the Ottoman Land Code was almost tailored to suit the needs of the Zionist movement, whose land purchasers, equipped with relatively substantial amounts of money, could only deal effectively with large landowners, especially landowners willing to reap handsome profits on investments that were speculative in the first place. The result shows clearly on the map: The plains fell largely to the Zionists, whereas the mountainous region remained overwhelmingly Palestinian. This is further proof, if any is needed, that the land regime in the mountainous regions of Palestine remained to the 1930s characterized by small and largely independent peasants.

The meager signs of radicalization that are observable in the Palestinian revolt may be understood in these terms. Most of the guerrilla band members and leaders were drawn from the mountainous region, and as no major class of agrarian exploiters existed in this area, there was nothing that could add a social undertone to the nationalist ideology propelling the campaign. It may even be that there is a connection between the fact that the clearest signs of radicalization appear in Jaffa—that is, in the heart of the region where a major agrarian problem did exist. But, for obvious topographical reasons, the coastal plain was hardly the place to carry out serious subversive activity, so radicalization remained necessarily limited there as well.

To what degree were the meager signs of radicalization attributable to some sort of "failure" of the Palestinian Communist party? This question is, of course, particularly interesting in light of the Albanian experience. In fact, the Communists were quite aware of the rising tension in 1935 and 1936 and were not slack in addressing the matter in various ways.[41] As soon as the revolt broke out, the Communist party hailed it enthusiastically, its members joined the rebel activities, and some Communist leaders were given important functions in the campaign.[42] This, however, was about the extent of their participation. The party never attained any position of influence in the revolt and remained entirely in the shade. When, years later, party leaders tried to account for this, they gave several explanations, such as this one:

> The lack of leadership in the Arab National Movement, the egotism and opportunism of the leaders . . . the decentralization of the guerrilla command, which allowed hooligans to enter the ranks of the partisans, and last but not least, the weakness, especially the numerical weakness, of the Communist Party.[43]

This explanation does not seem convincing at all. It is hardly likely that the objective situation of the Albanian Communist party was substantially different than that in Palestine. In Albania the party was initially no more than a chip of marginal power. It was what the Albanian Communists had to offer to the landless Albanian peasants in the south that made the difference. Its Palestinian counterpart could offer the peasants only a bunch of theoretical slogans that they were unable to comprehend anyway. Herein, I belive, lies the reason for the complete lack of Communist imprint on the Palestinian Arab Revolt.

CHAPTER SEVEN

Summary and Conclusions

In this study I have tried to provide answers to several questions, lying at different levels of abstraction. On one level, we examined the relationship between Islam and communism, posing the question, Is Islam receptive to communism or not? On a higher level of abstraction, we were interested in clarifying the question, Does an ideology have a life of its own, or is its rise or fall better understood in connection with the dialectics of changing social circumstances? Answers were sought through comparative analyses of a number of empirical case studies, each constituting a check and commentary on the others. Two basic case studies concerned Albania and South Yemen, both today avowedly Marxist countries with an overwhelmingly Muslim population. Analysis of these two case studies led me to develop a general theory, which I then tested against the background of several more cases—positive examples and some negative, in part or in total.

ALBANIA

In Albania, the Communist party came to power in November 1944, after several years of guerrilla warfare against the occupying German forces. Albania, a province of the Ottoman Empire until the eve of World War I and one of the last Ottoman possessions on the Balkan peninsula, became a fully independent state in the wake of World War I. After a few years of political wavering, including a period of toying with democracy, the country fell in 1924 under the rule of a tribal chieftain from the northern part of the country, Ahmed Zogu, who in 1929 crowned himself King Zog I. The leadership in Albania in this period was a closed elite composed of tribal chieftains and big landowners. On the whole, however, the Albanian central government was at this time characterized by great feebleness. The reason for this weakness was no doubt the minuteness of the tax base. The extremely mountainous nature of a large part of the country did not allow much space for sown agriculture, fostering instead rather extensive animal (mainly sheep) breeding and tribal social structure. There was very little economic surplus to be taxed, and tribal warriors and firearms made the life of any central government a nightmare.

The extreme and chronic weakness of the state in Albania opened the way to pervasive foreign influence—in this case, that of Italy, Albania's neighbor across the Otranto Pass. In contracts made in the 1920s, Italy received far-reaching economic concessions in Albania, which it used ruthlessly both economically and politically. When in 1939 King Zog refused to renew a contract, Italy reacted swiftly by invading Albania with full force (April 1939). The Albanian army, actually a token army, showed almost no resistance, and Albania fell to the Axis half a year before the beginning of World War II. Subsequently, when Italy surrendered in September 1943, a German army immediately entered Albania and the Axis's occupation remained uninterrupted.

Not long after the beginning of the Italian occupation, a popular resistance movement started, which for a number of years was irregular and small. In 1942, more organized political organizations decided to take hold of this activity and direct it. In September of that year the Front for National Liberation (LNC) came into being and assumed leadership of the guerrilla campaign. The LNC initially comprised all the political groups in the country, at least on paper. But after a few months it became clear that Communist leaders were overwhelmingly predominant. Before long, this situation and the public perception of the LNC as a Communist organization pushed the remaining non-Communists out. But the overwhelming thrust of the evidence indicates that this was neither an outcome of prior planning nor to the liking of the Communists. Rather, it was an outcome of sociological dynamics.

At the same time, two other important facts became clear. First, it soon transpired that only the LNC was engaged in guerrilla war. The non-Communist elite failed to carry out actual guerrilla activities and, in the course of time, began more and more to side with the Germans against the guerrilla movement. Second, it became clear quite early that the partisans were only active in the south of the country—that is, south of the Shkumbi River. North of that river they had no popular support, and, naturally, no guerrilla activity took place there. Such was the situation until the summer of 1944, when the LNC completed its takeover of the entire southern part of the county and, after some wavering, crossed the Shkumbi River to the north. The south was friendly terrain, but the north was controlled by the anti-Communist elite; crossing over meant fighting on two fronts—against the Germans and in a civil war. The partisans had, of course, to take this risk if they wished to control the entire country. The Communists also had amassed a sufficient number of supporters and warriors for the task. Their ranks had swelled during the fighting in the south to several tens of thousands.

What threatened to become a bloodbath rather than a civil war turned out to be a rather easy undertaking (although the German military challenge proved formidable). It is clear that even on paper the nationalist elite of the north had little chance against the partisans, as the number of warriors they could put into the field was much smaller and their weapons much inferior. The Allies were supplying the partisans with weapons. But, in fact, the nationalist leaders were not even able to unite and put forward the best defensive line they might have marshaled. They were deeply divided, each leader fiercely independent in his own small area. Thus, the resistance showed by the northern elite was quite intermittent and sporadic, always in small forces that were easily defeated by the Communists. At this stage, the partisans already constituted a real army; one last major German drive to destroy them failed in September. The Germans realized that with the relatively meager and probably second-grade forces that they could afford to keep in Albania they would be unable to keep the country—hence, their total evacuation of Albania in November 1944, amidst ongoing heavy fighting with the partisans. The traditional elite of the country was wiped out. Those members of this elite who were caught were summarily tried as war criminals and executed, although a large number made good their escape. The Communist revolution was now complete.

This is the general outline of the course of the Albanian revolution. But an explanation of why it happened is still lacking. Two smaller but fundamental questions are crucial to such an explanation: Why did not the traditional elite take part in the guerrilla campaign? And why did the guerrilla movement originate and blossom only in the south? Answers to these questions lie in the preexisting social structure of Albania. It must be remarked also that nothing in the prewar situation hinted at even a near success for the

Communists. The party did not so much as exist formally; there were only some traces of political activity on the part of a small number of intellectuals; and no lower-class support seemed forthcoming. The success of communism in Albania was rather an outcome of a combination of propitious circumstances and the prewar social structure.

The immediate fact that is thrown into relief is the sharp division of the country into two halves: the south and the north. This division corresponds entirely to the division observed in the conduct of the guerrilla war, and for good reasons. In the north the region is extremely mountainous, little accessible to outsiders, such as government officials, and an ancient tribal social structure held sway, probably in a more pure form than anywhere else in Europe. The south was much more flat, hence more agricultural in nature and also easily accessible to foreign intrusion. Whatever the southern ecology left undone in terms of wreaking havoc to the old tribal social structure, the fierce ruler Ali Pasha of Yanina had completed at the beginning of the nineteenth century. The area thus became a classic one of absentee large landlordism. The landlords lived in the big towns, while the lands were held by sharecroppers, who had reason to hold grudges against the landlords for the high rents they were made to pay.

When the anti-Axis guerrilla movement was engrafted onto this social structure, several outcomes ensued. In the first place, members of the country's elite did not join in. Hard life and personal sacrifice were simply not for them. Also, they were too well known. The enemy would soon single them out for destruction. Only a totally unknown elite could succeed in remaining anonymous. Thus, very few of the elite—that is, non-Communists—joined the guerrilla campaign. The situation wherein the guerrilla movement assumes a somewhat pinkish character is self-reinforcing, as it pushes out some leftover non-Communists who are reluctant to be associated with the Left. Also, local tribal rulers in the north, whose rule was plainly incongruous with Communist teachings, began to object to guerrilla activities in their areas, which relates to a second fundamental factor: that the south was a political no-man's-land. The landlords were absent, and there was no local overlordship in daily life. It was only in the south that an oppositional urban elite could freely propagate, amass supporters for the nationalist cause, and later start to inject into the nationalist cause subtle social messages.

To sum up, it seems quite clear that the success of communism in Albania was a result neither of the mysterious super abilities of this or that leader nor of some kind of chance. It was caused by the combination of a two-class agrarian social structure and an antiforeign guerrilla war. In Albania, this success was further enhanced by the fact that the Albanian guerrilla campaign was part and parcel of the war against the Axis in World War II. This meant that the resistance movement in Albania received substantial quantities of supplies (including weapons and ammunitions) from the Allies, especially in 1942 and after. The partisans naturally put these weapons to excellent use in their internal wars as well.

SOUTH YEMEN

South Yemen is outwardly a completely different story. Here we have a country that had been a British colony since 1839. The motivation to capture the place had been connected with the introduction of the steamship in the 1820s. England urgently needed a coaling station en route to India, and Aden, with its excellent natural harbor, seemed a perfect choice. It was conveniently situated in terms of distance from India and England, and it belonged to a small desert principality that was unable to show any substantial resistance. Its original and basic function as a bunkering post remained Aden's main function for the next century and continued even after oil eclipsed coal as the source for ships' energy, for by sheer luck, Aden was superbly situated close to the main sources of oil in the Gulf. This successful shift from coal to oil was completed in the 1950s, when the British Petroleum Company established a £45-million refinery there.

Aden after World War II assumed an added importance when, following Kenya's independence in 1954, it became Britain's last remaining possession in the Middle East and its periphery. Britain chose Aden as the new site for its Middle East Command; this move was completed in 1960, and thousands of military personnel were transferred there with their families. Aden thus became a place of major importance in the rapidly disappearing British empire. Britain was entirely carefree about its future control of Aden, and for a seemingly good objective reason. Whereas Arab nationalism was fiercely chasing Britain from everywhere else in the Middle East, Aden appeared almost entirely unaffected by this sentiment. In retrospect, Britain's carefree attitude was based on a mistake. There was a good reason for the late arrival of nationalism to South Yemen: Most of the country was materially on a much lower level than the rest of the Arab world.

When Great Britain wished to take hold of Aden in 1839, it needed the Aden harbor alone, but Aden did not come alone but with a loose hinterland of a large semidesert, very sparsely populated and politically controlled by twenty-odd small principalities. With Aden, this area was culturally part of Yemen. South Yemen was politically a residual category, comprising those areas where the authority of the imam, Yemen's ruler, could not reach and which detached themselves from Yemen at the beginning of the eighteenth century. Beyond Aden, the region could be inhabited only in those few oases where a permanent source of water existed. Especially notable was the easternmost Wadi Hadramawt, several hundred kilometers long. Initially, Britain did not want anything to do with this area: It was too destitute, sparsely populated, and entirely devoid of exploitable natural resources. However, because this area constitutes Aden's defensive hinterland, Britain was forced to become involved with it. Several series of defense pacts were signed between the rulers of these principalities and Great Britain, and Britain increasingly participated in the management of the area. But South Yemen must have been one of the few colonies that were truly more a liability than an asset to the colonial power. After World War II Britain somewhat naturally hit upon the idea of uniting all the area into one federal state, tied closely, needless to say, to Great Britain. However, when the idea was finally put into effect, in 1958, a vociferous nationalist movement already existed in Aden and parts of the protectorate, which viewed the prospects of a federal state with horror. Such a state meant the subjugation of Aden, with its relatively open and liberal social structure, to a sociopolitical regime based openly on caste; a federation would also degrade Aden economically.

Indeed, the social structure in preindependence South Yemen was characterized by a rigid form of stratification, quite akin to a caste system. It is interesting that these characteristics were most far-reaching in Hadramawt, also the most urban corner in the hinterland. The higher caste level was composed of sayyids, living saints. This unique social structure was an outcome of the special combination of, on the one hand, a vast stretch of semiarid area, which could not support a peasantry and hence taxation and which was very weakly governed, and, on the other hand, oases, which allowed for quite developed urban structure. How could these cities survive in such a violent and hostile surrounding environment? The solution that was found (obviously an unconscious solution) was that the upper class in the urban settlements became a class of holy men. This holiness, no doubt, served the tribes by providing neutral mediators. But most important, holiness scared off the tribes in case they coveted urban riches. In the extremely loose political regime prevailing in the area, holiness could be preserved and monopolized only by making of it something immutable, ideologically and legally—hence, the castelike rigidity of the social system. This ruling class, composed as well of rulers and their families not enjoying sayyid status, also relied on large landlordism.

Britain's position in South Yemen seemed secure until the 1950s, when the first mild nationalist demands were voiced. Mild demands got mild response, and the area did not seem to be heading toward independence. But a turning point came with the North Yemeni republican revolution of September 1962, which touched off a bloody civil war of tremendous emotional magnitude. This revolution found ready echo in the hearts of many South Yemenis, some of whom became involved as volunteers in this war, mostly on the republican side. A group of such activists convened in June 1963 and established an organization for armed struggle against the British in South Yemen, to help divert British attention from helping the royalists in North Yemen—a quite unpretentious beginning for what eventually became one of the most rigid Marxist regimes in the world.

On the whole, the scale of the guerrilla activity in South Yemen was modest compared with that in Albania, not to mention bigger countries. But this does not mean that the sociological mechanism was necessarily different or diametrically opposed. The resistance to the occupation in South Yemen was carried out by a middle-class urban elite, and the warriors were mostly tribesmen and peasants from the hinterland. The traditional social elite of the country did not join the struggle and was opposed to it from the start. The old nationalist oppositional leadership of Aden also did not join, though they were at heart opposed to the occupation. The guerrilla organization was led by completely anonymous figures, whose initial avowed ideology was pure Arab nationalism. But in the course of 1965, there suddenly sprang up among the activists a large radical sector. In some democratically run congresses held that year, this sector showed a possible majority of votes within the guerrilla organization. The growth of the influence of this organization, the NLF, attracted attention, as well as competition, and thus FLOSY came into being, representing mainly the traditional Adenese elite. Such competition was all in vain: The formative two first years had proved essential in building popular support for the NLF, which became a legitimate body for the common people.

The fact that Cairo Radio completely ignored the NLF and its activities (causing a nearly total contemporary ignorance of it) did not affect what was going on in the field. One is struck by a similar eventuality in Albania and South Yemen—the failure of the upper social elite to join the guerilla movement, a failure that was unavoidable and that seems to have been of crucial importance in both cases. No less crucial was the quiet build-up of a guerrilla force more and more imbued with radical ideology, which at first nobody noticed and later nobody could stop.

A THEORY OF GUERRILLA WAR
AND POLITICAL RADICALISM

The theory I have suggested, based on the revolutions in Albania and South Yemen, sets out to find the connections between guerrilla war and political radicalism, and may be summarized as follows:

1. A precondition for the radicalization of a guerrilla movement is for it to take place in a society riven by class differences and conflicts, preferably of agrarian nature. In the two societies in question this was certainly the case, more purely so in Albania but also true in South Yemen. Moreover, the logic behind the requirement that the two classes pitched against each other be landlords and landless peasants applies quite as perfectly to the empirical situation that obtained in South Yemen. The history of the twentieth century shows that most, if not all, of the radical social revolutions were carried out in societies with an overwhelmingly peasant majority. It is surprising that this fact has not attracted more research than it actually did. Possibly the explanation is to be sought in terms (largely suggested by Moore) of the visibility and reasonableness of the expropriation of the surplus. In the case of a peasant population of sharecroppers who live for generations on land they consider their own, yet have to pay a substantial proportion of the produce to city-based landlords who perform no function connected with the land, the potential for resentment is understandably great. The expropriation of a surplus in the case of an industrial concern, even if it exists, is much less visible, and there is rarely a popular doubt that the entrepreneur is fulfilling a positive role of certain nature. For the peasant sharecropper, the land is eternal and is alone sufficient to make the concern an ongoing one. An industrial plant, however, often ceases to exist when something happens to the owners. This is probably the reason why a class society based on sharecropping is potentially more revolutionary than one based on large-scale industry. In so far as South Yemen is concerned, the role of the sayyids was quite similar to that of big absentee landlords: By 1960, the lower classes viewed the sayyids as

largely superfluous, parasitic, and fulfilling no positive function connected with them.

2. When a guerrilla war starts, the following process is set in motion. The ruling upper class finds itself unwilling—and, in fact, also unable—to take part in it. Because of its special life-style, this class finds the life of the guerrilla warriors too arduous. Moreover, the upper class is too detached mentally and socially from the lower class to share with them years of extreme hardship. But most important perhaps, members of the upper class are too well known to the foreign ruler and would be immediately destroyed.

3. Consequently, a situation comes into being in which only the lower class takes part in the guerrilla activity, which is led by an anonymous urban middle-class elite. In a sharply defined two-class society, this middle-class elite finds itself in effectual tactical control of a population normally client to the upper landed class. It is only natural that the members of this middle-class elite at this particular juncture add some social drops to the nationalist beverage that they present to "their" people. If this social overtone is modest enough not to arouse the peasants' natural sense of loyalty to accepted authority, these social messages may soon become part and parcel of the peasants' spiritual world and may forge a strong alliance between the peasants and the middle-class elite even after the nationalist pretext for the guerrilla war vanishes.

4. The old social elite does not take actual part in the guerrilla activity, although initially it may think the venture commendable, for the driving force seems purely nationalist. This hiatus in the alertness of the traditional elite proves decisive for enlisting sufficient support for the new force.

THE VIABILITY OF THE THEORY: THE CASE STUDIES

I tested the viability of this theory in relation to a number of guerrilla wars that took place in the twentieth century. It should be noted that although this theory, as I have just presented it, may seem transhistoric, the actual historical record shows that never before the twentieth century did a guerrilla campaign actually radicalize. One important case that may help clarify what was missing before the twentieth century is the Spanish guerrilla war against Napoleon in 1809–1813. This guerrilla war showed clear signs of radicalization, but these did not lead to any institution of a new social order, and in the last phase of the war the guerrilla bands deteriorated and became an army of bandits, looting and killing indiscriminately. As I see it, the reason for the difference between the campaigns in Spain and, say, Albania, was that the Spanish guerrilla movement was led by peasants, whereas the Albanian movement was led by a middle-class elite with a certain purpose and the self-discipline to enforce it. An explanation of this difference may be sought in the fact that a middle-class elite with modern education only came into being in the twentieth century. As apparently no country had any such educated elite before the late nineteenth century, and as every country apparently has such a group in the twentieth century, the theory put forward here may be true only for the twentieth century.

The most important test of my theory is the Algerian war of independence of 1954–1962. This war was conducted in the form of guerrilla war, one of the fiercest in the post–World War II period and one that cost the lives of 1 million Algerians. The story in Algeria began in 1830, with the unplanned French conquest of parts of that country. Algeria was until than an Ottoman province, though an autonomous one. A Turkish social elite, privately recruited in Turkey, headed the province, but the Algerian government was not very subservient to that of Istanbul. However, there was no question of independence: Ottoman rule was not considered an alien rule in any Muslim province of the empire until the beginning of the twentieth century, and even then such stirrings of nationalism were accompanied by a great deal of guilt. The political culture of Algeria was no doubt greatly influenced by that of the Ottoman Empire; among other things, a relatively strong central government, in principle and ideology, sitting astride a relatively autonomous group of popular institutions, without trying to coerce these institutions beyond exacting taxation.

As throughout the Ottoman Empire, in Algeria there was no cooperation between the central government and a landed upper class to ensure compliance by the peasantry. There also were no ecological pressures to create landed estates, as most regions of the country were semiarid and hence inappropriate for settlement by peasantry. A substantial peasantry existed only in the Berber areas of Aurès and Kabylia, where a well-known set of ecologically based constrictions (difficulty in uniting pieces of land; the military toughness of mountain dwellers in resisting a would-be upper landed class, etc.) prevented the creation of large estates. It is not surprising that especially in these mountainous areas the land was generally considered freehold, or fully private. In short, a combination of political-cultural and ecological reasons created in Algeria before 1830 a land regime of small landowners or else tribal ownership in which the individual family held a piece of land on a basis similar to small ownership. A landed upper class was conspicuous by its absence.

France initially had no clear policy concerning Algeria. However, after a number of years a policy slowly emerged of encouraging French popular settlement of Algeria, thereby turning that country into an integral part of France. The relationship between Algeria and France was imbued with this policy to the end. Only with tremendous difficulty could France realize the necessity of letting go of Algeria. As nineteenth-century France was not particularly a poor or densely populated country, it goes without saying that French colons who emigrated to Algeria did not do so for a piece of land that would merely ensure their subsistence. What attracted these colons was the prospect of getting good land to produce wine. Most of the lands in Algeria are quite arid, and thus the French colons were bent on having only Algeria's best lands. Indeed, in the course of the next century, the French administration of Algeria was quite successful in getting hold of these lands, through a variety of measures—mainly, confiscation following insurrection; seizure of religious endowments; appropriation of lands that did not belong to any particular person and were, therefore, quite defenseless, etc.

Thus, in the nineteenth and twentieth centuries, the small traditional landed elite that had existed (to the slight degree that it existed at all) became even weaker, and a new landed elite appeared that employed tens of thousands of Algerian agricultural workers, whose pay is said to have been unusually meager. At the same time, hundreds of thousands of French nationals inhabited Algerian cities and the best lands, thereby blocking the way up of any nascent Algerian middle class. All in all, then, the French occupied the position of an upper class that was bound to arouse resentment and rebellion. Such resentment and resistance showed a noticeable increase after the turn of the century and continued to increase throughout the first half of the twentieth century. Finally, in 1954 underground resistance broke out and rapidly became a widespread guerrilla campaign. The main success consisted—in Algeria, as elsewhere—in the ability to survive, and given the circumstances in Algeria, this was a great deal, and hardly something to be reasonably expected at the outset of the revolt. The survival of the Algerian resistance has to be attributed to the large number of direct participants and even greater number of indirect supporters who were involved. But unlike the case of South Yemen, where British rule was half-hearted, in Algeria the French were so resolved to hold on that they almost managed to wipe the guerrilla movement out. Luckily for the Algerian guerrilla campaign, the severe internal

French conflict that came into being in response to the tough measures of repression in Algeria eventually brought France to the brink of civil war, which it managed to avoid only by granting Algeria full independence.

Thus, the Algerian revolt, which in any case had as its main target independence rather than military victory, came to a successful end, and the leaders of the guerrilla movement came to power. When the smoke lifted, the purposes of the ruling elite turned out to be purely middle-class ones, contrary to expectations in many quarters. In fact, throughout the war of independence the Algerian movement showed no radical signs whatsoever. In line with the theory I have suggested, I would argue that the lack of radicalism in Algeria was a result of two factors: First, there was no clear two-class division of the indigenous society; and, moreover, the occupying power also filled the role of a landed upper class, whereby the national revolution and the social revolution converged. Small wonder that the main radical-looking act of the Algerian guerrilla movement after coming to power was to carry out a nationalization of the French estates. The Palestinian Arab Revolt of 1936–1939 against the British mandate is another example of a negative relationship between guerrilla war and political radicalism. The relevance of this case may be only partial. Not only was the Palestinian guerrilla campaign unsuccessful in terms of its final outcome; but also the phase that may reasonably be construed as guerrilla war lasted for only two to three months, and I am not entirely positive that the typical guerrilla social processes can come to fruition in such a short period. Bearing these reservations in mind, I believe that this case nevertheless tallies with the theory I have put forth in this book.

The Arab Revolt in Palestine broke out because of inadequate British responsiveness in yielding to Arab demands for self-rule and for a stop to Zionist immigration and land purchases. Throughout the country, several hundred bands of warriors appeared, mostly led by villagers, who started to conduct guerrilla activities against Jews and Britons. The British government was entirely unprepared, and the army stationed in the country was too small to quell the rebellion. Before major reinforcements arrived, a large part of Palestine actually passed into the hands of the insurgents. At this stage, some semiradical features appeared: Bands in Jaffa and in some other towns terrorized the urban folk, decreeing a moratorium on debts owed by villagers to city moneylenders, abolition of rents, and the like. When large reinforcements arrived and the British put a tough policy of repression into effect, these measures combined with heavy and bloody internal conflict to bring this phase of the revolt to an end by the close of the summer of 1938. The slight signs of semiradicalism make this case worthy of comparative analysis—however partial this comparison may be. It is symptomatic, in my view, that the radicalism that actually occurred was not directed against an upper landed class but, rather, against urban citizens. It seems to me that the reason for this was that most of those engaged in guerrilla activities came from the mountainous areas of central Palestine, where the traditional and modern land regime was one of small landowners, and where Zionist land purchases were almost nonexistent.

If Algeria and, to a lesser extent, Palestine, are two good negative examples affirming the validity of my theory, the best positive example is the case of China. China resembles Albania in a quite striking way. The Chinese Communist party tried for years to propagate its teachings in China, but with very little success. At the beginning of the 1930s, the prospects of the Chinese Communist party looked bleak indeed—the power of Chiang Kai-shek's government, despite it deficiencies, seemed too formidable for the Communists to handle. But then an unexpected development took place. In 1937 a Sino-Japanese war broke out. China's regular forces were swiftly defeated, but Japan's army was too small to handle China's vast areas, and the inevitable outcome was guerrilla war. In those northern areas where the Communists had a foothold, it soon became clear that the Communist guerrillas were the only force who were actually engaging the Japanese. The landlords shunned the countryside altogether and preferred the security of the city. Only then—and because of nationalist, not socialist, propaganda—did millions start to follow the Communist leadership in earnest. The initially moderate social policies that they proposed and propagated created a gap between the peasants and the landlords. The success of the Chinese revolution thus resulted neither from a night coup by a small group of militants nor from the rational conversion of millions of people to Marxist doctrines. It emanated from the special sociological dynamics created by a guerrilla war conducted in a society riven by class conflicts.

ISLAM AND COMMUNISM

It is proper at this point to conclude my view on Islam and communism according to the material presented in this book. We have seen that in the case of Albania and South Yemen the radical ideology won out without any resistance from institutions or people usually associated with Islam. And since their revolutions, no sign of Islamic resistance has come to light in these two countries.

But is it not possible that the lack of any resistance on the part of Muslim institutions is a result of the enormous prestige gained by the revolutionary party as the nation's leader in the struggle for independence? No doubt, this is a powerful argument but not entirely convincing: For if Islam per se *is* an all-powerful force, able to move the masses irrespective of existing social circumstances, would such prestige be enough to overcome its supposedly independent authority? Obviously not. Still, events of recent years have offered an excellent opportunity to test this point empirically rather than just logically. I refer to the anti-Communist resistance waged by the Afghan people after 1979. Outwardly at least, this movement was dominated by Islamic forces, and there is a widespread belief that the cause of this rebellion is Islam, pure and simple.

Careful investigation of this claim belies the argument. Pre-1978 Afghan society was an extremely decentralized society, with weak central government and strong local communities, many still tribally organized. The Communist revolution of April 1978 was carried out by a small group of insurgents and had no social base of support. The effort of this government to enforce far-reaching reforms in the countryside was bound to spark a rebellion, and there is no need to resort to religious factors to explain the process. It is only natural that later on Islam was chosen as a symbol and mode of expression for the rebellion. On the whole, then, the Afghan case definitely does not lend support to the argument that Islam is inherently a bulwark against radical left-wing ideology.

CHRONOLOGY AND THEORY IN REVOLUTIONS

In Chapter 1, I presented in some detail various theories of revolution that seemed to me the best available ones to explain the empirical case studies. It is time now to spell out more specifically exactly how these theories are relevant.

The first important point had to do with the role of leaders. Popular wisdom has it that this role is crucial. This book argues that in fact the role of the leader is not crucial; this claim has been corroborated by the cases of the revolutions we have studied. It can be observed clearly that in both Albania and South Yemen it was the special circumstances obtaining at the time—rather than what the leaders did—that determined the course of events. Far from making the revolution single-handedly, these leaders did not even know until late in the day that an actual revolutionary process was in the making.

A second point of importance was the place of formal ideologies in social revolutions. We have found that such ideologies are not supremely important to the understanding of such events. This was also found to be true for both Albania and South Yemen. In the case of South Yemen in particular, but even in that of Albania, Barrington Moore's theory on the reluctance of oppressed classes to adopt revolutionary stands was admirably corroborated. Consequently, the transfer of allegiance from the ruling elite to the revolutionary elite was a slow and smooth process, which was closely connected to the fact that the new elite had led a successful national struggle for independence. The radical social ideology played a marginal role at best.

A third point of importance had to do with the role of the masses in the revolution, as against the role of the revolutionary party. Skocpol underscores the fact that the role of the masses in revolutions is usually much greater than is popularly thought, and this analysis, too, finds ample corroboration in the cases of Albania and South Yemen. The masses wanted independence and a piece of land in Albania, independence and an end to the caste system in South Yemen. It may be argued that these masses, for the most part, were unaware that the leaders they followed were to go much further than just independence and a piece of land. In that sense, the revolutions were in an important way made by unintending masses.

We are thus forced to conclude that the two main revolutions studied here fit admirably the modern sociological theory of revolution, despite the fact that we are dealing with Islamic culture, often said to be a subject inappropriate for the tools of analysis of the social scientist. But when carefully and sensitively applied, it is appropriate to apply historical sociology crossculturally.

Notes

CHAPTER 1

1. B. Moore, *Social Origins of Dictatorship and Democracy: Lord and Peasant in the Making of the Modern World* (Boston, 1966.)
2. G. Geertz, *Islam Observed* (Chicago, 1968).
3. B. Lewis, "Communism and Islam," *International Affairs* 30 (1954): 1-12.
4. M. Halpern, *The Politics of Social Change in the Middle East and North Africa* (Princeton, 1962), p. 156.
5. W.Z. Laqueur, *Communism and Nationalism in the Middle East* (New York, 1956), p. 3.
6. Ibid., pp. 27ff.
7. Ibid., p. 277.
8. Ibid.
9. Ibid., pp. 277ff.
10. See, e.g., E. Sivan, *Radical Islam* (New Haven, 1985), Chapter 1.
11. Moore, *Social Origins of Dictatorship and Democracy*; T. Skocpol, *States and Social Revolutions* (Cambridge, 1979).
12. J. Paige, *Agrarian Revolution* (New York, 1975).
13. B. Moore, *Injustice: The Social Bases of Obedience and Revolt* (New York), 1978.
14. R. Aya, "Theories of Revolutions Reconsidered: Contrasting Models of Collective Violence," *Theory and Society* 8 (1979): 39–99.
15. Skocpol, *States and Social Revolutions*, p. 4.
16. I see as formalistic and unacceptable the widespread views claiming that Middle Eastern society (traditional and modern) lacks classes. It is quite possible that such classes were loose, lacked any sort of self-consciousness, and were much less worthy of that lofty name than were their European counterparts. Yet, meaningful groups such as merchants, artisans, tax farmers, religious dignitaries, state officials, peasants, and landlords did exist. Such groups often had divergent socioeconomic interests, whether they

were conscious of these or not. I see no reason, therefore, to refrain from calling such groups classes, unconventional though such a usage may sound.

17. T. R. Gurr, *Why Men Rebel* (Princeton, 1970). For an effort at applying some of these ideas to the Middle East, see I. W. Zartman, J. A. Paul, and J. P. Entelis, "An Economic Indicator of Socio-Political Unrest," *International Journal of Middle East Studies* 2(1971): 293–310.

18. It is to be remarked that although in Skocpol's book this idea appears as part of a more or less coherent theory, it is fully expressed in Moore's *Injustice* (Chapter 10, which deals with the Russian Revolution). As Skocpol had been Moore's student, real credit for this idea should probably go to Moore.

19. Despite Eric Wolf's statement to the contrary, that peasants are isolated and hence weaker than city folk. E. R. Wolf, *Peasant Wars of the Twentieth Century* (New York, 1973), p. 289.

20. Paige, *Agrarian Revolution.*

21. Ibid., p. 23.

22. Ibid., pp. 64–66.

23. Skocpol, *States and Social Revolutions*, p. 17.

24. Ibid.

25. L. Kochan and R. Abraham, *The Making of Modern Russia* (Harmondsworth, 1983), Chapter 14.

26. Ibid., p. 288.

27. Ibid., p. 307.

28. A. W. Gouldner, *The Future of Intellectuals and the Rise of the New Class* (New York, 1979), p. 9.

29. Moore, *Injustice*, pp. 371ff.

30. S. Hook, *The Hero in History* (Boston, 1943).

31. Moore, *Injustice*, Introduction, but especially pp. 15ff.

32. Ibid., p. 22.

33. Ibid., p. 100.

34. Ibid., p. 124.

35. Ibid., p. 161.

36. Ibid., pp. 352–353.

37. E. Ben-Rafael and M. Lissak, *Social Aspects of Guerilla and Anti-Guerilla Warfare* (Jerusalem, 1979).

38. Skocpol, *States and Social Revolutions*, p. 115.

CHAPTER 2

1. For general introductions to the modern history of Albania see R. Marmullaku, *Albania and the Albanians* (London, 1975); N. C. Pano, *The People's Republic of Albania* (Baltimore, 1968); S. Skendi, *Albania* (New York, 1958); S. Skendi, *The Albanian National Awakening, 1878–1912* (Princeton, 1967); H. Hamm, *Albania: China's Beachhead in Europe* (New York, 1963). For a good short account, see I. Whitaker,

"Tribal Structure and National Politics in Albania, 1910–1950," in I. M. Lewis, ed., *History and Social Anthropology* (London, 1970), pp. 253–293.

2. Skendi, *The Albanian National Awakening*; Marmullaku, *Albania and the Albanians*.

3. M. Belegu, "La Révolution de Juin 1924—un événement marqué pour l'Albanie et les Balkans," in *Actes du premier congrès international des etudes sud-est européennes*, vol. 5 (Sophia, 1969), pp. 137–149.

4. Public Record Office, London (hereafter, PRO), Foreign Office (hereafter FO) 371/18338, p. 107.

5. PRO, FO 371/15887, p. 11.

6. PRO, FO 371/19476.

7. PRO, FO 371/21112.

8. PRO, FO 371/23710, pp. 182ff.

9. PRO, FO 371/21112, p. 151.

10. Ibid., p. 152.

11. PRO, FO 371/19476, p. 64.

12. S. Peters, "Ingredients of the Communist Takeover in Albania," in T. T. Hammond, ed., *The Anatomy of Communist Takeovers* (New Haven, 1975), p. 273.

13. J. Amery, *Sons of the Eagle: A Study in Guerrilla War* (London, 1948).

14. This is more than may be said for an Albanian scholarly account of the war of liberation by N. Plasari, which gives the exact dates and events (overlooking entirely, however, the Allies' help to the partisans) but does not really explain anything. The revolution, according to this version, emanated from the heroism of the Albanian people, from the determination of the Albanian Communist party, and from the fact that the Albanian peasantry and townfolk became convinced that the Communists were right. This is a classic case showing that a problem-oriented study not cast in a true comparative framework cannot really advance understanding. Was Albania really different on all these counts from other nations? It would be surprising if this were so and would certainly call for a very strong explanation. See N. Plasari, "Caractéristiques de la lutte de libération nationale du peuple Albanais contre les occupants Fascistes (1938–1944)," *Actes du premier congrès international des études sud-est européennes* 5 (Sophia, 1969): 459–468.

15. Enver Hoxha, *Twenty-Five Years of Struggle and Victory on the Road to Socialism* (Tirana, 1969), pp. 5–6.

16. On this subject in general, see E. Barker, *British Policy in South-East Europe in the Second World War* (London, 1976).

17. Peters, "Ingredients of the Communist Takeover," p. 288.

18. PRO, FO 371/37144, p. 34.

19. Ibid., p. 25.

20. Ibid., pp. 29ff.

21. Ibid.

22. Ibid.

23. PRO, FO 371/43550, p. 113.

24. Ibid., p. 115.

25. PRO, FO 371/37144, p. 86.

26. E. Mandel, *From Stalinism to Eurocommunism* (London, 1978), p. 19.

27. E. F. Davies, *Illyrian Venture* (London, 1952). The mission was attacked in January 1944 by a unit of Balli Kombetar, and most of its handful of members were killed or wounded. Davies himself was wounded and spent the rest of the war as a prisoner of the Germans.

28. Ibid., pp. 77–78.

29. Ibid., p. 78.

30. For example, PRO, FO 371/43549, p. 110.

31. Ibid., p. 100.

32. Ibid.

33. PRO, FO 371/37444, p. 98.

34. PRO, FO 371/74145, p. 91, cable dated December 17, 1943.

35. PRO, FO 371/43550, p. 5.

36. PRO, FO 371/43551, p. 88.

37. PRO, FO 371/43549, p. 171.

38. PRO, FO 371/43551, p. 114.

39. PRO, FO 371/43576, p. 4.

40. Ibid.

41. PRO, FO 371/43550, p. 130.

42. PRO, FO 371/43551, p. 4.

43. PRO, FO 371/43561, p. 19.

44. PRO, FO 371/43553, p. 82, cable dated September 29, 1944.

45. Ibid., p. 101, dated September 23, 1944.

46. Ibid.

47. PRO, FO 371/43549, p. 107.

48. Ibid., p. 104.

49. Ibid., p. 109.

50. PRO, FO 371/43550, p. 133.

51. Ibid., p. 130.

52. Ibid., p. 133.

53. PRO, FO 371/37144, p. 35, dated July 16, 1943.

54. PRO, FO 371/48078.

55. PRO, 371/43549, pp. 99–100.

56. J. Bourcart, *L'Albanie et les Albanais* (Paris, 1921), p. 37.

57. On Ali Pasha, see L. Mile, "Sur le caractère du pouvoir d'Ali Pacha de Tépélène," *Actes du premier congrès international des études sud-est européennes* 4 (Sophia, 1969): 97–109; J. C. Hobhouse, *A Journey Through Albania and Other Provinces of Turkey in Europe and Asia* (London, 1813), passim. A good popular account is W. Plomer, *The Diamond of Jannina* (London, 1970).

58. W. M. Leake, *Travels in Northern Greece*, vol. 1 (London, 1835), pp. 16–17.

59. Ibid., vol. 4, pp. 222–223.

60. H. F. Tozer, *Researches in the Highlands of Turkey*, vol. 1 (London, 1869), p. 229.

61. C. S. Coon, *The Mountains of Giants: A Racial and Cultural Study of the North Albanian Mountain Ghegs* (Cambridge, Mass., 1950), pp. 30–31; Bourcart, *L'Albanie*, p. 178. On the tribal social structure, which has attracted substantial attention during the first half of the twentieth century, see M. Hasluck, *The Unwritten Law of Albania* (Cambridge, England, 1954); M. F. Durham, *High Albania* (London, 1959); M. E. Durham, *Some Tribal Origins, Laws and Customs of the Balkans* (London, 1929). Whitaker's "Tribal Structure and National Politics" is a good short introduction.

62. Coon, *The Mountains of Giants*, p. 30.

63. Ibid.

64. P. Bartl, "Die Mirditen: Bemerkungen zur nordalbanischen Stammesgeschichte," *Müncher Zeitschrift für Balkan Kunde* 2 (1979): 27–69.

65. PRO, FO 371/5730, p. 155; PRO, FO 371/5731, p. 131.

66. Coon, *The Mountains of Giants*, p. 31.

67. PRO, FO 371/43553, pp. 34ff.

68. Hasluck, *The Unwritten Law of Albania*, pp. 118–119.

69. For a review of relevant studies, see J. S. Kahn, "Marxist Anthropology and Segmentary Societies: A Review of the Literature," in J. S. Kahn and J. R. Llobera, *The Anthropology of Pre-Capitalist Societies* (London, 1981), pp. 57-88.

70. Amery, *Sons of the Eagle*, pp. 226ff.

71. Tozer, *Researches in the Highlands of Turkey*, vol. 1, p. 312.

72. R. Busch-Zantner, *Albanien* (Leipzig, 1939), p. 25.

73. Bourcart, *L'Albanie*, pp. 43, 178.

74. Ibid., p. 42.

75. C. Chekrezi, *Albania Past and Present* (New York, 1919).

76. Ibid., p. 149.

77. Ibid., p. 174.

78. Bourcart, *L'Albanie*, p. 209. For biographic accounts of big landlords, see Ekrem Vlora, *Als Berat und vom Tomor* (Sarajevo, 1911); ibidem *Lebenserinnerungen*, 2 vols. (Munich, 1968–1973). The latter book contains as an appendix an extensive genealogical list of the traditional Albanian elite, mostly composed of big landlords, with numerous cases of intermarriages between them.

79. See Whitaker, "Tribal Structure and National Politics," pp. 276, 286.

80. M. S. Stavrou, *Etudes sur l'Albanie* (Paris, 1922), pp. 27–28.

81. Chekrezi, *Albania Past and Present*, pp. 196–197. Much of this information is duplicated by Stavrou, *Etudes sur l'Albanie*, pp. 56–59.

82. School Statistics in PRO, FO 371/21112.

83. T. Myrdal and G. Kessle, *Albania Defiant* (London, 1978), p. 141.

84. Amery, *Sons of the Eagle*.

85. Ibid., p. 126.

86. Ibid., pp. 114–115.

87. Plasari, "Caractéristiques de la lutte de libération," p. 459.

88. Amery, *Sons of the Eagle*, p. 244.

89. Ibid., p. 256.

90. PRO, FO 371/43551, p. 43.

91. PRO, FO 371/43550, p. 86.
92. PRO, FO 371/43553, pp. 34ff.
93. Amery, *Sons of the Eagle*, p. 252.
94. Ibid. p. 255.
95. Ibid.
96. Davies, *Illyrian Venture*, passim.

CHAPTER 3

1. See, for example, A. Yodfat and M. Abir, *In the Direction of the Persian Gulf* (London, 1977), Chapter 8.

2. A good short account is J. E. Peterson, *Conflict in the Yemens and Superpower Involvement* (Washington, D.C., 1981), which describes South Yemen's turning into an actual if not formal Eastern bloc member.

3. On Hong Kong see, for example, R. Hughes, *Hong Kong* (London, 1968); S. G. Davis, *Hong Kong* (London, 1949).

4. The best general introductions to the history of South Yemen, which were consulted in writing this short summary are R. W. Stookey, *South Yemen: A Marxist Republic in Arabia* (Boulder, Colo., 1982); R. J. Gavin, *Aden Under British Rule, 1839–1967* (London, 1975); R. Bidwell, *The Two Yemens* (London, 1983); F. Halliday, *Arabia Without Sultans* (New York, 1975), Part 3; J. Kostiner, *The Struggle for South Yemen* (London, 1984).

5. Great Britain, Admiralty, Naval Staff, *A Handbook of Arabia* (London, n.d.), pp. 196–197.

6. Gavin, *Aden Under British Rule*, pp. 256ff.

7. Ibid., pp. 276ff.

8. As this analysis seems to evince a strong stand that smacks of ecological determinism, I would like to make my stand on this issue more explicit. It does seem evident to me that under certain circumstances ecological determinism seems to hold. As a general rule, the lower he material culture of a society, the greater the degree of ecological determinism. But sometimes, under special circumstances, human activities overpower that determinism. And, in fact, there is no better proof of this than South Yemen itself. After all, with the same set of ecological conditions (dictating the most feeble of political centers), South Yemen developed a most powerful political center. I do not think that this, or similar, transformations have been conceptually analyzed, but such an analysis is clearly beyond the bounds of the present study.

9. A. S. Bujra, *The Politics of Stratification* (London, 1971), pp. 1ff.

10. Cited in E. Gellner, *Muslim Society* (Cambridge, 1981), p. 37.

11. Ibid., p. 191.

12. Ibid., p. 118.

13. Ibid., p. 119.

14. Ibid., p. 118.

15. J. G. Hartley, "The Political Organization of an Arab Tribe of the Hadhramaut," Ph.D. dissertation, London University, 1961, pp. 103ff.

16. Ibid., pp. 82–84.

17. Ibid., pp. 175–176.

18. Ibid., p. 76 and passim.

19. Ibid., pp. 87ff.

20. Ibid., pp. 90–91.

21. Ibid., pp. 46ff.

22. R.A.B. Hamilton, "The Social Organization of the Tribes of the Aden Protectorate," *Journal of the Royal Central Asian Society* 29 (1942): 239–248, 267–274.

23. Ibid., pp. 240–241.

24. Ibid., p. 241.

25. Ibid., p. 267.

26. An anthropologist who conducted a field study of the structure of the tribes of North Yemen came up with conclusions quite in line with those I reached concerning South Yemen. Dresch found that although this structure was on the whole segmentary, this did not detract from the fact that tribal chieftains had much political power: "The tribal structure is emphatically not 'like the various parts of a wrist-watch.' The people within it are not automata. Great shaykhs in particular, and great shaykhly houses, have powers of their own which are an important part of the world in question." See P. Dresch, "The Position of Shaykhs Among the Northern Tribes of Yemen," *Man* 19 (1984): 46.

27. D. Van Der Meulen and H. von Wissmann, *Hadramaut: Some of Its Mysteries Unveiled* (Leiden, 1964), Introduction.

28. PRO, Colonial Office 725/79/2, no. 291, dated 1941.

29. PRO, CO 725/79/12, no. 298.

30. Ibid., no. 343. The reference is to Bin 'Abdat.

31. PRO, CO 725/79/13.

32. Ibid., no. 804, dated 1942.

33. PRO, CO 725/79/14, no. 2090, dated 1943.

34. PRO, CO 725/79/12, no. 299, dated 1941.

35. For an example, see PRO, CO 725/79/13, no. 803, dated 1942.

36. Bujra, *The Politics of Stratification*, p. 35.

37. PRO, CO 725/79/13, no. 1054.

38. Ibid., no. 1171.

39. The indispensable source on this institution (and in fact on South Yemeni social structure in general) are the studies of R. B. Serjeant, of which the most important are: *The Saiyids of Hadramawt* (London, 1957); "South Arabia," in C.A.O. van Nieuwenhuijze, ed., *Commoners, Climbers and Notables* (Leiden, 1977), pp. 226–247; "Hud and Other Pre-Islamic Prophets," *Le Muséon* 67 (1954): 121–179; "Haram and Hawtah, the Sacred Enclave in Arabia," *Mélanges Taha Husain* (Cairo, 1962), pp. 41–58.

40. PRO, CO 725/79/12, no. 178.

41. Serjeant, "Hud and Other Pre-Islamic Prophets," p. 151.

42. Ibid., p. 157.

43. A good example is the case of Hurayda. See Bujra, *The Politics of Stratification*, pp. 13ff.

44. Van Der Meulen and von Wissmann, *Hadramaut*, p. 108.

45. T. Gerholm, *Market Mosque and Mafraj: Social Inequality in a Yemeni Town* (Stockholm, 1977) passim.

46. Bujra, *The Politics of Stratification*, pp. 17–18.

47. PRO, CO 725/80/11.

48. Van Der Meulen and von Wissmann, *Hadramaut*, pp. 130ff.

49. Ibid., p. 181.

50. Bujra, *The Politics of Stratification*, p. 62.

51. Great Britain, *Handbook of Arabia*, p. 226.

52. Muhammad 'Umar al-Habashi, *Al-Yaman al-Janubi* (Beirut, 1968), pp. 181–185.

53. PRO, CO 725/90/13, p. 2.

54. Ibid.

55. PRO, CO 725/69/2.

56. PRO, CO 725/846/26, p. 1.

57. PRO, CO 725/8/11.

58. PRO, CO 725/90/13.

59. Ibid.

60. PRO, CO 725/69/2.

61. PRO, CO 725/86/1, no. 44, dated 1944.

62. A.M.A. Maktari, *Water Rights and Irrigation Practices in Lahj* (Cambridge, England, 1971), pp. 50–51.

63. H. Ingrams, *A Report on the Social, Economic and Political Conditions of the Hadhramaut* (London, 1934), pp. 145ff; L.W.C. Van Den Berg, *Le Hadhramout et les Colonies Arabes dans l'Archipel Indien* (Batavia, 1886); J. Kostiner, "The Impact of the Hadrami Emigrants in the East Indies on Islamic Modernism and Social Change in the Hadramawt During the 20th Century," in R. Israeli and A. H. Johns, eds., *Islam in Asia*, vol. 2 (Boulder, Colo., 1984), pp. 206–237.

64. Ingrams, *Conditions of the Hadhramaut*, p. 146.

65. Ibid., p. 142.

66. Van Der Meulen and von Wissmann, *Hadramaut*, p. 64.

67. Ibid., p. 93.

68. H. Ingrams, *Arabia and the Isles* (London, 1952), p. 190.

69. For an example from Hurayda, see Bujra, *The Politics of Stratification*, p. 76.

70. F. Stark, *Southern Gates of Arabia* (London, 1936), pp. 54–55.

71. F. Stark, *A Winter in Arabia* (London, 1940), p. 186.

72. Stark, *Southern Gates*, p. 105.

73. Bujra, *The Politics of Stratification*, pp. 19ff.

74. Ibid., pp. 34–37, 116–118.

75. Ingrams, *Conditions of the Hadhramaut*, p. 9.

76. Stark, *Southern Gates*, p. 105.

77. *Handbook of Arabia*, p. 236.

78. Ingrams, *Conditions of the Hadhramaut*, p. 80.

79. Ibid., pp. 80ff.

80. Great Britain, *Handbook of Arabia*, pp. 194–195.

81. Ibid., p. 185.
82. Ibid., pp. 195–196; A. Grohman, *Südarabien als wirtschaftgebiet*, vol. 1 (Vienna, 1922), p. 72.
83. Ingrams, *Conditions of the Hadhramaut*, p. 85.
84. For an example of such a contract, see PRO, CO 725/79/13.
85. For example, Van Der Meulen and von Wissmann, *Hadramaut*, p. 66.
86. Ibid., p. 141. See also Ingrams, *Conditions of the Hadhramaut*, p. 86.
87. Van Der Meulen and von Wissman, *Hadramaut*, pp. 96–97.
88. Stark, *Southern Gates*, p. 194.
89. Ibid., p. 196.
90. PRO, CO 725/80/11.
91. Ibid.
92. PRO, CO 725/80.
93. Ingrams, *Conditions of the Hadhramaut*, pp. 93–94.
94. Ibid., pp. 91ff.
95. Bujra, *The Politics of Stratification*, pp. 125ff.
96. Stark, *Southern Gates*, p. 217.
97. Ibid., p. 221.
98. Stark, *A Winter in Arabia*, p. 99.
99. Ibid., p. 235.
100. PRO, CO 725/79/12, no. 180.
101. PRO, CO 725/80/11.
102. Ibid.
103. PRO, CO 725/79/13, no. 1168.
104. Ibid., no. 1006.
105. PRO, CO 725/89/5.
106. Ibid.
107. Ibid.
108. PRO, CO 725/100/3.
109. Ibid.
110. PRO, CO 725/106/2.
111. Ibid.
112. Ibid.
113. Bujra, *The Politics of Stratification*, pp. 167ff.
114. Ibid., pp. 172ff.
115. Ibid., p. 172.
116. Ibid.
117. Ibid., pp. 134–135.
118. Ibid., p. 173.
119. M. Gilsenan, *Recognizing Islam* (New York, 1982), p. 10.
120. R. J. Gavin, *Aden Under British Rule, 1839–1967* (London, 1975), p. 319.
121. Ibid., p. 321.
122. Ibid., p.322.
123. G. King, *Imperial Outpost: Aden* (London, 1964), p. 10.
124. Gavin, *Aden Under British Rule*, p. 320.

125. D. C. Watt, "Labor Relations and Trade Unionism in Aden, 1952–1960," *The Middle East Journal* 16 (1962): 443–456.

126. The account of the war of independence in South Yemen is based mainly on the following sources: J. Bower Bell, *On Revolt* (Cambridge, Mass., 1976), a study of the last major insurrections that brought down the British empire and probably the first effort to uncover real, day-to-day details on the guerrilla campaign in South Yemen; Fred Halliday, *Arabia Without Sultans* (New York, 1975), which remains the most important account, despite its being overloaded with unusually ultra-Marxist rhetoric. The unique merit of this account is that it is based on rare interviews with people who had taken part in the war of independence; Joseph Kostiner, *The Struggle for South Yemen* (London, 1984), is important for presenting the full picture as it can be reconstructed from the Arab press and radio broadcasts. Arab accounts, especially by those who took part in the events, are very disappointing as far as concrete details are concerned. The best that we have to date are several virtually identical accounts by 'Abd al-Fattah Isma'il, the undisputed ideologue of the Left in South Yemen and president between 1978 and 1982. Accounts used were 'Abd al-Fattah Isma'il, *Hawl al-Thawra al-Wataniyya al-Dimuqratiyya wa Afaqiha al Ishtirakiyya,* (Beirut 1979); *Al-Taqrir al-Siyasi lilqiyada al-'ama ila al-mu'tamar al-'am al-khamis . . .* (Beirut, 1972). The only other useful Arabic accounts that were found were Naif Hawatima, *Azmat al-Thawra fi Janub al-Yaman* (Beirut, 1968); and Makram Muhammad Ahmad, *Al-Thawra Janub al-Jazira: 'Adan wal-Yaman* (Cairo, 1968).

127. Kostiner, *The Struggle for South Yemen,* p. 26.

128. Ibid., pp. 26–27.

129. Ibid., pp. 27–28.

130. S. Harper, *Last Sunset* (London, 1978), p. 68.

131. Ibid., p. 69.

132. Ibid., p. 133.

133. J. Paget, *Last Post: Aden 1964–1967* (London, 1969), p. 113.

134. Ibid., p. 115.

135. Ibid., pp. 222–223.

136. Ibid., p. 123.

137. Harper, *Last Sunset,* p. 128.

138. Ch. Tilly, *From Mobilization to Revolution,* (n.p., 1978), pp. 190ff.

139. Makram Muhammad Ahmad, a North Yemeni who stayed with South Yemeni guerrilla fighters for a month and a half, narrates that four of them subsisted on a daily ration of one loaf of bread and a can of sardines. See Ahmad, *Al-Thawra Janub al-Jazira,* p. 96.

140. Ibid., p. 181.

141. For the radicalization in Hadramawt, see Hawatima, *Azmat al-Thawra fi Janub al-Yaman,* especially pp. 71ff.

142. J. Stork, "Socialist Revolution in Arabia," *MERIP Reports* 15 (March, 1973): 14.

143. Halliday, *Arabia Without Sultans*, p. 225.

144. Harper, *Last Sunset*, p. 65.

145. Ibid. p. 20.

CHAPTER 4

1. E. Hermassi, *Leadership and National Development in North Africa* (Berkeley and Los Angeles, 1972), p. 131.

2. Ibid.

3. For a general introduction to Algerian history under French rule, see Ch.-A. Julien and Ch.-R. Ageron, *Histoire de l'Algérie Contemporaine*, 2 vols. (Paris, 1964).

4. P. von Sivers, "The Realm of Justice: Apocalyptic Revolts in Algeria (1849–1879)," *Humaniora Islamica* 2 (1973): 47–60.

5. The most important book on this subject is no doubt H. Aleg et al., *La Guerre d'Algérie*, 3 vols. (Paris, 1981). Other studies include A. A. Heggoy, *Insurgency and Counterinsurgency in Algeria* (Bloomington and London, 1972); M. C. Hutchinson, *Revolutionary Terrorism* (Stanford, 1978); E. O'Ballance, *The Algerian Insurrection, 1954–62* (London, 1967).

6. P. Braestrap, "Partisan Tactics Algerian Style," in F. M. Osanka, ed., *Modern Guerrilla Warfare* (New York, 1962), p. 390.

7. Ibid., p. 377.

8. E. Wolf, *Peasant Wars of the Twentieth Century* (New York, 1973), pp. 240–241.

9. For the Ben Bella period in Algeria, see Hermassi, *Leadership*, passim; D. Ottaway and M. Ottaway, *Algeria: The Politics of a Socialist Revolution* (Berkeley and Los Angeles, 1970); W. B. Quandt, *Revolution and Political Leadership: Algeria, 1954–1968* (Cambridge, Mass. 1969).

10. R. Vallin, "Muslim Socialism in Algeria," in I. W. Zartmahh, ed., *Man, State and Society in the Contemporary Maghrib* (New York, 1973), pp. 50-64.

11. R. King, *Land Reform, A World Survey* (London, 1977), p. 427.

12. Ibid., p. 434.

13. W. H. Lewis, "The Decline of Algeria's F.L.N.," *Middle East Journal* 20 (1966): 169.

14. Wolf, *Peasant Wars of the Twentieth Century*, Chapter 5.

15. Original credit for this brilliant idea really goes to Eric Wolf. But he seems to have given it a somewhat unwarranted twist by claiming that peasant uprisings have been really a matter for small independent peasants enjoying tactical autonomy. However, as I have shown in the case of Albania, and as Paige has shown extensively, tactical autonomy has also been enjoyed by peasants subject to absentee landlordism, who in addition have had other grounds for dissatisfaction.

16. W. Z. Laqueur, *Guerrilla* (London, 1977), p. 297. See also Braestrup, "Partisan Tactics," p. 382.

17. J. Ruedy, *Land Policy in Colonial Algeria* (Berkeley and Los Angeles, 1967), p. 17.

18. Ibid., p. 6.

19. Ibid., p. 8.

20. Ibid., pp. 9–10.

21. Ibid., p. 12.

22. Ibid., pp. 11–12.

23. L. Valensi, *On the Eve of Colonialism* (New York, 1977), p. 26.

24. Ibid., p. 26.

25. Ibid., p. 30.

26. P. von Sivers, "Les plaisirs du collectionneur: capitalisme fiscal et chefs indigènes en Algérie (1840–1860)," *Annales (E.S.C.)* 35 (1980): 679.

27. T.M. Houston, *The Western Mediterranean World* (London, 1964), pp. 667–668.

28. F. Colonna, "Saints furieux et saints studieux ou, dans l'Aurès, comment la religion vient aux tribus," *Annales (E.S.C.)* 35 (1980): especially pp. 653ff.

29. B. Moore, *Social Origins of Dictatorship and Democracy* (Boston, 1966), pp. 469–471.

30. R. Dumont, *Types of Rural Economy* (London, 1970), pp. 182–183.

31. Ibid., p. 184.

32. Ibid., pp. 181–182.

33. R. Maunier, *Mélanges de sociologies Nord-Africaine* (Paris, 1930), pp. 57ff.

34. Ibid., p. 69.

35. Ibid., pp. 75–76.

36. Ibid., pp. 67–69.

37. Ibid., p. 68.

38. Dumont, *Types of Rural Economy*, p. 171.

39. P. von Sivers, "Insurrection and Accommodation: Indigenous Leadership in Eastern Algeria, 1840–1900," *International Journal of Middle East Studies* 6 (1975): 259–275.

40. Ibid., p. 263.

41. P. von Sivers, "Algerian Landownership and Rural Leadership, 1860–1940: A Quantitative Approach," *The Maghreb Review* 4 (1979): 58–62.

42. Ibid., p. 61.

43. J. Berque, *French North Africa* (London, 1967), p. 136.

44. Ibid.

45. M. Launay, *Paysans Algériens* (Paris, 1963), pp. 223–224.

46. L. Binder, *In a Moment of Enthusiasm* (Chicago, 1978), p. 62.

47. Ruedy, *Land Policy*, pp. 6–8.

48. Ibid., p. 58.

49. O.F.. Colonna, "Cultural Resistance and Religious Legitimacy in Colonial Algeria," *Economy and Society* 3 (1974): 240–241.

50. Wolf, *Peasant Wars of the Twentieth Century*, p. 217.

51. Launay, *Paysans Algériens*.

52. Ibid., pp. 16–17.

53. Ibid., pp. 70–71.

54. Ibid., pp. 56ff.
55. Ibid., p. 82.
56. J. Paige, *Agrarian Revolution* (New York, 1975), p. 8.
57. Ibid., p. 328.
58. Ibid., pp. 326ff.
59. R. Descloitres, C. Descloitres, and J. C. Reverdy, "Urban Organization and Social Structure in Algeria," in Zartmann, *Man, State and Society in the Contemporary Maghrib*, p. 425.
60. E. Gellner, *Muslim Society* (Cambridge, 1979), p. 152.
61. Quandt, *Revolution and Political Leadership.*
62. Ibid., passim.
63. Ibid., p. 227.
64. Ibid., pp. 85–86.
65. Colonna, "Cultural Resistance".
66. E. Gellner, "A Pendulum Swing Theory of Islam," in R. Robertson, ed., *Sociology of Religion* (Harmondsworth, 1969), pp. 127–138.

CHAPTER 5

1. The literature on the Afghan revolution is by now enormous. Some good accounts are the following: B. Sen Gupta, *Afghanistan* (Boulder, Colo., 1986); J. J. Collins, The Soviet *Invasion of Afghanistan* (Lexington, Mass., 1986); F. Halliday, "Revolution in Afghanistan," *New Left Review*, no. 112 (1978), pp. 3–44; idem., "War and Revolution in Afghanistan," *New Left Review*, no. 119 (1980), pp. 20–41; H. Bradsher, *Afghanistan and the Soviet Union* (Durham, N.C., 1983).

2. General good introductions to the geography and history of Afghanistan are L. Dupree, *Afghanistan* (Princeton, N.J., 1973); H. H. Smith et al., *Area Handbook of Afghanistan* (Washington, D.C., 1969); D. N. Wilber, *Afghanistan* (New Haven, 1969).

3. The following summary of Afghan history is based on Dupree, *Afghanistan*; Smith, *Area Handbook*; Wilber, *Afghanistan.*

4. Smith, *Area Handbook*, 85.

5. J. W. Anderson, "How Afghan Tribes Define Themselves in Relation to Islam," in M. N. Shahrani and R. L. Canfield, eds., *Revolutions and Rebellions in Afghanistan* (Berkeley, 1984), 273.

6. See especially Collins, *The Soviet Invasion*, and Bradsher, *Afghanistan and the Soviet Union.*

7. See H. Beattie, "Effects of the Saur Revolution in the Nahrin Area of Northern Afghanistan," in Shahrani and Canfield, *Revolutions and Rebellions*, pp. 184–208.

8. Many of the rebellions are described in a group of excellent anthropological studies assembled in Shahrani and Canfield, *Revolutions and Rebellions.*

9. As is claimed by some writers, for example L. Dupree, "The Marxist Regimes and the Soviet Presence in Afghanistan: Ages-Old Culture Responds

to Late Twentieth-Century Aggression," in Shahrani and Canfield, *Revolutions and Rebellions*, pp. 63ff.

10. Shahrani and Canfield, *Revolutions and Rebellions*, passim.

11. M. N. Shahrani, "Introduction: Marxist Revolution and Islamic Resistance in Afghanistan," in Ibid., pp. 3–57.

12. Ibid., p. 9.

13. R. F. Strand, "The Evolution of the Anti-Communist Resistance, in Eastern Nuristan," in Shahrani and Canfield, *Revolutions and Rebellions*, p. 79.

14. E. Gellner, "A Pendulum Swing Theory of Islam," in R. Robertson, ed., *Sociology of Religion* (Harmondsworth, 1969), pp. 127–138.

15. B. Spooner, *The Cultural Ecology of Pastoral Nomads* (Reading, Mass., 1973), p. 41.

16. Anderson, "How Afghan Tribes Define Themselves," p. 266.

17. Cited from Peters in Shahrani, Introduction, p. 30 (emphasis added).

18. B. Tavakolian, "Sheikhanzai Nomads and the Afghan State: A Study of Indigenous Authority and Foreign Rule," in Shahrani and Canfield, *Revolutions and Rebellions*, pp. 249–265.

19. Ibid., p. 262.

20. Ibid.

21. Ibid., p. 263.

22. See R. L. Keiser, "The Rebellion in Darra-i Nur," in Shahrani and Canfield, *Revolutions and Rebellions*, pp. 119–135; Strand, "Eastern Nuristan."

23. Beattie, "Effects of the Saur Revolution."

24. Ibid., p. 203.

25. Ibid.

26. J. W. Anderson, "How Afghan Tribes Define Themselves," pp. 266–287.

27. Ibid., p. 276.

28. Ibid., p. 266.

29. R. L. Canfield, "Islamic Coalitions in Bamyan: A Problem in Translating Afghan Political Culture," in Shahrani and Canfield, *Revolutions and Rebellions*, pp. 211–229.

30. Ibid., p. 228.

31. Ibid., p. 229.

32. It was also a comparative perspective that led Sen Gupta to say that "Islam *per se* has not been an inseparable barrier to Communism. The Indonesian Communist Party (PKI), the largest party outside the Communist world in the early sixties, consisted of millions of Muslim peasants." See Sen Gupta, *Afghanistan*, pp. 63–64.

33. O. Roy, *Islam and Resistance in Afghanistan* (Cambridge, 1986).

34. Ibid., pp. 65ff.

35. Ibid., pp. 54ff.

36. See, e.g., D. Taylor, "The Politics of Islam and Islamization in Pakistan," in J. P. Piscatori (ed.), *Islam in the Political Process* (Oxford, 1984) pp. 181–198.

37. Roy, *Islam and Resistence*, p. 3.

38. Dupree, *Afghanistan*, p. 104.

39. Keiser, "The Rebellion in Darra-i Nur," p. 135.

40. Wilber, *Afghanistan*, p. 3.

41. Smith, *Area Handbook*, p. 257.

42. Wilber, *Afghanistan*, p. 226.

43. Dupree, *Afghanistan*, p. 147.

44. Ibid., p. 153.

45. F. Halliday, "Revolution in Afghanistan," p. 33. The figure is derived from Halliday's data.

46. Wilber, *Afghanistan*, p. 76.

47. Ibid., p. 81.

48. Keiser, "The Rebellion in Darra-i Nur."

49. J. W. Anderson, "There Are No *Khans* Anymore: Economic Development and Social Change in Tribal Afganistan," in *Middle East Journal* 32 (1978): 167–183.

50. L. Dupree, "The Changing Character of South-Central Afghanistan Villages," *Human Organization* 14, no. 4 (1956): 26–29.

51. Ibid., p. 28.

52. R. Tapper, "Ethnicity and Class: Dimensions of Intergroup Conflicts in North-Central Afghanistan," in Shahrani and Canfield, *Revolutions and Rebellions*, pp. 230–246.

53. Ibid., p. 245.

54. Wilber, *Afghanistan*, p. 80.

55. The pattern is nicely described by Anderson, "There Are No *Khans* Anymore."

56. See B. Moore, *Social Origins of Dictatorship and Democracy* (Boston, 1966), pp. 468ff.

57. T. Skocpol, *States and Social Revolutions* (Cambridge, England: 1979), p. 115.

58. Halliday, "War and Revolution," p. 24.

CHAPTER 6

1. T. Skocpol, ed., *Vision and Method in Historical Sociology* (Cambridge, England, 1984).

2. As cited in V. E. Bonnell, "The Uses of Theory, Concepts and Comparison in Historical Sociology," *Comparative Studies in Society and History* 22 (1980): 162.

3. Ibid., p. 173.

4. D. B. Rutman, "History and Anthropology: Clio's Dalliances," *Historical Methods* 19 (1986): 120–123.

5. D. Quataert, *Social Disintegration and Popular Resistance in the Ottoman Empire, 1881–1908* (New York, 1983).

6. D. F. Eickelman, *The Middle East: An Anthropological Approach* (Englewood Cliffs, 1981).

7. Ibid., pp. 228ff.

8. C. Geertz, *Islam Observed* (Chicago, 1968).

9. D. I. Kertzer, "Anthropology and Family History," *Journal of Family History* 9 (1984): 204.

10. Geertz, *Islam Observed*, p. 7.

11. Ibid., p. 9.

12. Ibid., pp. 10–11.

13. For an assessment of this effort, see D. Chirot, "The Social and Historical Landscape of Marc Bloch," in Skocpol, *Vision and Method in Historical Sociology*, pp. 33ff.

14. E. H. Carr, *What is History* (Harmondsworth, 1975).

15. Ibid., p. 63.

16. Ibid., p. 87.

17. W. Z. Laqueur, *Guerrilla* (London, 1977).

18. Y. Harkabi, ed., *On Guerrilla* (Tel Aviv, 1983), p. 11.

19. Laqueur, *Guerrilla*, Chapter 5.

20. Ibid., pp. 29–41.

21. R. Carr, *Spain, 1808–1939* (Oxford, 1966), p. 88.

22. K. Marx and F. Engels, *Revolution in Spain* (New York, 1939).

23. Ibid., p. 55.

24. Ibid., pp. 46–47.

25. Carr, *Spain*, p. 109.

26. Marx and Engels, *Revolution in Spain*, p. 54.

27. Ibid.

28. The main sources I have used for the Chinese revolution are: L. Bianco, *Origins of the Chinese Revolution, 1915–1949* (Stanford, 1971); T.L. Skocpol, *States and Social Revolutions* (Cambridge, 1979); B. Moore, *Social Origins of Dictatorship and Democracy* (Boston, 1966); M. Meisner, "The Chinese Communist Revolution," in L. Kaplan, ed., *Revolutions: A Comparative Study* (New York, 1973), pp. 315–354.

29. Meisner, "The Chinese Communist Revolution," p. 330.

30. Bianco, *Origins of the Chinese Revolution*, p. 148.

31. Ibid., p. 151.

32. Ibid., p. 150–151.

33. Ibid., p. 149.

34. Moore, *Social Origins of Dictatorship and Democracy*, p. 223.

35. On Vietnam, I have used mainly J. Paige, *Agrarian Revolution* (New York, 1975), Chapter 5.

36. Y. Porath, *The Palestinian Arab National Movement*, vol. 2 (London, 1977).

37. Ibid., p. 238.

38. Ibid., pp. 267–268.

39. Ibid., p. 265.

40. H. Gerber, *Ottoman Rule in Jerusalem, 1890–1914* (Berlin, 1985), Chapter 9.

41. W. Z. Laqueur, *Communism and Nationalism in the Middle East* (London, 1961), p. 96.

42. Ibid., p. 97.

43. Ibid., p. 98.

Index

About the Book
and the Author

Haim Gerber addresses the phenomenon of radical revolution within Islam, seeking both to understand a certain type of revolution and to discover whether there is a typical Muslim response to Communism.

Gerber first investigates the 1944 Marxist revolution in Albania and the 1967–1969 Marxist revolution in South Yemen. He finds, in conformity with the sociological theory of revolution, that these two revolutions were due not to the sway of ideologies nor to the extraordinary abilities of leaders, but to objective circumstances that were beyond the control of any individual.

The theory he builds to explain the cases of Albania and South Yemen is then tested in several other cases—notably that of the Algerian war of independence (1954–1962)—leading to the conclusion that Islam per se has little to do with the revolutionary potential of social movements. To check this conclusion in a more direct manner, he dwells at some length on the anti-Communist Afghan resistance dating from 1979. Contrary to widespread views, Gerber finds that Afghanistan's guerrilla movement should not be seen as a specifically Muslim resistance. His more general conclusion is that the tools of social history can, indeed, be applied cross-nationally.

Haim Gerber is senior lecturer in the Department of Islam at the Hebrew University of Jerusalem. He is author of *The Social Origins of the Modern Middle East* (a *Choice* Outstanding Academic Book for 1987).